Selling Style

Selling Style

Clothing and Social Change at the Turn of the Century

ROB SCHORMAN

PENN

University of Pennsylvania Press

Philadelphia

10 9 8 7 6 5 4 3 2 1

Published by
University of Pennsylvania Press
Philadelphia, Pennsylvania 19104-4011

Library of Congress Cataloging-in-Publication Data

Schorman, Rob.
   Selling style : clothing and social change at the turn of the century / Rob Schorman.
   p. cm.
   Includes bibliographical references and index.
   ISBN 0-8122-3728-5 (cloth : alk. paper)
   1. Fashion merchandising—United States—History—19th century. 2. Clothing
trade—United States—History—19th century. 3. Social change—United States—
History—19th century. I. Title.

HD9940.U6S36 2003
687'.068'8—dc21   2002043042

For Judi, my guiding star

Contents

Introduction

"The Influence of Clothes"

Herein may be found an invincible argument against the development of mannish tendencies in feminine costume. The influence of clothes is so strong, so irresistible, that few women can wear masculine garments without losing something of the charm of womanliness, while on the other hand, effeminacy in man's attire has nearly always proved indicative of a corresponding emasculation of character.

—*"The Individual Significance of Clothes,"* Godey's Magazine, *1893*

The commentary by the fashion editor of *Godey's* suggests much about the "significance of clothes" in the 1890s.[1] The writer considers clothing to have unmistakable masculine or feminine qualities and goes even further to suggest that garments not only mark gender consciousness but make it. According to the author, "the influence of clothes" is so powerful that the wrong apparel diminishes a person's status as "woman" or "man." Furthermore, the article assumes the virtue of maintaining sharply divided realms for men and women despite (or perhaps because of) the manner in which middle-class women increasingly pushed against the boundaries of the Victorian ideal of separate spheres. The passage hints at the manner in which the ongoing construction of gender roles, particularly evident in the 1890s as part of an overall reformulation of middle-class values, became visible, accessible, fiercely contested, and, to a certain extent, manipulable through clothing.

A clear sense of broad social change, of more specific challenges to gender boundaries, and of clothing's important role in articulating both is apparent in the magazine articles, advertising copy, etiquette manuals, trade journal reports, newspaper stories, fiction, diaries, and memoirs from this period. Consider a short story called "The Right Man" that appeared in the *Woman's Home Companion* in 1898. The heroine is Miss Deland, a young woman who has begun a successful career as a writer and editor for a weekly magazine. Her employment represents something of a departure from the middle-class domestic ideal for women, but a coworker, Mr. Gates, focuses his discomfort not on her job but on her clothing. "I wish she would try to be a little more feminine," he says to himself. "Somehow it irritates me . . . the severely plain way in which she dresses, in spite of the fact that she always looks neat. . . . It isn't exactly masculine, but neither is it feminine. I don't like her, and yet there is something about her that attracts me." Mr. Gates's conflicted feelings are resolved when he visits Miss Deland at her home. As if demonstrating the truth of the *Godey's* commentary, a change of clothes restores the "charm of womanliness" to the story's heroine: "She seemed a different person, in a dress of soft gray ornamented by ribbon, bows, a film of white lace about her neck, with a pink flower or two at the throat." She notices his surprise: "'Perhaps I ought to be introduced,' she said. 'At the *Weekly Recorder* office I am Miss Deland, reader of manuscripts—a mere business woman. Here I am myself. I like to keep the two personalities distinctly separate.'" At the end of the story Mr. Gates, having discovered the real Miss Deland, offers a proposal of marriage, which she accepts.[2]

Significantly, this story grants its central female character a role outside the home, but just as significantly, it does so in rather grudging terms. While she is clearly competent in the workplace, this fictional female stresses her desire to keep life at work and at home "distinctly separate," and she is clear about which represents the "real" Miss Deland. She describes her office role as that of a "mere" business woman, but at home, she says, "I am myself." The author of this story described the tension between these two roles primarily through references to Miss Deland's clothing, confident that the magazine's readers would understand the significance of dress, as Miss Deland herself obviously did. This strategy reiterated a frequent theme of the mass-circulation magazines. As the *Ladies' Home Journal* asserted in a column of fashion advice: "We know that many a gown has told its owner's story, and my dear general woman, what I want is that your house gown shall tell a story of contentment and love."[3]

This book examines the intersection of gender, mass media, and consumer culture at the turn of the twentieth century. Clothing—and mass-produced images of clothing—constituted a symbolic system that worked not only in fiction but in life to help people deal with changes in American society at large and in gender roles in particular. What *Godey's* called "the influence of clothes" played a crucial role in the creation and maintenance of social norms, even channeling the expansion of mass market capitalism according to cultural expectations for sex differentiation. At the same time, attitudes toward attire did not mold belief systems rigidly or inevitably. Nor was fashion's expressive capacity restricted to definitions of gender ideals, for clothing habits also influenced individual and collective responses to a host of issues including class, national identity, and change itself.

Therefore we can interpret fashion advice, fashion advertisements, and fashion styles within the context of social transformation to see how a segment of society, in this case the American middle class, coped with broad shifts in American culture, attempting to manage the process of change by welcoming its material and psychological benefits while maintaining a comforting continuity with traditional values that, not coincidentally, would help preserve the sources of their own status and power. The *Woman's Home Companion* represented this process explicitly when it described Miss Deland as shifting back and forth "from the new woman to the old-fashioned one."[4] In advice columns and advertisements, this cultural dynamic appeared more subtly but with enough clarity to demonstrate how material culture and mass media provided reference points that people used to generate meaning about the nature of society and their own relationship to it. The interplay of fashion and advertising provides a fine-grained picture of attitudes toward gender and reveals those attitudes as both constrained and flexible in ways historians have not always noted. The relation of the two also shows the advance of consumer culture as more piecemeal and conflicted than many histories of the era imply. It also demonstrates how issues of class and citizenship were integrated with—or overlaid upon—this emerging dynamic of personal identity and mass consumption, and it reveals the extent to which cultural values are continually made and remade through everyday acts of consumption.

The final years of the nineteenth century offer a particularly rich slice of history for observing these trends. Americans at this time lived against the backdrop of a nationalizing economy that was dominated by giant corporations, fell under the influence of the first true mass media, and maintained a sometimes uneasy relationship with a rising tide of immigration, the spectacular growth of cities, and an expanding national appetite for imperialistic adventurism. Technological breakthroughs and the growing power and productivity of large corporations produced a sense of both energy and unease that was noted by contemporary observers and historians alike. The *Ladies' Home Journal* referred to "the restlessness of the age" and "the rush of American life."[5] Looking backward, historians called this cultural unrest "weightlessness" and described turn-of-the-century America as "a society without a core."[6]

For middle-class Americans, the changes of this era brought unprecedented levels of material abundance and confirmation of the righteousness and progress of American life. Between 1870 and 1900 the gross national product of the United States more than doubled and the value of manufactured goods exceeded the value of agricultural commodities for the first time in the nation's history. Americans benefited from a host of new products and technologies. By the turn of the century, a visitor reported that life in the United States was a "perpetual whirl of telephones, telegrams, phonographs, electric bells, motors, lifts, and automatic instruments."[7]

At the same time, many people perceived threats as well as benefits in the new era because aspects of urbanized, industrial society challenged conventional notions of personal autonomy, changed the rules for workplace and community, and tested the gender roles that underwrote much of the social, economic, and political structure of the time. In particular, the growth of corporations, cities, and the foreign-born population represented serious threats to the control, status, and stability that middle-class Americans valued so highly in their lives. The uncertainty and hardships caused by the onset of a severe economic depression in 1893 further exacerbated this unease. Writing in 1900, Brooks Adams recalled, "During the summer of 1893 I became convinced that the financial convulsion which involved so many widely separated communities could only be due to some profound perturbation which extended throughout the world." Before the depression was over, a violent confrontation of union railroad workers and the U.S. Army during the Pullman Strike unleashed what one historian called "the most destructive civil violence since the Civil War," adding to fears that society was out of control. Also in 1893, Frederick Jackson Turner's essay on the closing of the American frontier offered the disquieting suggestion that a great source of individual opportunity had been eliminated and the wellspring of American democratic institutions had dried up. Adams concluded that "in 1890, a new period of instability opened. Civilization . . . seems to have entered upon a fresh epoch of unrest."[8]

In the most literal way, Americans began to *see* these changes in different terms at this time, thanks to the explosive growth in the type and supply of visual images circulating through society. Kinetoscope galleries, comic strips, home cameras, and picture postcards appeared in the United States during this era, which also saw the emergence of halftone photo reproduction, the poster craze, and enhanced appreciation of the display potential of artificial light and new kinds of color. On top of this, magazines and newspapers began for the first time to merit the description "mass media," expanding the scope of daily life in remote towns as well as bustling cities. Thus people confronted not only a multitude of new consumer goods but also a multitude of new representations of them. Indeed, they even embraced new ways of talking about objects—words such as "gadget," "thingamajig," and "dingus" entered the language at this time as descriptions of things in general.[9] As the era of mass communications began, new objects, images, people, and ideas increasingly became part of the everyday experience of many Americans.

Susan Snow, wife of a civil servant in Junction City, Kansas, offers a small-town example. In a letter to her family, she mentioned that when the latest copy of her favorite magazine arrived, "it seemed like an old friend and I sat right down and read it through." She referred to the magazine in numerous letters as she tried to stay current with social etiquette and fashion: "I forgot to mention that my bonnet was a new one for the occasion. I got a shape half turban and half bonnet . . . it is something like Fig. 4 in April *Delineator.*" Throughout her correspondence, Snow often couched her observations of other people in terms of clothing: "While I have been writing here by the window I have seen all sorts of people going by. . . . All kinds of styles, some have hats same as mine. A Miss Wright quite tony wore one like my best." Likewise, she described social occasions in terms of her attire: "I wore my blue and brown and the lace coiffure Mrs. Howes gave me"; "It was quite informal so I wore my green"; "I did not eat but a little for fear it would fly over my blue silk." The story of Miss Deland or the "invincible argument" of the *Godey's* editor would be instantly comprehensible and meaningful to Mrs. Snow, as it would be to hundreds of thousands of the magazine's readers across the country.[10]

The clothing habits of the middle class had some distinctive characteristics in the 1890s. By this time, most American men wore ready-made clothing, but a great deal of women's clothing was still custom-made. Contemporary observers claimed that 90 percent of men wore ready-made clothing, and the available evidence supports this assertion, even though the rhetoric surrounding men's clothing continued to stress a custom-made ideal. Some historians suggest that by the 1870s or 1880s, the ready-made revolution had overtaken the women's market as well, but I believe this overstates the acceptance and influence of women's ready-made garments.[11] *Ladies' Home Journal* editor Edward Bok was surprised in 1899 when a woman reader wrote the magazine and questioned its continued attention to home dressmaking. The reader asked: "Do you not know . . . that the vast majority of women have their dresses made outside their home?" Bok responded in one of his monthly columns: "As a matter of fact, although this woman may not know it, more than three-fourths of the dresses worn in this country are the deft handiwork of the wearers."[12] Note that neither Bok nor his correspondent thought ready-made clothing merited any consideration at all. Their debate was between clothes made-to-measure by dressmakers and clothes made-to-measure at home.

This book focuses primarily on the 1890s because it is the decade when the contrast between men's and women's clothing was sharpest.[13]

The basic questions I have tried to answer are: What accounts for this contrast? Why did it seem so sharply defined right before the turn of the century? What connection do clothing and the making of clothes have to broader cultural issues such as gender?

The discrepancy in the development of men's and women's clothing does not sit squarely with the conventional wisdom about increasing mass production. Most standard sources for industrialization—technology, labor, raw materials, transportation—would have been equally available to both men's and women's manufacturers and so cannot explain this divide. It is especially remarkable that ready-made clothes seem to have met their main resistance among women because, by this time, social commentators and advertisers were already constructing a stereotype of women as the prototypical consumer.[14]

The root cause of this schism in the clothing industry was cultural, not economic, and a main task of this book is to describe the various meanings and symbolic uses clothing had for men and women and thereby to link fashion and clothing manufacture to the gender politics of this era. The rhetoric that surrounded fashion suggests the intensity with which changes in gender roles were debated and provides a glimpse at the way dominant gender ideals were worked into the everyday experiences of men and women of the time. Even the juggernauts of mass production and mass consumption had to accommodate their bottom-line mentality to the cultural imperative for gender definition.

Another distinguishing characteristic of fashion in the 1890s was that information about it began to reach people in new ways. Advertising, which was just assuming recognizably modern form, provided a powerful new medium for conveying the meaning of clothes. Ads for men's and women's clothing differed significantly at this time, with men's clothing ads focusing on ready-made goods and women's ads focusing on sewing aids. However, these advertisements shared many other attributes, most notably their increasing pervasiveness. During the 1890s, magazines and newspapers in the United States experienced enormous growth, in some cases achieving circulations that approached or exceeded 1 million.[15] The simultaneous emergence of a separate advertising industry as an important economic and social force accompanied this expansion of print media. William Dean Howells, taking note of one of the earliest advertising how-to manuals in 1896, commented that advertising "can't keep increasing at the present rate. If it does, there will presently be no room in the world for things; it will be filled up with the advertisements of things."[16]

Some historians contend that advertising did not develop a sophisticated and deeply symbolic cultural role until the late 1910s or 1920s, but in fact advertisers deployed a wide array of sociopsychological advertising strategies before the turn of the century. Although such tactics may have been relatively unrefined, at the very least it is oversimplified to argue that "advertising between the 1890s and 1910s was dominated by rational appeals that sought to persuade chiefly by attracting readers' attention and informing them that goods were available."[17] An additional attraction of the 1890s, then, is that here we can observe, for the first time in a mass market context, how advertising had begun to shape meaning in everyday life and provide a symbolic code of common reference for a broad spectrum of Americans.

Under the influence of advertising, the cultural context of consumption entered a new phase at the end of the nineteenth century, just at the time when the phrase "ready-to-wear" began to supplant the earlier label "ready-made" in descriptions of manufactured clothing.[18] This linguistic shift of emphasis to a "consumed" item from a "produced" item supports the idea that an American consumer culture originated in this era, but historians have made solid claims for dating consumer culture both earlier and later.[19] Indeed, the term "consumer culture" is misleading, for all societies are consumer cultures in the sense that they all consume goods and all consumption is both social and symbolic.[20] Nonetheless, several important features distinguished the consumption patterns that began to develop in the late nineteenth century. First and foremost was a dramatic change in scale. An unprecedented range of goods was mass produced in equally unprecedented volume at the end of the nineteenth century. This goods explosion meant not only that people possessed new things, but also that objects existed in newly standardized, almost infinitely replicable form. In addition, the relationship between buyer and seller much more frequently assumed a less personalized, less localized character in which consumers no longer knew the producer, met the seller face to face, or had firsthand knowledge of an object's history or construction. Thus advertising assumed a new importance in communicating information and attitudes about the world of goods. The result was a culture distinguished not simply by an emphasis on "consumption" but by the high-intensity, high-volume circulation of symbolic goods.[21]

The dawning of an era of large-scale consumption, national markets, and mass communications required not only products and technology but also symbols that would make that transition intelligible and accessible to ordinary people. Clothing and advertising supplied such symbols, assuming forms particularly suitable to changing attitudes toward gender and other social relations.[22] Recent scholarship has suggested that gender roles both influenced and were influenced by the emergence of consumer culture and that the resulting tension around the meaning of gender became especially prominent in periods of transition and social distress.[23] At certain times, such as the 1890s, economic or political circumstances may shake the cultural kaleidoscope with exceptional force, and the history of clothing habits not only reveals the complex contours of this transformed cultural landscape but also suggests how Americans navigated through it.

In this book, the term "fashion" refers to both the clothing everyone wears and the symbolic system inevitably connected to any choice of clothing. Some writers have restricted the term to elite fashion or haute couture, but every act of dressing engages the communicative function of clothing. Even "unfashionable" and "utilitarian" garments such as work clothes or athletic apparel convey and constitute cultural attitudes. Rather than make distinctions among terms such as "fashion," "costume," "dress," and "style," I presume that even when these words are not exact synonyms, they exist in such a tight network that they cannot be studied separately.[24] I will treat "fashion," "dress," and "clothing" as essentially interchangeable terms throughout this work. Similarly, "clothing habits," "dress code," and "fashion system" all refer in a general way to the broad realm of clothing practices and the symbolic networks they create.

Notably, this definition of fashion requires attention to the clothing of both men and women. By the late nineteenth century, writers typically characterized fashion as a concern exclusive to women, and many subsequent books on the subject all but ignore men's clothing. Florence Howe Hall, a nineteenth-century etiquette writer, captured this attitude: "Whether Woman is behind Man in civilization because she pays an attention to dress which he has long ago disused, or whether her devotion to it is because man requires her to be robed in gay attire, is a question which I shall not here enter into. Suffice it to acknowledge that women are expected in this age to pay more attention to dress than men do, and that they are therefore justified in so doing—within limits."[25] Hall's reference to the progress of civilization alludes to a belief in sexual differentiation so firm as to be accepted as a law of nature based on Darwin's theory of evolution: the more advanced the society, the more specialized the sexes. Clothing, as the passage suggests, helped provide the terms for delineating and maintaining this differentiation. But Hall wrongly implies that men were exempt from fashion. As I will demonstrate, male gender roles and ideal masculine body types were also subject to the symbolic power of clothes.[26]

The most common weakness in theories of fashion stems from their efforts to find a single mechanism or pattern by which dress performs its cultural work. Depending on the theory, changes in fashion are linked almost exclusively either to autonomous cycles, business influences, aesthetic factors, class emulation, sexual attraction, or marketing magic.[27]

However, fashion incorporates multiple meanings and responds to many influences, even to the point of incorporating contradictory points of view or a paradoxical conjunction of divergent attitudes. In the late nineteenth century, clothing could embody older middle-class concerns, such as the maintenance of social hierarchy, the survival of the individual in a corporate world and avoidance of the unhealthy side effects of material prosperity, while simultaneously reflecting a modern engagement with new forms of body ideals, increased commodity production, and emerging modes of mass communications. Fashion is inherently both ambiguous and ambivalent, providing the means of creating identities that juggle opposing values and competing perspectives.[28] Both clothing and advertising juxtaposed old and new values and allowed people to try out various syntheses and strategies of personal accommodation to the transformation of American society. Although fashion and advertising may not actually have resolved the cultural contradictions an individual faced in changing times, they offered a symbolic means of managing these contradictions in day-to-day life.

For the nineteenth-century middle class, the connection between fashion and a wide range of sociological and psychological issues constituted practical knowledge, not academic abstractions. Etiquette writers constantly reminded readers to seek "suitability to age and times and seasons," "consistency in regard to station and fortune," and "costume appropriate to the occasion."[29] In doing so, they linked dress with a host of categories, including gender, marital status, age, class, time of day, specific occasion, and personal temperament. Furthermore, etiquette advisers insisted on a personal, even moral, equation between garment and wearer, offering injunctions such as: "Indifference and inattention to dress is a defect of character" and "refinement of character is said never to be found with vulgarity of dress."[30] In Kansas, Susan Snow took this to heart, worrying frequently about matching her clothing habits very precisely to specific circumstances. Recalling one social engagement, she wrote: "I learned that when cards read 'At Home' it was meant to be informal. No bonnets, some kept on their gloves. I think all should have. . . . I saw hats, gloves, and bonnets lying on the dressing table, so I thought they all must have taken them off. . . . I wished I had kept them on after I had gotten among the company. The people amongst them had on gloves but no bonnets."[31]

Still, one cannot explain new fashion trends simply by considering their cultural implications. Fashion is a business and an art form, and the styles worn by women like Miss Deland and Susan Snow were available to them only by virtue of elaborate networks of design, production, and distribution that closely tracked business interests and aesthetic trends. However, no authoritarian business cabal or marketing machine could simply impose fashion on the public. In the 1890s, for example, fashion mongers spent the first half of the decade attempting to revive the crinoline and the last half attempting to squelch the popular appeal of the shirtwaist, a blouselike woman's garment. Despite controlling the levers of design, production, and promotion, they could do neither. The *Chicago Dry Goods Reporter* summed up the situation in 1899: "While every year there has been talk against the shirt waist, and not infrequently strong efforts to bring into notice some other style of dress to take its place, the shirt waist still survives."[32] Through admissions such as this, fashion writers and trade publications acknowledged that new styles were subject to some sort of popular ratification. For this reason, advice manuals warned consumers not to jump on a fashion trend too early in the season.[33]

A new clothing style starts with designers and manufacturers, but among their offerings only those having a particular resonance with the cultural moment take hold.[34] The development of specific networks of production, advertising, and distribution created necessary but not sufficient conditions for the adoption of fashion styles—social and cultural factors wielded decisive power in the development of fashion and its meaning.[35] Some scholars contend that certain formal properties of design—constricting clothes, for example—equate naturally with certain social meanings, such as female oppression. At the other end of the spectrum are those who believe fashion symbolism is so arbitrary that it may assume a limitless array of meanings.[36] In reality, fashion's cultural meaning at any historical moment is neither intrinsic nor arbitrary. Although a particular fashion detail could assume any one of a number of cultural meanings in the late nineteenth century, the dress code had inherent properties that shaped and limited the range of messages it could offer. In particular, fashion tended to reinforce a cultural emphasis on change, body politics, and highly visible social interactions. Each offered important opportunities and restraints for fashion's expressive potential.

The consumer advice that appeared in catalogs and magazines under headings such as "The Newest Spring Gowns" or "The Newest Design in Bodices" is testimony to fashion's bias toward change.[37] As large-scale change represented one of the most striking social facts of the era, adapting and manipulating fashion provided an important way people could integrate the "restlessness of the age" into their lives. Some writers have seen the succession of styles as nothing more than a lure to trap people on a consumer culture treadmill.[38] Others detect a subversive quality to this process, arguing that fashion provides a space in which the exploration of alternatives is not only sanctioned but expected.[39] Indeed, clothing practices provided opportunities both to welcome and to stand apart from change. In line with its paradoxical and flexible structure, fashion provided both submissive and subversive means of orienting oneself amid the tendencies of the day.

Besides its focus on change, fashion is inescapably about the body and about the body's relationship to individual identity and social power— Miss Deland expressed as much when she distinguished between her appearance as a modern businesswoman and that of a sentimental Victorian. Fashion descriptions that moved methodically from sleeve to neck to bodice to skirt were characteristic of a time when the strategies of mass production suggested that social control could involve the discipline of individual bodies through regulation of their component parts.[40] The inch-by-inch demarcations of the human figure in catalog measuring diagrams evoke this type of bodily discipline, as do fashion illustrations in which sleeves, collars, and bodices float unattached through space, awaiting reassembly into a personage (Figures 1, 2). The pieces provide a sort of "identity kit" one could use to assemble a corporeal self, even if only from a prescribed range of options.[41] Once again, however, the incessant change of fashion offered the possibility of continual

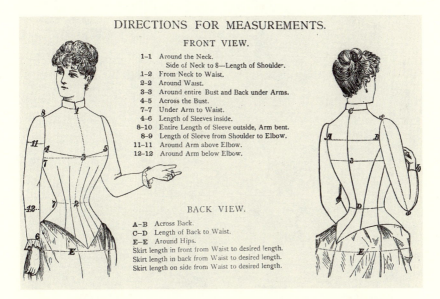

DIRECTIONS FOR MEASUREMENTS.

FRONT VIEW.

1–1	Around the Neck.
	Side of Neck to 8—Length of Shoulder.
1–2	From Neck to Waist.
2–2	Around Waist.
3–3	Around entire Bust and Back under Arms.
4–5	Across the Bust.
7–7	Under Arm to Waist.
4–6	Length of Sleeves inside.
8–10	Entire Length of Sleeve outside, Arm bent.
8–9	Length of Sleeve from Shoulder to Elbow.
11–11	Around Arm above Elbow.
12–12	Around Arm below Elbow.

BACK VIEW.

A–B	Across Back.
C–D	Length of Back to Waist.
E–E	Around Hips.

Skirt length in front from Waist to desired length.
Skirt length in back from Waist to desired length.
Skirt length on side from Waist to desired length.

Figure 1. This measuring chart from an 1890s mail-order catalog asks the customer to supply eighteen measurements with her order. It shows the precision with which the bodily image had to be constructed to fulfill the requirements of fashionable dress. Deutsch & Company, *Catalogue: 1891 Fall and Winter* (New York, 1891): 25. Reproduced courtesy of the Winterthur Library: Printed Book and Periodical Collection.

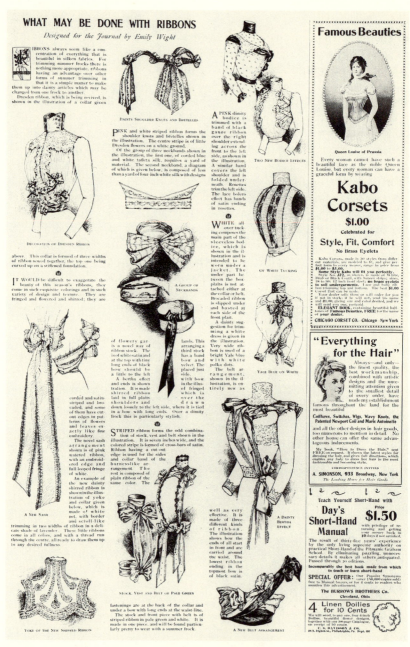

Figure 2. The idea of clothing as an "identity kit" is represented in layouts such as this one, which suggest a sense in which the individual is fashioned through the skillful combination of component parts. Emily Wight, "What May Be Done with Ribbons," *Ladies' Home Journal* (June 1899): 25. Reproduced courtesy of the Winterthur Library: Printed Book and Periodical Collection.

reinvention, and thus the logic of fashion could serve both as a force for control and as an impetus to creativity, could afford opportunities both for conforming and rebelling, and could lead to both repression and expression. The fashion system controlled the body *and* offered it the opportunity to act out.[42]

Dress is also inextricably linked to the social presentation of the self and highly visual forms of social interaction.[43] A concern for appearances, a consciousness of being judged, and an emphasis on reading interior truths from surface details all held special meaning for people at the end of the nineteenth century. As the United States urbanized, throwing large numbers of strangers into daily contact, and as market relations covered greater distances with increasing impersonality, the importance of managing and interpreting presentations of the self increased. Susan Snow's concern for dress and etiquette showed her clear understanding of this process: "We appeared 'out' Sunday in our all finery. . . . I guess we made an impression. J[unction] C[ity] is quite a dressy place. I have begun to receive callers. Yesterday I had five, and I have received a number before. All the tony folks are calling."[44] A presumed relationship between personal appearance and personal character is deeply embedded in Western thought, but in the late nineteenth century the proliferation of visual media and the need of an increasingly urbanized population to deal each day with "a world of strangers" created a new emphasis on self-presentation and the interpretation of visual culture. This fascination for determining the essential qualities of an individual from available surface clues affected cultural enterprises as diverse as art criticism, psychology, and detective fiction, which all fixated at this time on the effort to discern an inner truth from external, often seemingly irrelevant, details.[45] For etiquette writers and fashion watchers, this was validation of their work. Advice manuals often exhorted people to understand that dress and physical appearances were not only important, they were the essence of interpersonal contact: "The outward garb is usually indicative of the inward personality of the wearer; and our first impressions of those we casually meet are more often formed on the fit of their clothes and their manner of wearing them than upon anything they do or say."[46]

This book focuses mainly on gender, but such a focus by itself oversimplifies the cultural work of fashion. By looking at patterns in the rhetoric and imagery that surrounded clothing practices, I will also show how contested ideologies of class, citizenship, and individualism figured in the consumption of clothing at this time. Members of the middle class, seeking to maintain status amid a variety of threatening circumstances, repeatedly used dress to define themselves against the upper class (by their dress you would see they were decadent) and the lower class (by their dress you would see they were unrefined). For instance, in an 1898 article Edward Bok unfavorably compared men in "frock coats and silk hats going to teas and receptions" with those men "at their places of business, dressed as is most suitable for the purposes of business." Bok addressed class relations by suggesting the idleness and unproductiveness of the rich, and he tied this to gender roles in hinting at a certain effeminacy in the tea-party men. Bok deliberately overlapped the two criticisms and cultural categories, conveniently using dress as a means of doing so. In the same article, he derogated the lower classes, again using dress as a medium, when he warned readers that "to overdress one's station in the world is always in poor taste." He added, "When a young man wears clothes beyond his means he invariably shows it." Working-class aspirations to fashionable dress—and workers' success at achieving a reasonable facsimile thereof—irritated and alarmed etiquette writers throughout the last part of the nineteenth century.[47]

Another aspect of personal identity examined in this book is national identity, a subject of intense debate at the turn of the century as the United States became a colonial power controlling territory from Puerto Rico to Guam at the same time that foreign-born immigrants and their children began to comprise a majority of the population in many American cities.[48] Both developments raised questions about what it meant to be an American, and the established middle class responded positively to recommendations that "the American woman's dress may bear the stamp of patriotism" while regarding uneasily the working-class immigrant's self-satisfaction in attaining "a proud sense of being dressed like other Americans."[49]

Consumption of goods was not a separate, sideline activity that existed apart from an individual's effort to construct an identity based on certain ideals of gender, class, or citizenship. Rather, consumer goods provided the resources out of which an individual could fabricate such an identity.[50] Fashion is central to identity construction because it is inherently personal and social at the same time—literally serving as the boundary between self and society—and because it enables people to reconcile several categories of cultural identity simultaneously. Fashion distinctions detailed in advice literature of the late nineteenth century give physical presence to social definitions of masculine and feminine, public space and private space, business and leisure, to name just a few. All these distinctions were apparent in the actions of Miss Deland, and etiquette writers strove to establish them as the behavioral norm. For example, they maintained gender definitions by criticizing women who were "donning masculinity, not only in their garments but in their ideas"; guarded the distinction between public and private by warning that a woman should "not appear on foot upon the streets in a dress suited only for the carriage, nor . . . walk or drive in a costume appropriate alone for the home"; and distinguished labor and leisure by prescribing certain attire for work, advising that "ladies who are employed . . . [in] business of any kind should wear a dress different from the usual walking suit."[51]

These categories overlap in clothing, just as they do in individual life and society as a whole. Classifications of gender, class, self, and national identity manifested themselves concretely and recognizably through clothing in every person's daily routine, in every social interaction, in every glance. If we consider the way dress organizes different categories of social knowledge simultaneously, we might be able to ascertain how one set of relationships is overlaid upon others and why it is so difficult to disentangle them. By looking at the manner in which ideologies of gender, class, or citizenship emerge in categories of dress, we can see more clearly how these ideologies operate in society and upon individuals.[52]

To explore these issues of fashion and personal identity, this book relies heavily on four kinds of publications that achieved special prominence during the last part of the nineteenth century: popular magazines, trade publications for advertising and clothing, mail-order catalogs, and etiquette manuals.

Magazines, particularly the new breed of women's magazines, began at this time to circulate on a scale never before contemplated by periodical publishers. By the mid-1890s, magazines such as *Ladies' Home Journal* and *Delineator* had circulations well above a half-million. Total magazine circulation in the United States jumped from 4 million in 1865 to 18 million in 1890 to 64 million in 1905. These publications not only made changes in fashion much more accessible, they also pioneered many editorial and advertising strategies that came to characterize the mass media. Indeed, they were among the first publications underwritten primarily by advertisers rather than subscribers, and their extensive use of drawings and photographs set the early standard for mass-produced visual images.[53]

Trade journals devoted to a wide variety of business interests appeared in the last part of the nineteenth century. As one journalist commented in 1890: "The multiplication of trade and class papers during the past ten years has been something enormous. Almost every line of industrial endeavor has one or more organs which represent, or misrepresent, its interests."[54] *Clothing Gazette*, the first journal to give extensive coverage to ready-made clothing, began publishing in 1881. *Printers' Ink*, the first major advertising journal, was founded in 1888. Their pages suggest that by the mid-1890s they had broadly dispersed readership, including many subscribers in small towns far from major markets.[55] Such publications offer insight into the emergence of a mass marketing mentality, showing upon close examination just how ambivalent and complex this phenomenon seemed, even to its creators.

Mail-order catalogs had existed for centuries, but it was in the 1870s, according to one historian, that they "abruptly became major marketing tools." In the 1890s, a surge in the scale of mail-order operation further boosted the circulation of these catalogs. In 1884 Montgomery Ward, then in its twelfth year of catalog sales, had sixty-five employees. By 1899, the company employed two thousand. Sears, Roebuck and Company did not even exist before the late 1880s, but by 1899 the company had two thousand employees and sales of $8.5 million. Aided in the last third of the century by an expanding population, transportation and communications breakthroughs, the increase in mass-produced goods, and friendly government action (such as the start of the Rural Free Delivery postal system in 1896), hundreds of manufacturers and big-time retailers established immense and profitable mail-order divisions. Catalogs provided a working model for long-distance customer relations, standardized goods, and pictorial advertising, reflecting the new regime of business interaction and social relations that took hold during this period.[56]

Etiquette books also enjoyed a publishing boom in the late 1800s. The best (though by no means complete) bibliography of this genre indicates that approximately seventy new titles appeared between 1885 and 1900. Such works struck a special chord with readers of the time, as further indicated by the enormous number of people who wrote seeking advice from etiquette writers at magazines such as the *Ladies' Home Journal.* Daily newspapers also began to feature advice columns starting in the mid-1890s. Most etiquette books carried a strong subtext of social conservatism, and their contents (not to mention their appearance as mass-market commodities) demonstrate various ways in which the middle class attempted to deny, deflect, or take control of trends that challenged its established position.[57]

All these sources frequently asserted the close link between individual identity and clothing, as did newspaper articles and advertisements, contemporary fiction, diaries, letters, and memoirs. This linkage was a well-recognized motif in stories people told about themselves, in stories advertisers and etiquette writers told to their readers, in stories that literary artists told about fictional characters. Thus a young immigrant girl in Cleveland who worked alongside the boss's children in an 1890s sweatshop saw class distinctions develop in specific ways as the business made the boss more prosperous: "Soon, his children underwent a remarkable change. They dressed differently from the rest of us, and looked with scorn upon our poor clothing, and our poor lives." An advertiser in 1890s Chicago published an illustration that showed a dapper man making a favorable impression on a young woman and asked its readers:

"Don't it beat all what a difference good clothes make?" An etiquette writer reported that "he never yet met with a woman whose general style of dress was chaste, elegant and appropriate, that he did not find her on further acquaintance to be, in disposition and mind, an object to admire and love."[58]

In an ambitious literary effort to capture the transformation of American culture, Theodore Dreiser used clothing descriptions on page after page to describe people's attitudes and attributes in his novel *Sister Carrie*, first published in 1900. As the title character moves to the city and confronts new objects, images, people, and ideas, her regard for others is frequently expressed by her observations of their clothing. Within the first few dozen pages, she meets a stranger and finds that "there was something satisfactory in the attention of this individual with his good clothes," imagines the rich and powerful as "counting money, dressing magnificently, and riding in carriages," and walks down the street and feels "ashamed in the face of the better dressed girls who went by." Throughout the book, characters are introduced by specific fashion details ("His suit was of a striped and crossed pattern of brown wool, new at that time, but since become familiar as a business suit"), and Carrie soaks up detailed fashion advice ("Why don't you get yourself one of those nice serge skirts they're selling at Lord & Taylor's? . . . They're the circular style, and they're going to be worn from now on"). Her rise in the world is marked by a progression from "a worn shirt-waist of dotted blue percale" to a "little tan jacket with large mother-of-pearl buttons which was all the rage that fall." Dreiser characterizes the expressive properties of clothing as "the voice of the so-called inanimate." Indeed, in a chapter titled "The Persuasion of Fashion," Carrie imagines she can hear her fashion accessories actually speaking to her:

"My dear," said the lace collar she secured from Partidge's, "I fit you beautifully; don't give me up."
"Ah, such little feet," said the leather of the soft new shoes; "how effectively I cover them."[59]

Many writers have characterized fashion as fundamentally irrational. Even its advocates, such as an 1890s writer in the *Woman's Home Companion*, have suggested that "fashion is the absolute despot whose capricious behests make thousands upon thousands do her bidding whether it pleases their own sweet will or not."[60] My contention to the contrary is that the essential importance of clothing lies in its capacity to make sense. Clothing is a daily factor in our ability to comprehend the world. By examining the meaning of clothes in the 1890s, one sees the conflicted, contradictory way a culture changes, moving inexorably forward while remaining embedded in its past. [61]

Chapter 1

Men's Clothing
"A Ready-Made Look"

In 1895, when the editorial committee for a proposed encyclopedia of American industry needed someone to write a history of clothing manufacture, they turned to the head of a company that claimed to be "the largest manufacturers and retailers of fine clothing, ready to wear, in the United States." The man, William C. Browning, proudly wrote: "If it be true, as I think it is, that the condition of a people is indicated by its clothing, America's place in the scale of civilized lands is a high one. We have provided not alone abundant clothing at a moderate cost for all classes of citizens, but we have given them at the same time that style and character in dress that is essential to the self-respect of a free, democratic people." Browning was an eminent merchant whose firm, Browning, King & Company, had a seven-story factory in New York, a warehouse in Chicago, and fifteen retail stores scattered from Boston, Massachusetts, to Lincoln, Nebraska. Despite his claims, Browning remained acutely aware of how tenuous and recent the respectability of his product was: "To-day one can hardly fancy what an uphill road the early manufacturers traveled before the high quality of their wares was recognized."[1]

Although Browning asserted that prejudice against ready-made clothing had "altogether disappeared," his firm still felt compelled to state in advertisements in the 1890s that its clothes were "as good . . . as you can get from the tailor shop." A monthly publication the company sent to customers included humorous anecdotes and sales pitches arguing that ready-made suits were "undeniably superior" to custom clothes and refuting "the unconscionable advertisements of the small tailor" who claimed otherwise. One blurb asserted that Browning, King clothes presented "a significant exception to a pretty general rule" that ready-made clothing lacked style. The boastfulness and lingering defensiveness in these claims underscore both the considerable progress of the ready-made industry and its continued insecurity.[2]

Historians have usually described the success of men's ready-made clothing as occurring much earlier than 1895 and meeting little resistance. They have advocated every decade from the 1820s to the 1850s as the period when ready-mades triumphed.[3] These claims have merit with respect to sales, but examining the terms under which manufactured clothing gained acceptance sheds a different light on the ready-made revolution. At the end of the century, many clothing manufacturers besides Browning took pains to promote their wares as "equal to custom made" and tried to distance themselves from the industry's past. In 1893, the *Clothing Gazette* recalled that "previous to the late civil war the product consisted of little else than cheap, plain stuffs . . . and anything like a fit was a rarity. Moreover, there was a pretty solid prejudice, not altogether unfounded, against both the product and the producers." Clothiers in the 1890s betrayed continued self-doubts with such carefully hedged advertising claims as: "We guarantee each of our garments to be as near 'merchant tailor standards' as is possible to manufacture in ready-to-wear clothing."[4]

Although men's ready-made clothing may have achieved a certain marketplace success by the 1850s, the values and standards associated with the custom trade continued to exert influence for a long time thereafter. Ready-made clothing finally achieved acceptance not simply because it offered a convenient and less expensive alternative to custom clothing but because it also managed to appropriate some of the older values associated with made-to-measure garments. Fashion and advertising helped establish a new norm for middle-class masculinity that attempted to maintain old prerogatives of dignity and individualistic autonomy while embracing the new efficiencies and comforts of standardization and large-scale enterprise.

Examining men's ready-made clothing reveals how social tensions of the 1890s—between a longing for stability and a belief in progress, for example, or between male ideals of self-control and those of physical aggressiveness—were at least partially contained, if not resolved. A garment or an advertisement could embody contradictory impulses in a seemingly unified whole. The materiality of the garment and the seeming naturalness of an advertising image masked social contradictions and rendered them manageable in everyday life, providing both an index and example of a new amalgam of middle-class American values (Figure 3). Ambivalent acceptance of factory clothing paralleled a simultaneous redefinition of masculinity; male attire provided a ubiquitous representation of this redefined masculine role and even (in the case of ideal body types) helped constitute it.

Historians have offered a variety of explanations for the growth of the manufactured clothing industry. Those who see ready-made clothing as a democratizing force cite the political influence of Jacksonian democracy in the 1830s. Others cite urbanization, which not only supplied a concentrated labor force but also produced a new population of white-collar

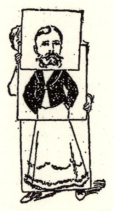

Much of the ready-made clothing makes a man look ridiculous.

They sound well in the advertisements, look first rate in the window, and the prices are regular "bankrupt sale" "forced-to-the-wall" figures.

But goodness! when you've worn 'em a week they look like "an assortment," they're all out of shape.

These Rogers, Peet & Co. Men's Spring Suits are the opposite of all this—fit, style, tailoring right.

"Money back if you want it" is your "satisfaction-insurance" policy here.

F. M. ATWOOD,
N. W. Cor. Madison and Clark Sts.

Figure 3. This advertisement's odd illustration suggests the elements of self-presentation and gender anxiety that the clothing system embodied in the 1890s. The ad also demonstrates the still tenuous acceptance of ready-made apparel, opening with the words: "Much of the ready-made clothing makes a man look ridiculous." F. M. Atwood advertisement, *Chicago Tribune* (May 18, 1898): 5.

workers who expanded the market for ready-made clothing. Still others look to the enormous expansion of the United States in the rural areas of the South and West as crucial to the industry's development. The aggressiveness and business acumen of the New York merchants also have been highlighted.[5] To some extent all these factors influenced the rise of ready-made clothing, although none satisfactorily explains why men's clothing developed so differently from women's with regard to ready-mades.

William Browning's background and career exemplify much of the history of men's clothing in the United States. After a couple of false starts running general stores in Connecticut, his father established himself in the early 1830s as a dry goods jobber in New York. In 1848 he opened a branch store in California that soon specialized in selling cheap ready-made clothing to gold-rush miners. Browning joined his father's firm in 1850 and branched out a few years later with a different partner, selling mostly to southern markets. He managed to recover from the loss of $500,000 in confiscated assets at the start of the Civil War by landing a government contract to supply $1.25 million worth of Union military uniforms. After the war, thanks to its manufacturing expertise, aggressive expansion, and heavy advertising, Browning, King grew into the enterprise that the *Clothing Gazette* would designate "the premier clothiers of America." A *New York Tribune* reference work in 1895 described Browning himself as "among the leading merchants of this generation."[6]

The Browning family bypassed one part of the industry's development: the early sale of clothes to sailors from shops near the waterfront, where the first American ready-mades appeared in the late eighteenth or early nineteenth century. These garments were given the disparaging name "slops," a term referring to sailors' garments. This may be the origin of the term "sloppy dresser," since "slops" soon came to designate all cheap, ill-fitting clothes, but especially those that were ready-made. The first ready-made clothing stores, known as "slop shops," thus catered mainly to seamen and others in need of a quick and cheap set of clothes. These shops "were used only by those who either had little concern for size and fit or placed a premium upon a quick change."[7]

The manufactured clothing industry grew substantially in the second quarter of the nineteenth century, but its markets were mostly downscale: rural Southerners, including slaves; soldiers from the Mexican-American War; and rootless frontiersmen such as California gold rush adventurers or railroad workers. Entrepreneurs in the Northeast, who were close to a growing immigrant labor pool, flourishing textile mills, and ports that could be used to import raw materials and export finished products, organized manufacturing operations in the major cities and shipped products south and west to markets that were as yet undeveloped industrially.[8] New York, Boston, Philadelphia, and Baltimore became primary clothing centers, accounting for the majority of production in the country.[9]

After the Civil War, an increasing number of companies began to manufacture suits as well as work clothes, and more men began to consider these suits acceptable substitutes for custom-tailored clothing.[10] One historian estimated that in 1880 less than half of men's clothing was purchased ready-to-wear, but by the mid-1890s the figure had grown to more than 90 percent. Census figures show the total value of the men's clothing industry output climbed from $48.3 million in 1849 to $414.5 million in 1899.[11] This increase undoubtedly reflects the dramatic rise of the ready-made industry, although various problems with census techniques make exact assessments—or closer comparisons with the custom trade or with women's clothing—virtually impossible.[12] By the mid-1890s, however, William Browning could justifiably claim that "though progress was slow, little by little the early prejudice, founded upon the character of the 'slop' clothes, was overcome."[13]

Technology seems to have played a relatively minor role in the industry's development. The manufacture of sewing machines began to take off in the 1850s, but their impact was small before the Civil War and cannot be regarded as decisive during the period when the men's ready-made industry took root. The weak influence of technology was underscored by the fact that the adoption of the sewing machine did not substantially increase the output of women's ready-made clothing. Quite the contrary, it primarily increased the standards of complexity expected in custom and home production because a woman could produce more elaborate tucks and trimming with a machine than she could without one.[14]

The early industrialization of the textile industry also had a remarkably slight impact on garment production. As Jesse Pope wrote shortly after the turn of the century: "Despite the fact that the introduction of machinery made it possible to supply an abundance of raw material that would bring it practically within reach of all, half a century went by before the fruits began to be realized in so far as our wearing apparel was concerned, and the industry of furnishing such apparel did not become of great importance until almost an entire century had lapsed." Indeed, as late as 1904, most men's clothing manufacturers in Baltimore still used foot-powered sewing machines and pressed clothes with a "goose," a hand iron that had changed little over centuries.[15]

Some trends associated with industrialization, such as the division of labor, did affect the clothing business. When Edwin Freedley, author of a number of books on business practice and history, visited one of New

York's largest clothing companies in 1856, he declared that the "operations of this establishment are thoroughly systematized." The system he described was fairly rudimentary, but it was a large step from a process in which an individual tailor created a garment single-handed. A few years later Charles Cist reported on a Cincinnati business that had subdivided the work of making a pair of pants among seventeen people. At the end of the century, Jesse Pope reported on a company that used thirty-nine steps—and thirty-nine workers—to manufacture a man's coat.[16]

In broader terms, men's clothing did reflect the changes that made late nineteenth-century consumption patterns distinctive: large-scale production, mass media advertising, and impersonal selling relationships. The upsurge in clothing manufacturing contributed to the "avalanche of factory-produced goods" that swept over the country during this time.[17] In addition, clothiers came to embrace wholeheartedly the power of both the mass media and visual images. As the *Clothing Gazette,* a leading trade periodical for men's clothing, proclaimed in 1895: "Snappy advertisements that will catch people's attention, awaken their interest, and extract their cash, are necessary nowadays. You can't do business without them." One clothing merchant argued that striking advertising illustrations were essential because they communicated more quickly, provided a message understandable to an urban population still learning English, and made ads more difficult for a competitor to copy.[18] Finally, the expansion of Browning, King's clothing empire to more than a dozen cities reflected the trend toward less personalized, less localized relationships between buyers and sellers. To handle the enormous quantity of goods, new systems of marketing developed; department stores, mail-order companies, and advertising all became big businesses during this period. Standardization of goods made a one-price policy possible; the scale of the urban marketplace made it necessary, further changing the context of acquisition. In earlier transactions the buyer knew the seller, negotiated the price, and sought a product that was custom-made or custom-measured. Increasingly by the 1890s, such transactions involved a payment to a stranger, a fixed price, and a pre-made product.[19] The division of labor within industry, coupled with long-distance marketing and a more impersonal retail setting, meant that neither manager, nor worker, nor consumer could form a complete picture of the object's "career." A commodity's capacity to incorporate symbolic meanings for such categories as gender, class, or national identity could thus no longer depend on the user's firsthand acquaintance with the object's producer or the method of its production. Instead, fashion and advertising assumed an increasingly pivotal role in providing shared names and social categories—that is to say, meaning—for the goods.[20]

As the turn of the century approached, white, middle-class men sought to create an identity congruent with the changing economic and social world while retaining older ideals that promoted their own privilege and self-esteem. The social and cultural dimensions of this effort are revealed in clothing consumption. To understand these gender dynamics, however, one must appreciate the extent to which men did *not* unreservedly accept ready-made clothing by midcentury—or for a long time thereafter. The uniformity of standardized clothing apparently did not mesh with the consumer's self-image because a preference for custom-made goods haunted suit manufacturers and retailers throughout the nineteenth century.[21]

It is true that industry commentators offered testimony for the early, widespread adoption of ready-made clothing, but these accounts require serious qualification. In 1849, the "Mercantile Miscellanies" section of Freeman Hunt's *Merchants' Magazine and Commercial Review* claimed that manufacturers had begun producing ready-made clothing for "all markets and for all classes of men, from the humblest laborer to the fashionable gentleman." When Edwin Freedley surveyed the American business scene in the 1850s, he concluded: "Within the last quarter of a century a most important and complete revolution has been effected in the ancient and respectable occupation of tailoring, as well as in a branch of the Dry Goods Trade, by the introduction of ready made clothing."[22]

The boosterish tone of such evaluations invites skepticism, as does their placement in publications avowedly aimed at serving business interests. Hunt's self-proclaimed purpose was "to represent and advocate the claims of Commerce."[23] Opposing viewpoints offered by other observers raise further doubts. In the same year that Hunt touted the widespread acceptance of ready-made clothing, a newspaper journalist sarcastically described the clothing "revolution": "You may have experienced some difficulty and vexation in getting your tailor in Broadway to fit you? Pshaw! Step into the nearest clothing store on Chatham-street and slip on a coat—any coat—and we'll wager our wedding suit that it is a 'splendid fit.' There is no such thing as an ill-fitting coat in Chatham-street. Every coat there fits everyone." He went on to describe the interior of the typical clothing store: "Stooping, as you enter the low, dark doorway, you find yourself in the midst of a primitive formation of rags, carefully classified into vests, coats, and pantaloons."[24]

A clothing store at this time might well have had a "puller-in" standing in the doorway to drag business in off the street, sometimes literally. Inside the store, no effort was made at display or enticement. Customers encountered the goods heaped on tables and faced high-pressure sales tactics rather than courteous service. The journalist's encounter with the ready-made clothing store was all too typical, as was his disdain for the goods.[25]

Thus, although in the late 1850s Charles Cist declared Cincinnati to be "the largest market for ready made clothing in the country," it comes as no surprise to find that throughout that decade, listings and advertisements in the city directory indicated that tailoring establishments far outnumbered ready-made stores, and that most "clothiers" specified that they also did custom work or sold dry goods. Although manufacturers had the advantage of offering lower prices, the prices had limited appeal if they only reinforced the notion that such goods were low class. More than thirty years later, the Cincinnati Chamber of Commerce still trumpeted the *future* capture of the custom market by ready-made clothing by asserting that the quality of manufactured clothes continued to improve and that "the product of the manufacturer is becoming more and more a dangerous competitor to the tailor."[26]

By the last decade of the century, the *Clothing Gazette* estimated that 80 percent of men wore ready-made clothing, and it pointedly distinguished the industry's output from that produced only a few years before: "It must be admitted that, in comparison with the garments of to-day, the ready-made clothing of 1875 was not much to boast of."[27] In 1916, the U.S. Department of Commerce averred that the rapid development of the clothing industry did not begin until at least 1880; in 1926, Harvey Morris, writing at the behest of the Hickey-Freeman Clothing Company of Rochester, New York, claimed that even in the 1880s ready-made clothing was "totally lacking in style, quality and tailoring"; in 1950, *Men's Wear* suggested that in 1890 "ready-to-wear clothing, was, not withstanding all the progress which had been made in its manufacture and distribution, still in general disrepute."[28]

Of course, these writers' connections to the industry suggest certain vested interests of their own. It was good business to claim the superiority of the current product, as well as a sign of allegiance to the gospel of progress that characterized this age of technological innovation and business expansion. Yet such comments reflect the image problems that dogged ready-made clothing, problems that only began with the quality of standardized garments. Popular agitation against sweatshop conditions and other exploitive labor practices also brought disrepute. Furthermore, the industry's reliance on a foreign-born workforce ran counter to growing feelings of nationalism and concerns about racial purity.

Custom-made clothing represented more than superior workmanship; it also symbolized social status, belonging, and identity. The alternative designations of the custom-made business—"bespoke tailoring" and the "order trade"—imply a mastery of circumstances and security of position. In contrast, ready-made clothes (whether they were secondhand or not) were known as "hand-me-downs" throughout the nineteenth century.[29] Custom-made apparel provided a better fit, both physically and psychologically; it guaranteed one was in step with fashion and offered a one-to-one relationship between buyer and seller that reaffirmed an individual sense of self. An 1885 book on men's dress stressed that "when sufficiently cultivated, the young man feels that his wear must be custom made, instead of a hap-hazard selection from those great stocks of alleged clothing which flood the country from establishments patterned, as it were, on the manufactories of Birmingham and Manchester, making goods for the colonies with every implication that the inhabitants were savages." According to the author, one must seek out those tailor shops where "a man is not dressed in a minute, but his peculiarities of frame are made the subject of careful study, and his adaptability to special styles and colors is seen in the light of experience and cultivated judgment."[30]

For men, the most significant fashion developments of the era were the nearly universal adoption of the sack suit for almost all occasions and the modification of these suits into something close to the form they have carried into the twenty-first century (Figure 4). These changes marked the eclipse of a careful Victorian bourgeois etiquette of sack coats, frock coats, cutaways, and tails—each with its appropriate usage according to the time of day or the protocols of a specific occasion. By

No. 281. $1.00   No. 266. $1.00   No. 294. $1.00   No. 297. $1.00

Figure 4. The men's sack suit gained increasing acceptance as appropriate attire for a variety of occasions. The generic advertising illustrations pictured above were available at $1 each to merchants who wished to use them in advertisements. Thus not only the garments but also the images of them came under the sway of mass production and mass communications. *Gibson's Clothing Gazette* (September 1895). Reproduced from the collections of the Library of Congress.

the early 1900s, a well-equipped wardrobe could have consisted entirely of sack suits.[31] This fashion development had considerable symbolic significance because by the turn of the century, the three-piece suit had clearly become the lowest common denominator in male attire. Even working-class men often owned at least one suit, and for middle-class men it was virtually a uniform.[32]

The sack suit illustrates how a successful clothing style must accommodate business conditions and aesthetic desires but must also embody broader cultural needs. Its boxy shape suited large-scale manufacture better than its form-fitting predecessors, and its appearance showed a discernible stylistic connection to earlier garments.[33] Just as important, however, the sack suit fit the cultural moment in other ways, providing symbolic resources to balance competing ideals of progress and stability, society and the individual, self-control and self-expression. Issues of gender were also prominent, as when trade publications distinguished "manly" from "effeminate" styles of overcoats.[34] The focus on gender definitions in clothing echoed an emphasis on gender definitions in the wider culture, where the sack suit served a new ideal of middle-class masculinity.

Although historians have often applied the phrase "crisis of masculinity" to the late nineteenth century, the phrase downplays the extent to which gender roles are continually in the process of reconstruction and has ominous connotations that are perhaps overwrought. Nonetheless, the basic assumption underlying use of the term—that masculinity was in transition during the period as the result of widespread economic and social changes—remains sound.[35] The effects of this transition, and the eventual configuration of old and new values that emerged, can be traced in men's clothing habits. As the concern with "manly" style shows, the political economy of clothing presented itself forthrightly as an arena for struggles involving the political economy of gender.

Historians have identified various models of masculinity available to men through the nineteenth century and developed a variety of typologies and chronologies to explain them.[36] Virtually all agree, however, that the Victorian middle-class male ideal of the last half of the nineteenth century emphasized strength achieved through self-mastery. The middle-class stress on gentility, respectability, and dignity echoed this principle, reflecting an effort to maintain or reassert control in the face of disruptive social influences.[37]

A variety of challenges threatened these men with loss of control as the century drew to a close. The increasing dominance of corporations and their vast managerial bureaucracies threatened republican ideals of economic independence and individuality; political and workplace challenges from women and immigrants threatened middle-class male power in those realms; new scientific concerns about the degeneration of the species and "race suicide" created further anxiety. Self-reliant, autonomous individualism—a prevalent masculine ideal in America since the founding of the republic—seemed far less attainable. The sense of threat became palpable as middle-class and upper-class Americans interpreted insurgent labor and political movements as harbingers of chaos and ruin. In 1896, the Populist political push so unnerved these classes that they launched a fear-mongering publicity effort that characterized Populist candidate William Jennings Bryan as an anarchist, revolutionary, blasphemer, and madman, arguing in apocalyptic terms that his candidacy represented the most dangerous menace to the nation since the beginning of the Civil War in 1861.[38]

American middle-class men responded to these pressures by cultivating a sense of virile self-assertion. The increased popularity of dude ranch visits, recreational hunting, and athletic competition all attest to an effort to revitalize the frontier spirit through outdoor activities. A pronounced effort to link militarism and masculinity accompanied the Spanish-American War in 1898. In America's new imperialistic agenda, "empire figures as the site where you can be all that you can no longer be at home—a 'real live man'—where you can recover the autonomy denied by the social forces of modernization."[39] Teddy Roosevelt's persona and his promotion of what he called "the strenuous life" served as both an example and an impetus for these developments.[40] In addition to these aggressive assertions of masculine identity, a new sharpness and insistence characterized attempts to draw lines of exclusion for women, for immigrants, and for homosexuals.[41]

Perhaps the most striking assertions of strenuous-life masculinity had to do with the body itself. A new, much more muscular male body ideal emerged, along with sports crazes for boxing, football, and bodybuilding. Men prized vigor, prowess and strength not only in one's character but also in one's physique. Theodore Roosevelt received this advice from his father: "Without the help of the body the mind can not go as far as it should. You must *make* your body." And the sickly, asthmatic young man followed this exhortation and through exercise regimens did essentially *make* his body into an emblem of manly strength. Yet though men were adapting to changed circumstances, embodying the exuberance and forcefulness of America's industrial rise and emergence as a world power, they did not want to forfeit their traditional sources of power and pleasure in the process. Thus the emerging masculine ideal, though embracing the future in many ways, also attempted to preserve many older values, including the steadfast dignity and individual self-mastery that traditionally equated with male privilege.[42]

The adoption of ready-made clothing provided perfect cover for this project. Taking possession of the ready-made business suit implied that the upheaval of industrialization had been mastered, while the relatively unchanging and unadorned styles provided comforting symbols of stability and continuity. The industry touted the ready-made suit as a testament to American industrial prowess and democratic freedom—an appealing claim during a decade when masculinity came to be ever more closely associated with militant American nationalism. Not coincidentally, ready-made suits strongly differentiated men's clothing from that of women in terms of its production, its aesthetic values, and its symbolic meaning.

Unlike other suit-coat styles—frock, cutaway, or tails—the sack coat had neither a cutaway nor a waist seam to soften or sculpt its outline. The *Clothing Gazette* explained the contrast in highly gendered terms. "Your 'paddocks' and other street-sweeping abortions may find favor with the sweet little five o'clock tea set, but real men don't like the long coats and that ends the matter. The 'covert' is a manly, sensible and dressy topcoat. Its *re-entre* means the death of the effeminacies of the beskirted school." The "beskirted school" mentioned by the *Clothing Gazette* columnist in his condemnation makes reference specifically to the flaring lower portion of a traditional frock coat, which the writer associated with "the ladylike school" of men's fashion. In contrast, the broad shoulders and padded chest of the sack suit created a massive, rectilinear form that corresponded to the new male body ideal. The 1890s fashion of wearing such coats buttoned all the way to the top further emphasized a big-chested, solid figure. This image-making extended into slang metaphors of the era; to call another man "square" was a high compliment, for the term denoted a sense of honor, courage, and dignity that was considered distinctly male. Teddy Roosevelt once commented how much he disliked a man "with shoulders that slope like those of a champagne bottle."[43]

The sack suit did not *have* to represent new ideas of masculinity, it was enough merely that it *could* represent them, gaining significance not through its intrinsic properties but because of its difference from the fashionable styles of coat that preceded it and because of its applicability to contemporary cultural needs.[44] If the male body was rediscovered at the turn of the century as a site for masculine assertion, then maximum differentiation of male and female body types—made culturally visible in dress—would be a logical means of demonstrating masculinity. Advice manuals at the time made this idea explicit: "Don't—we address here the male reader—wear anything that is pretty. What have men to do with pretty things? Select quiet colors and unobtrusive patterns, and adopt no style of cutting that belittles the figure." Indeed, any male too overtly interested in stylish attire risked ridicule. For example, the effeminate "dude" emerged as a stock character and object of derision in magazine cartoons during the 1880s. One publication in 1896 satirically described "the narrow sloping shoulders that made the dude immortal." The dude always wore old-fashioned, occasion-specific, probably custom-tailored clothing; his body was slender and his silhouette curved gracefully. His counterpart, the square-jawed, square-shouldered Rough Rider type, began to appear in magazine illustrations of the mid-1890s— and he was wearing a business suit (Figures 5, 6). In a speech at the Republican convention of 1900, Sen. Chauncey Depew praised Theodore Roosevelt's self-fashioned manliness by proclaiming that "the dude had become a cowboy, the cowboy had become a soldier, the soldier had become a hero."[45]

Although separate spheres for men and women may have been more of an ideological than a physical construct, the contrast between men's and women's clothing provided a portable and omnipresent metaphor for attempting to maintain the power relations of separate spheres in an era when the sexual division of labor faced increasing challenges.[46] The persistent, indeed sharpening, distinctions between men's and women's attire in the 1890s testifies to the continued potency of middle-class Victorian ideals of sex differentiation. These issues emerged in clothing discussion, sometimes in direct statements and other times in more subtle details of word usage and illustration. For instance, one Browning, King advertisement asserted outright that "it's only a dude who goes to the merchant tailor now-a-days to get his clothes," and a well-known New York clothier advertised: "Your boy will be manly according to the way he's treated. Put him into one of our 'mannish' topcoats; see how pleased he'll be, and you too, at him." One writer cautioned men to avoid anything flashy in the way of cufflinks, rings, or watch chains: "The charge of effeminacy is so repulsive to most men that many fly to the opposite extreme, and avoid every kind of adornment that savors of luxury of display." Another warned sales clerks that "the men you meet in business do not as a rule respect the loudly-dressed namby-pamby individual. . . . Manliness, gentility and honesty are to my mind the most requisite attributes of successful salesmanship."[47]

The posture and figure of men in advertisements tended to reflect the new body ideal—in more than one case the robust advocate of the strenuous life and his sack suit come to the foreground while other body types in other types of suits recede from view (Figures 7, 8). Another example emerges in the bulging biceps used to advertise the "Sandow suit" (Figure 9). The Sandow suit was named to capitalize on the popularity of Eugen Sandow, the most famous bodybuilder of the era, who first toured the United States amid a whirlwind of publicity in 1893 and 1894. Sandow was a popular culture phenomenon who inspired songs and physical culture disciples, became a best-selling author, and consulted

"GOD KNOWS I'M NOT THE THING I SHOULD BE!"

Figure 5. The "dude" was almost always dressed in older-style clothes and had a slender, sinuous body shape when he appeared in drawings and cartoons. He emerged as an object of ridicule late in the nineteenth century. *Life* (March 1896): 196.

Figure 6. The sack suit, which increasingly displaced frocks, cutaways, and tails at the end of the century, presented a massive, rather monolithic silhouette that corresponded to the new ideal body type for men. Hays, Goldberg & Company advertisement, *Gibson's Clothing Gazette* (April 1895): 23. Reproduced from the collections of the Library of Congress.

with luminaries including Theodore Roosevelt. The popularity of his muscle-bound figure itself indicates the development of a new ideal body type for men.[48] The middle-class man took pains to appear physically powerful, perhaps to compensate for real power that was eroding.[49] At the same time, he could insist that by purchasing ready-made clothes he had lost none of his self-respect, dignity, or command.

Clothing advertisements—like clothing styles—mixed older values of character associated with custom-made clothing with a more modern celebration of industry and progress. The clearest evidence of the continued allure of custom-made clothing is the clothiers' advertisements at the end of the nineteenth century, which show that custom tailoring remained the standard by which all clothes were measured. "Ours are equal to the creations of the exclusive merchant tailors," ran one ad for ready-made suits. "The kind that looks like custom-made and costs about half as much," said another. "Ask a man we have converted from custom garments, and he can give you but one answer—that our clothes are precisely as good as he has ever worn, and his year's bill surprisingly reduced," said a third. One Chicago clothier boasted in 1898 that his customers sometimes asked to have the labels removed from delivery

No. 232.	No. 233.	No. 234.	No. 235.
Fine Overcoat.	Elegant Sack Suit.	Cutaway Sack Suit.	Full Dress Suit.
Price, $10.00.	Price, $12.00.	Price, $9.00.	Price, $15.00.

Figure 7. The increased dominance of the sack suit demonstrated in displays such as this mail-order catalog, in which the men in top coat, sack suit, and "cutaway sack suit" appear solid and self-confident, while the figure in tails fades into the background. Simon Heyman, *Season of Fall 1891, Spring 1892* (Newark, N.J., 1891): 16. Reproduced courtesy of the Winterthur Library: Printed Book and Periodical Collection.

Figure 8. This company is promoting its ability to fit all body types, but the large, athletic figure on the left, who even looks a little like Theodore Roosevelt, dominates with his enormous size and aggressive stance. The other men, whose more rotund and slender body types had enjoyed their own vogues in the past, are smaller and turned away from the reader. Their suits also have a much more pronounced cutaway, and therefore old-fashioned, look. Lesser Brothers advertisement, *Gibson's Clothing Gazette* (January 1895): 29. Reproduced from the collections of the Library of Congress.

·· ·· The ·· ··
Sign of Success
···
··· The ···
Sandow
Suit.

SOLD ALL OVER THE LAND BY THE UP-TO-DATE DEAL-
ERS, BECAUSE THE MAKE, FIT, STYLE AND SELLING
POWER OF THE "SANDOW" IS SUPERIOR TO ANY
SUIT MADE. A LARGER AND HANDSOMER SELECTION
OF STYLES THAN WE HAVE EVER BEFORE SHOWN.

The Victory

Combination

CONSISTS OF AN EXTRA PAIR PANTS AND CAP.
SEWED, MADE AND FINISHED IN SUCH A MAN-
NER THAT WE CAN GUARANTEE THEM TO
THE MOST CRITICAL BUYER. THE STYLES
ARE MOST ATTRACTIVE AND WILL RETAIL AT
A GOOD PROFIT FOR $3.00. SEND FOR SAMPLES.

THE "SANDOW" KNEE PANTS ARE SUPPLIED WITH DOUBLE SEAT,
DOUBLE KNEES, PATENT BUTTONS AND EXTENSION WAISTBAND.

B. SCHLEESTEIN, 215=217 Greene Street, NEW YORK.

Figure 9. Sandow suit advertisements underscored the male ideal of a muscular
physicality, traits embodied in the person and performances of strongman
Eugen Sandow. B. Schleestein advertisement, *Gibson's Clothing Gazette* (January
1895): 71. Reproduced from the collections of the Library of Congress.

packages because without the labels no one would know they were buying ready-made. Sometimes clothing advertisements conveyed these attitudes more indirectly. A mass-produced "personalism" began to characterize ads, which increasingly struck a conversational tone and addressed the reader in the second person to simulate a one-to-one relationship: "It is worth your while to look into the merits of the best ready-made clothes before turning to a cheap tailor—in fact to any tailor. The old bugaboo tale, 'a ready-made look,' no longer applies to the rightly-made kind."[50]

Clothing retailers took other steps to accommodate the desire for an individual fit, offering a large and continually expanding variety of options to the consumer. A customer of the 1895 Montgomery Ward catalog could select from nearly 100 versions of the basic sack suit, while a few years later Rogers, Peet & Company advertised 325 styles. Early in the 1900s William Browning's organization pioneered the merchandising of half sizes and cuts for different body shapes—regular, regular short, stout, long, extra long. Shortly after World War I, one manufacturer offered forty-three different models of sack suits, each available in three styles of lining construction, three combinations of lining material, and nearly 1,100 varieties of cloth—a total of 278,000 possible combinations, resulting in the production of 400,000 suits a year in batches that rarely exceeded twenty. The desire to embody individual identity and social relationships in clothing did not give way; it persisted in a reformulated, ready-made incarnation.[51]

The multiplicity of clothing choices suggests that men at this time were not indifferent to fashion, but instead were pursuing an alternative dress code of their own. Recall Edward Bok's injunction that men avoid "frock coats and silk hats" in favor of more modern, businesslike attire. Such prescriptive writing did not exempt men from fashion except in the narrowest sense of the word, for it actually urged men to pay careful attention to the details of their clothing and to match it to the norms of middle-class masculinity. Advertisers understood this. One clothier's advertisement in the 1890s sought to "call your attention to the neat adjustment of the collars and lapels; the fine work on buttonholes and pockets, the excellent tailoring throughout." And if there were any doubt that such fashion savvy was perfectly compatible with the current embodiment of manliness, the same ad also promised a free football to any customer who spent at least $3.50 in the children's department.[52]

Ready-made manufacturers did not fight a purely defensive battle. They also sought to counter the attractions of custom clothing by capitalizing on whatever allure the modern age offered. Price was one advantage they often trumpeted at the direct expense of custom tailoring. Indeed, the mere existence of fixed-price retailing represented a significant change and major accommodation to the spreading culture of mass consumption.

Somewhat more subtly, the ads sought to convey a progressive and up-to-date image: "Gentlemen formerly patronising high-grade tailors come to us for *advanced* ideas in everything, and they're not disappointed." They promised to deliver the miracles of modern science—"it stands to reason pants made by steam power machines have no equal"—at a tempo that suited a hustling age: "Wait two weeks after you're measured and a few days more for vexatious alterations, pay a big price, and what have you got to show for it? A 'made to order' suit no better than we can sell you for half the cost or thereabout, and fit you in five minutes." Some ads encouraged progressivism and modernism for their own sake, stating simply: "Progression is the order of the day—it used to be tallow dip; now it's the electric light. So with Clothing. The old made-to-order method is superseded by the modern ready-to-wear idea." The ads suggested there was comfort in standardization—"no guess work; no tailor's say so"—and promoted pride in American achievement and advancement: "There never was a time in the history of this country when a man could dress so well for so little money as he can to-day." Advertisers, in other words, sought both to promote their goods as progressive products while at the same time claiming for them the time-honored appeal of custom work.[53]

In 1894, a David Marks & Sons ad offered "The New Declaration of Independence"—freedom from custom tailors: "Know all men by these presents that We, the well-dressed men of the United States do hereby declare our Independence of merchant tailors, having found ready-made clothing that is Equal to Custom made" (Figure 10).[54] Claiming traditional virtues for a nontraditional product has become a familiar advertising tactic. The David Marks ad, which associates a still-emerging industry with foundational elements of American heritage, provides an early example of this reconciliation of opposites. The ad also offers a rich visual text, another sign of the maturing advertising discourse. It depicts an elegantly attired, ready-made man aggressively thrusting his cane forward as he reads the declaration. He has appropriated both the modishness and prestige of fashion as well as a prideful nationalism and advocacy of the strenuous life characteristic of the day. In contrast, the merchant tailor—rotund, in shirt sleeves, outmoded cutting shears hanging at his side—assumes a deferential pose, perhaps vaguely indicating ethnic or European submissiveness. The ready-made side of the street has smooth concrete sidewalks, plate glass windows, and skyscrapers; the tailor's side of the street has flagstones and a row of shops more reminiscent of the bygone artisan age. Note, once again, that the ready-made side attempts not merely to assert the values of modernity and progressiveness but to absorb the qualities of tradition and fashionable identity previously associated with custom-made clothes.

THE NEW DECLARATION OF INDEPENDENCE
DAVID MARKS & SONS, 687 AND 689 BROADWAY, N.Y.

Figure 10. Ready-made clothiers were still taking pains to assert their "equality" with custom tailors in the 1890s, even though practically all men were already purchasing their goods. Through advertisements, ready-mades were associated with traditional values and American virtues, while still standing for progress and modernity. David Marks & Sons advertisement, *Clothing Gazette* (July 1894): 3. Reproduced from the collections of the Library of Congress.

Despite the meek posture of the tailor pictured in the David Marks ad, the custom clothing trade did not stand idly by while the ready-made merchants advanced their claims. In 1890, the *Custom Cutter,* a journal "published in the interests of merchant tailoring exclusively," noted the "alarming fact that the ready made trade is gradually and surely eating like a cancer into the very vitals of merchant tailoring."[55] In various ways, custom tailors joined the battle on their side with the same sense of imminent change and their own mixture of old and new values, but neither their garments nor their business practices could match the cultural moment in the same way that the ready-made sector did. Their suits and outmoded self-image did not imbibe enough of the modern, and custom tailors were noticeably reticent to use advertising, a medium that might have allowed them to recast their cultural position.

Nonetheless, the trade journal pronouncements of the custom trade reflected in their own way the transitional mix of old and new values. The *Custom Cutter,* for example, stated that tailoring on the one hand "embodies the scientific" and on the other was "high art." Thus, the tailor's work aspired to modern standards of efficiency and aggressiveness and deserved consideration as a profession, yet it also represented the honorable trade of "the artisan classes who are the sinews of any republic." The *Custom Cutter* emphasized its success in being able to "keep up in the march of progress" and gain its place in "this advanced age," but it also sought to restore the hereditary rights ("still practiced in European countries") by which sons naturally sought to follow their fathers into the business. The journal described women's designer Charles Frederick Worth as a romantic artist ("it has been reported that he did not design dresses, but that he dreamed them"), yet it also compared him to industrial geniuses like Fulton and Edison. In a single article, custom tailoring could be described as a science, an art, a trade, a profession, and a craft.[56]

Clearly, however, tailors' business sense owed more to artisanal practices than mass-market strategies. In the made-to-measure world, the tailor—not the customer or the marketplace—would decide what was desirable. The custom tailor would depend for his sales on the type of stylized, face-to-face interplay between buyer and seller that was being displaced elsewhere by mass merchandising. As one trade journal put it: "A cutter or tailor is not perfect in his art until in addition to the ability to make a fine fit he possesses the persuasive power which enables him to sell just what he thinks would look best on the man who patronises him." The *Practical Cutter and Tailor* commented on more than one occasion that perhaps the best way to deal with a complaining customer was merely to pretend to make requested changes and then assure the client that the desired alterations had been completed. One tailor related his success using this tactic in the following way: "The fact of the matter was . . . I never ripped out a blessed stitch in the coat or vest. I saw the garments were perfect in the first instance, and then I amused myself by humoring my patron, for the reason that he is a good customer and pays well."[57] Price, in this system, would not derive from the cost of materials or the lure of a mass market because tailors should charge according to their skill and artistry. The tailors bitterly denounced their colleagues who were "doing a discount business and advertising such" for lowering the "dignity and prestige" of the trade.[58]

Tailors' strategies for meeting the challenge of ready-mades included the promotion of fashion change that was so rapid that manufacturers would not be able to keep up. Tellingly, journals such as the *Custom Cutter* also suggested their subscribers switch to making women's clothing, which appeared more securely fixed in the realm of custom clothing: "Unlike men's tailoring, which has largely degenerated into the ready-made, the making of ladies' garments will always be a matter of individual skill and art." Although they praised "progress" and "staying up-to-date" on their own terms, the custom tailors' antimachine pronouncements ("a decline in natural ability inevitably follows the adoption of a machine") and ardent defense of the older, more elaborate dress etiquette (the idea that the sack suit might replace the frock and cutaway was "a threatened catastrophe") meant their garments clearly were oriented to the past rather than the future.[59]

Significantly, merchant tailors did not compete very effectively with the ready-made clothiers in the advertising arena. Charles Austin Bates, a self-styled advertising expert, noted that most tailors did not advertise and encouraged them to change their ways. Likewise, the advertising journal *Fame* took the tailors to task more than once for failing to realize the value of publicity. "If we look over the leading newspapers in the principal cities, and in the pages of the prominent magazines, we will find very few merchant tailors advertising," wrote one of its correspondents, "but not a paper or magazine we pick up is without a goodly share of ready-made clothing advertisements." The reason, according to the writer, was that the tailor believed "advertising was detrimental to his dignity." He urged them to rethink their priorities. Some months later another *Fame* writer noted the trade's aversion to advertising, which was again attributed to a misplaced sense of dignity, and urged tailors to abandon their longstanding reluctance and "kick over the traces of these mouldy traditions and do business in a businesslike way."[60]

Some custom tailors tried to adapt their business to the emerging retail world. Certain enterprising individuals established branch stores in different cities—in effect merchandising their names and reputations rather than their personal skills—and created advertisements similar to those of the ready-made manufacturers. Starting in the 1890s, a new branch of the industry called "tailor to the trade" began to adopt mail-order techniques. These tailors supplied local merchants in rural areas with sample books and measuring instructions and then filled their orders from a central location. By the turn of the century, hundreds of these operations inundated small-town retailers with solicitations for business. Sometimes the same company used different names so it could make "exclusive" offers to more than one merchant in the same town.[61]

The largest of these enterprises, the International Tailoring Company, sent out solicitations in 1903 that stated: "Formerly the small town men gave less consideration to the style of their clothes and were content with 'ready-mades,' but since the introduction of our goods in practically every town in the Union, the average well dressed man is wearing 'International' made-to-order garments." Among the company's promotional material was a brief piece of fiction distributed as a booklet called "The Label Mystery: Being a Short Story." In this story, a murderer is unmasked because he tried to frame an innocent man by sewing an International Tailoring label (which bears the innocent suspect's name) into a ready-made overcoat and passing it off as the made-to-measure original. An expert from the company cracks the case by proving the coat does not belong to the suspect and therefore has been planted at the crime scene. The suspect dons the overcoat in court and the company expert testifies: "'To the layman's eye it might seem all right, but all the same this coat was never made to the wearer's measurement. The shoulders are not correct, they do not fit properly; besides, the International never uses lining of this quality, nor do they use canvas like this for the coat fronts.'" Uncovering this deception leads investigators to the true perpetrator.[62]

A similar firm, the Spencer-Tracy Superior Tailoring Company, offered local merchants a brochure of "selling arguments" to use on those customers tempted by ready-made clothes. "Clothes *we* make to order outwear ready-mades because they are cut to *fit* a certain man's form and upon fit depends the wear," it said. Another argument in the brochure said, "Styles you know change twice a year, and all ready-made dealers have to carry overstock, and so about half the suits they sell are really *last year's* styles." And a third stated: "Impress your customer with the fact that his clothes are *not* made in sweatshops where disease is bred, but in great, well aired, well lighted workrooms where tailors and finishers can work to the best advantage."[63]

Such enterprises generated considerable business through the first part of the twentieth century, but they could neither compete with the perfect cultural fit of the ready-made industry nor establish themselves as a true custom product. When Alexander Nicoll, a pioneer of the multicity tailoring operation, died in 1895, a journal devoted to the custom trade memorialized him with complaints about his "demoralizing system of cheap tailoring that has always hurt the legitimate fine trade." The article explained that Nicoll got his start in New York and then spent his professional life "spreading the plague system to other prominent cities throughout the United States" (Figure 11). *Men's Wear* later described the overall quality of the tailor-to-trade segment as low and characterized it as "a cocksure, raucous, fumbling, reckless, careless industry."[64]

The tailors never seemed to master the merchandising environment and media in the same way as the ready-made manufacturers. Perhaps this was inevitable given their artisanal worldview. Tailoring trade journals were full of technical information, feature stories about the dress of "eminent men in history" (including Napoleon, Frederick the Great, and Andrew Jackson), news of their professional associations, advice about customer relations, and complaints about deadbeat clients, but scarcely a word about advertising. Instead, the journals argued that the only way a tailor could compete against "rowdy made clothing" was "to constantly demonstrate, *both by word of mouth and the appearance of his work* that only a tailor can make clothes fit for a man of taste to own."[65] At a time when manufacturers' trade publications had a section in each issue that dealt with advertising ("the foundation stone upon which rests most of great retail clothing houses of the day"), the custom journals all but ignored the subject.[66] This placed them at a severe disadvantage at a moment when advertising was beginning to provide an important means for organizing the values and perceptions associated with clothing.

Yet despite the success of the ready-made clothing trade, custom tailoring obviously continued to set the standard in many ways through the end of the nineteenth century. The values and cultural significance of custom-made clothing could not be replaced as easily as one could slip out of a frock coat into a sack suit. The continued allure of custom tailoring is revealing because many historians have depicted consumer society in a way that implies Americans adopted wholly new standards of behavior, shifted from a producer mentality to a consumer mentality or from an inner-directed to outer-directed personality type, and abandoned or obliterated the past in pursuit of a new kind of materialism.[67] The men's clothing example shows that the transition occurred differently. Encoded in the contest between ready-made and custom-made was a complex reorganization of cultural values. Newer goods were accepted only if they managed to incorporate some of the old values of individuality, respectability, command, craftsmanship, as well as the appeal of the new—hustle, progressiveness, science, and expertise. In addition, they needed to embody both newer definitions of masculine prowess and older values of

To Be Well Dressed—

Does not necessarily imply that you must be expensively dressed. But it *aoes* require that your clothes be made for *you*. And when you can have this advantage, together with unlimited variety of material from which t ﹥ select, and perfect fit, at no more cost than "hand-me-downs," why not have them?

Next time try

Your Money Back If Not Satisfied.

Clark and Adams-sts Branches in 11 Large Cities.

Figure 11. Nicoll the Tailor remained a presence in Chicago in 1898—three years after Nicoll the man had died. Although the firm's ads traded on the allure of the custom-made, arguing that being well dressed "*does* require that your clothes be made for *you*," other merchant tailors considered Nicoll's whole system a degradation of their trade. This ad uses the term "hand-me-downs," which was a denigrating designation commonly used for all ready-made clothes, whether they were secondhand or not. Nicoll the Tailor advertisement, *Chicago Tribune* (October 20, 1898): 7.

male prestige. Turn-of-the-century America was beginning to work out a new synthesis of cultural values in which older ideals were modified or repositioned to accommodate standardized goods, national markets, corporate capitalism, mass communications, the "new woman," the "new immigrant," and a host of other changed circumstances. For middle-class males, ready-made clothes offered a means and an emblem for the effort to reorient themselves to these modernizing forces. Only when clothiers, through their styles and advertisements, crafted a symbolic amalgam of old and new values and communicated it widely could they safely say that American men were ready for ready-made clothes.

Chapter 2

Women's Clothing
"What to Wear and How to Make It"

Edward Bok, editor of the *Ladies' Home Journal,* reflected frequently in the magazine's columns on "the woman question" of the late nineteenth century. "The sense of rush has taken hold of the American woman," he wrote in 1899, "and with her it is more dangerous because it is so far-reaching in its close application to the family life." Bok singled out women's expanding public role for specific criticism, inveighing against their involvement in clubs, the workforce, municipal reform, and the cause of female suffrage. These were areas in which the women of the *Journal's* idealized middle-class audience were pushing into formerly male enclaves, increasing the pressure on prevailing gender roles.[1]

The climate of change presented even women who welcomed it with a sort of identity crisis, but their dilemmas differed from those of men. Should women seek wider opportunity on the basis of equality with men or on the basis of their different capacities and needs? Did they want recognition of individual rights or of collective capability? Could they maintain a sense of female solidarity while becoming more and more engaged in previously all-male activities? Would they be able to reconcile increased participation in the public sphere with values of home and family that they continued to hold dear?

As with men, the era's cultural tensions and its provisional solutions for women took material form in clothing, and Bok seemed to recognize this. For him, the sewing needle held talismanic qualities for maintaining the female ideal: "The modern girl, in taking up her sewing, only comes back to first principles. But they are sturdy principles to which she is returning, and she will find them so. . . . So essentially feminine an art should never be allowed to die out, and when its possibilities, artistic and useful, are better understood by our girls, their own pride will keep it in its proper place: among woman's highest arts and truest accomplishments."[2] For Bok, clothing was no trivial matter, but rather "an indication of our inner characters." Consequently, he denounced women who wore "garments that were never intended for them" or, even worse, styles by which they "unsexed themselves." Dress was central to womanliness:

"It is woman's mission to make life gentler and more beautiful, to make the world a better place to live in, to elevate mankind and to develop certain instinctive traits in the young. Surely in her dress she cannot afford to forfeit the respect which has always been accorded her sex."[3]

Clothing could indeed convey female "difference" in a very tangible—and constraining—form, yet fashion also implied how unstable any such a definition of femininity was. After all, women's styles changed yearly, if not seasonally. The details of womanliness were never, finally, pinned down, which at least in theory provided space for women to attempt to remake themselves and provided them with a fashion vocabulary with which to do it. Fashion bowed to an overwhelming cultural emphasis on strict differentiation between men and women, but it also offered opportunities for individual expression and assertion.

While the men's clothing discourse of this time seemed to be trying to transport custom-made values to the new frontier of ready-made goods, discussions of women's clothing staked out completely different territory, one which presumed intimate links between a woman's identity, character, gender role, and *custom-made* garments. Just as clothing embodied and naturalized certain social contradictions for men, so it helped organize a variety of social facts for women, molding ambivalent impulses into a visible and coherent self.[4] The attributes of custom clothing offered a specific approach for preserving the past while facing the future, for balancing individual expression and female solidarity, and for overlapping gender identity and class consciousness. Although the ethos of mass production infiltrated the world of women's dress, women's fashion entered the mass-market age slowly and on very different terms than did men's clothing, embodying a host of attitudes required for the maintenance of gender roles that ready-mades could not yet provide. For women, gender ideology was enacted in everyday life not only in the style of certain garments but in the way such garments were made. Unlike the men's industry, which attempted to achieve symbolic equilibrium by grafting the attributes of custom-made clothing onto ready-made products, for women the very act of custom-making clothes was intimately tied to ideals of femininity, and so custom goods retained a much broader hold in the marketplace.

Popular women's magazines of the 1890s—both those most oriented to the hand-stitched past and those most in tune with the mechanized future—agreed that sewing and custom-made clothing were closely linked to a social identity as woman and mother. *Godey's,* by then a fading fashion journal only a few years from extinction, referred to "the tender thoughts that may be interwrought with every stitch . . . how the pleasure or pain of a lifetime may work itself in with the making of a single garment." The *Ladies' Home Journal,* one of the new breed of women's magazines whose seven-figure circulations would redefine mass communications, advised its readers: "Although all of the articles of which the layette is composed may be bought ready-made, it is usually a labor of love for the expectant mother to make the outfit herself. The seams, the tucking, etc., may be done on the machine, but most of the work should, when possible, be done by hand."[5]

Similar sentiments, shorn of their effusive language, can be found in the diary of Emily French, a divorced mother who eked out a meager and at times desperately poor existence in Colorado during the 1890s. The elliptical entries in her "dear little book" often document efforts to provide clothing for her children: "Commenced Ollie cream silk," she reported on May 22, 1890, when she started a new dress for her daughter, Olive. The next day she wrote, "I got Ollie's light silk dress out to see if I could do anything to it, there is so much needed to make it nice." And the day after that, "I showed her [Mrs. Corbin, an employer and friend] the silk I am fixing for Ollie, a light cream, 'twill be a lovely dress! Next Friday is Deckoration day, she wants to look nice sure." And finally on June 1, "Ollie wore her cream silk first time to day, it looks so nice."[6]

Almost all dresses—probably the key component in middle-class women's fashion discourse—were custom-made in the 1890s. Despite this, the ready-made industry had made inroads into the women's clothing trade, marketing cloaks, tailor-made suits, and shirtwaists in increasing numbers. Even in these areas, however, a made-to-measure bias remained prominent in a variety of ways.

Cloaks and capes were probably the first "public" garments (that is, not underwear or housedresses) sold in any quantity as ready-made goods. Several dozen manufacturers were listed in the 1860 census, and by the 1890s a number of relatively large firms had emerged in this sector, which according to one historian accounted for the bulk of ready-made sales to women as late as 1895.[7] Perhaps not coincidentally, some of these garments did not require a very close fit, either physically or psychologically. Capes (which remained popular well into the 1890s despite their stigmatization by some reformers as "pneumonia wraps") tended to blanket the wearer in loosely fitting, relatively inexpressive garments (Figure 12). This style conformed to the late Victorian prescriptions that women should reveal little of themselves in the street, advice that connected directly with a gender ideology that stressed respectability and attempted to restrict women from the public sphere. Sometimes etiquette writers even used clothing metaphors make this point: "The true lady walks the street, wrapped in a mantle of proper reserve, so impenetrable that insult and coarse familiarity shrink from her."[8] In this context, a factory-made product could find a niche without challenging the custom clothing's overall cultural work of providing self-expression and sex differentiation for women.

Notably, cloak manufacturers tended not to call attention to their products as ready-made. They rarely celebrated progress, modernity, standardization, or efficiency in the manner of men's advertising. Instead, cloak makers boasted that they pursued "the very latest Paris and Berlin novelties" and that the "distinctive grace" of their goods turned their customers into "artistically dressed women." In addition, fashion columns in the magazines indicated that many readers did not buy cloaks ready-made but rather made them or had them custom-made, a preference that some of the largest cloak-makers counted on.[9] The National Cloak Company, for example, was established in 1889 and built up a large trade selling made-to-measure cloaks by mail order. In 1895 the company promised that their goods would deliver "that perfection of fit and finish which is not to be found in ready-made goods"[10] (Figure 13). Even if purchased ready-made, cloaks were not necessarily ready to

Figure 12. Cloaks and capes were among the first ready-made garments sold for women because their loose-fitting cut made them easier to mass produce and their function as streetwear meant a high degree of individual expressiveness was not desired. Griswold, Palmer & Company advertisement, *Chicago Dry Goods Reporter* (October 26, 1895): 24.

Figure 13. Ready-made cloaks and suits for women competed with custom-
made versions until after the turn of the century, and even the ready-made
manufacturers used the custom-made language of distinction. Here, Chas. A.
Stevens & Bros. offers "distinctive grace" in its ready-made cloaks, while
immediately beneath it National Cloak promises made-to-measure garments
with "that perfection of fit and finish which is not to be found in ready-made
goods." Chas. A. Stevens & Bros. advertisement; National Cloak Company
advertisement, *Ladies' Home Journal* (September 1895): 29. Reproduced
courtesy of the Winterthur Library: Printed Book and Periodical Collection.

wear in a literal sense. In 1898 a writer describing a large department store observed: "In another room are found cloaks and wraps by the thousands and facilities for taking in or letting out the seams 'while you wait.'"[11]

Another garment sold ready-made to women by the end of the century was the "tailor-made suit," a special variant of women's outerwear that borrowed fabrics, cut, padding, pressing, and styling from tailoring techniques mostly associated with men's wear. In fact, men made most of these suits because the job required skills that dressmakers ordinarily did not possess. Perhaps because making them had never been within the normal scope of the homemaker or professional dressmaker, these garments gained earlier entrée into a factory system of production. Advertisements occasionally featured ready-made tailored suits in the 1880s, and they appeared more frequently in the 1890s, though they did not achieve widespread acceptance as ready-made goods until the early 1900s.[12]

As with cloaks, the tailor-made suit industry tended to market its product in custom-made terms. Advertisements stressed the excellence of the garments' tailoring to maintain a close association with a sense of personal craft, and trade publications urged dealers to follow fashion trends closely. The *Chicago Dry Goods Reporter* offered its subscribers a sample advertisement in 1896 that read: "The tailored suits have that stylish nattiness that you have to pay high for when you want a man tailor to do the work. These suits are in stylish, wearable fabrics, with *that made-to-order fit.*"[13] In another parallel to the cloak trade, some of the biggest tailor-made suit advertisers did not sell ready-made goods but instead offered made-to-measure garments by mail. One of them, H. C. F. Koch, noted in 1898: "These garments are not taken from a ready-made stock and altered, but are Made to Order from samples of your own selection." This comment indicates just how cloudy the distinction between ready-made and custom-made could be, with retailers often seeming deliberately to blur the line. In an 1898–99 catalog, one merchant specified that its tailor-made suits were ready-made, but then asked the customer to submit fourteen measurements with her order. The merchant concluded: "Should we not be able to fill measurements given us, we will make the same specially to order, at no extra charge." Once again, it was presumed that alterations would be necessary. A tasteful tailor-made suit required "a willingness to fit and refit," according to the *Ladies' Home Journal,* and a trade publication commented in 1898 that "the great difficulty in the way of a suit department is that it cannot be operated without an alteration department." The article estimated that forty-nine suits out of fifty needed alterations to achieve a proper fit and claimed that some stores employed more than one hundred people in their suit alteration departments.[14]

The breakthrough garment in the women's ready-made industry was the shirtwaist, a blouse fashioned along the lines of a man's shirt ("a man's shirt transformed into a thing of beauty," according to one observer).[15] The tailor-made suit had a removable jacket worn over such a waist, and in the 1890s it began to be acceptable to wear the waist and skirt as a complete outfit. This popular style had great advantages in terms of flexibility and economy, since skirts and waists could be mixed and matched in ways that would expand a woman's wardrobe options far beyond what was possible when each costume needed to be complete unto itself. The shirtwaist's popularity surged throughout the 1890s and 1900s, achieving its peak between 1909 and 1914. Industry observers estimated there were not more than a half-dozen shirtwaist factories in New York City in 1895, but by 1900 there were 472.[16] The shirtwaist owed its success in part to its ability to provide economical stylishness to the lower classes while offering variations that would still serve middle-class needs for distinction. It offered "something for everyone," according to one account, "there were tailored waists, semitailored waists, hand-embroidered waists, waists decorated with 'machine stitching cleverly done to resemble handiwork,' nursing waists, fancy lawn waists, very dressy taffeta silk waists, china silk waists, handsome novelty waists, stunning white lingerie waists and on and on."[17]

Yet reservations about ready-made goods remained steadfast in this sector too. Retailers felt obligated to warn people that certain shirtwaists lacked durability. One such warning emphasized that "this is true only of the waists that are ready-made, for the business in custom-made waists is almost entirely on heavier weight goods." Shirtwaist advertisements used the language of custom clothing, offering "exclusive patterns" and "individuality." The Chicago department store Carson Pirie Scott stressed that its shirtwaists were "finished inside, outside and all over in a way you'd expect only of the smart tailor-made product" (Figure 14). And many shirtwaists were in fact custom-made or homemade. The *Ladies' Home Journal* published articles offering "Shirt-waists which are not in the shops, because each one has been specially designed for the Journal by Emily Wight." In 1899, *McCall's* thought it could lure new subscribers by offering them a free pattern for a shirtwaist, which indicates that there must have been a large constituency still making these garments for themselves.[18]

The most complete resistance to ready-made clothing came in the making of dresses. Just as the three-piece suit was the lingua franca for men's clothing at the time, so the dress provided a fundamental symbolic basis for the middle-class woman's presentation of self. Although some ready-made dresses appeared in catalogs as early as the 1880s, women did not commonly buy them ready-made until the 1910s or later.[19] Articles and advertisements in women's magazines clearly reflected this situation, often focusing on fabrics rather than finished garments, giving specific instructions on sewing, on dealing with dressmakers, and on making over old gowns, promoting paper patterns that allowed home copies of the latest styles, and discussing the limitations of ready-made garments.

Magazine fashion writers assumed women shopped for the raw materials of garments rather than the garments themselves, and they offered

IT PAYS TO DO YOUR **SHOPPING BY MAIL** WITH **CARSON PIRIE SCOTT & CO.**

100 TO 112 STATE STREET, CHICAGO

Not Like Other Girls

They have an air at once distingué and characteristic—an individuality that bears the stamp of our Waist-energy! There's style and chic in every fold of the sleeves (that means about as much as even the modern garment can carry), but we think the reason folks prefer them is because they're finished inside, outside and all over in a way you'd expect only of the smart tailor-made product.

Scotch Wool Plaid Waists

Either Shepherd, Royal Stuart, Victoria or Gordon — blouse front, extra large interlined sleeves, velvet collar, and bodice with tight lining. All that care, skill and experience can lend the waist-builder has been sewn and shaped into these garments, and the result is unmatchable style at **$6.50**

In ordering state bust and sleeve measure. Pattern samples if you'd like them.

All-Wool Serge Waists

In Black, Navy, Brown or Cardinal—the new blouse front with three pleats, extra large interlined sleeves, velvet collar, and close-lined bodice. THEY KEEP THEIR SHAPE, for the finest that can be had, and form and fit are fashioned into honest wear at . **$4.50**

In ordering state bust and sleeve measure. We'd like to send you samples.

Figure 14. Carson Pirie Scott was advertising mass-produced shirtwaists by midcentury. The store assured buyers of this ready-made phenomenon that they were "not like other girls," however, because *these* garments "have an air at once distingué and characteristic—an individuality that bears the stamp of our Waist-energy!" Carson Pirie Scott & Company advertisement, *Ladies' Home Journal* (September 1895): 28. Reproduced courtesy of the Winterthur Library: Printed Book and Periodical Collection.

extensive advice on the selection of dress goods. Emma Hooper, one of the first staff writers for the *Ladies' Home Journal,* wrote an article in 1899 that suggested tasting, rubbing, burning, poking, shaking, unraveling, and using a pocket magnifying glass to check the quality of various fabrics.[20] Mary Katharine Howard, a *Woman's Home Companion* writer praised by her editors as one "who combines a knowledge of practical dressmaking with extraordinary facilities for obtaining fashion news," offered readers opinions such as: "Without question foulard is the reigning fabric for summer wear."[21] The level of production expertise and craft knowledge expected of readers was quite high. Advice such as "put not your money in moiré, you will regret it" was not directed at the dry goods buyer of a large retail store or the operator of a textile mill but to the general readership of the *Delineator,* one of the largest selling women's magazines of this era. *Good Housekeeping* ran a whole series of articles in 1899 under the heading: "Fashions and Fabrics."[22]

Magazine writers discussed dressmaking more directly as well. All the popular magazines included regular or occasional features—including articles by both Hooper and Howard—with titles such as "Hints on Home Dressmaking" or "Practical Lessons in Dressmaking." In the middle of the decade, the *Woman's Home Companion* regular fashion section ran under the title: "What to Wear and How to Make It." At the very end of the decade, this magazine assured readers it would continue furnishing "the most reliable fashion intelligence that can be obtained, with such practical hints as will enable women and girls to fit and construct their own gowns."[23]

At times the magazines seemed to take home sewing skills for granted: "A sketch is given of a little French dress that any artful woman can copy with her own needle." At other times they offered encouragement and pep talks, gave reassurance to the novice or insecure, warned about difficult projects, and offered suggestions as to tools and materials. They explained how to arrange the workspace and how to organize the work itself. Two different magazines explained how to build a sawdust-filled contraption that would serve as a dress form, a "prime necessity" for the home dressmaker. Writers also advised readers who employed outside sewing help not only how garments should be made but also how to deal with the people who would be making them. The *Ladies' Home Journal* discussed "the many arrangements necessary before and after the dressmaker comes," including what tools and materials to provide, how much to pay, how to offer suggestions, and what to do about providing meals.[24]

Such advice was eminently practical. Ethel Spencer, recalling her childhood in the 1890s, wrote that "though the great spurts of effort came in spring and autumn, dressmaking really went on in our house fairly constantly throughout the year." She also recalled her mother's continual struggle to find a competent seamstress to assist her during the semiannual "spurts." One December while at boarding school, Ethel received a letter from home that said: "Your poor sister Mary is still wearing summer dresses because I cannot get competent people to help me finish the garment begun long ago."[25] The hint of guilt over this perceived failure at mothering shows how the making of clothes was both practically and psychologically central to female gender roles.

For comfortably middle-class women, making clothes and dealing with the dressmaker was part of growing up. *Good Housekeeping* recommended that mothers "begin early to teach the little girls to do their own mending and to help with the easiest parts of the sewing." One day in the 1880s, Maud Rittenhouse, a high school senior in Cairo, Illinois, confided to her diary: "Yesterday morning my dress arrived [from the dressmaker] and I put it on. Such a fright you never saw in all your mortal days; didn't fit, drapery ungraceful, flounces uneven, lace whacked on and so tight that it looked like a string. . . . But Auntie Robbins (she's a born modiste) volunteered to fix it over and make it girlish and sweet. So they got a bolt of lace, ripped it up, and with Mrs. Menager are fast forming a fairy thing of it." Two days later she reported: "Had to pay [dressmaker] Mrs. James $5 for botching up my dress, but I gave her a talking to she's not apt to forget in a hurry." In 1889, Maud attended a friend's wedding as a bridesmaid. Ready-made clothes for this occasion, of course, were not mentioned. Instead, Maud bought some China silk by mail order from Mandel's department store in Chicago. She and her mother then sat down and together made a gown for the wedding party. The assumption that a woman's chief role was child rearing and that part of raising a daughter properly was teaching her to sew reinforced the links between separate spheres gender ideology and custom clothing. As a matter of course, Maud learned early how to deal with both dressmaking and dressmakers, and her mother offered a living example of the *Ladies' Home Companion* assertion that "every mother wants her daughters to learn how to cut and fit dresses. Even if they do not wish to make their own dresses, it cultivates their taste in dress and always causes them to look neat and stylish no matter what they wear."[26]

Equally removed from any idea of a ready-to-wear society were frequent references and advice concerning the remaking of old garments. The writers of these articles expected women to follow fashion through their own handiwork, rather than purchasing prepackaged chic. Readers learned renovation tips to keep a garment in style or to disguise worn and soiled areas and also how to recycle the fabric from an outmoded skirt into a new bodice or collar, how to use an old garment as the lining for a new one, and how to cut down adult clothing to make it over for children. Sometimes the changes were as small as adding new pieces of trim; sometimes they required ripping apart the entire garment and reassembling it in a different form.[27]

Emily French, struggling to make ends meet in Colorado, read the *Ladies' Home Journal* when she could and may have been taking its advice when she wrote, "She [her daughter Olive] does need a dress to wear on Arbor day, so I must try to look over the things & see if I have something. I found the old summer silk that mother sent to Abbie [another daughter], blue & white—shall I try to make a dress for her out of it, 'twill be a job."[28]

Further attention to the needs of the home dressmaker came in the ready availability of paper patterns.[29] Virtually all the popular magazines at least dabbled in the business of providing patterns to their readers, and some of the biggest successes in the field, the *Delineator, McCall's,* and *Pictorial Review,* began their publishing existence as little more than pattern company catalogs.[30] Merchants were advised to stock patterns as well as fabrics, if for no other reason than to keep up with the styles. During the Christmas season at the end of the decade, retailers made up special gift boxes that contained all the fabric needed for a particular dress—plus the pattern for it. The *Ladies' Home Journal* assured its readers this was one gift "that is always sure of a welcome."[31]

By and large, women incorporated the harbingers of mass consumption, such as the standard sizing of paper patterns, the adoption of the sewing machine, and emergence of large-circulation magazines, into familiar work patterns and prevailing concepts of fashionable dress. In other words, women attempted to devise strategies for accommodating such changes within an existing cultural context. The availability of patterns may have made fashionable dress accessible to more people, but it did not significantly alter the trajectory of the women's clothing industry with respect to ready-mades and in fact probably prolonged the reign of custom-made clothes.[32]

Even mail-order catalogs, which represented modern consumption patterns in so many ways, had to accommodate this home-sewn bias.[33] As late as the 1920s, customers continued trying to establish custom-made relationships with mail-order catalog companies and their offerings. Women made their own clothes using catalog illustrations as sewing guides in the same manner they used fashion plates. They bombarded catalog offices with queries seeking fashion advice, even asking how they could go about remaking their old dresses to look like the latest models offered for sale. Many presumed a conversational acquaintance with the recipient of their letters, even though they wrote at a time when a large mail-order house might receive more than 100,000 pieces of mail a day.[34] Catalogs that dealt in women's clothing catered to this attitude, stressing fashion talk, component parts, and made-to-measure garments along with frequent warnings or qualifications about their ready-made offerings. Many featured tidbits of advice that could have come straight from the pages of the fashion journals. Most continued to sell dry goods and sewing aids, some with the notation that they considered them "probably the most important departments in our store." Surveys by researchers at Harvard University indicated that the value for the sale of yard goods exceeded that of ready-made garments well into the twentieth century.[35]

In popular women's magazines, references to ready-made clothing were relatively rare and most often criticized such garments as overpriced and poor in quality, lacking in individuality and fit, and exploitive of sweatshop labor. A writer for *Good Housekeeping* warned that buying a good quality ready-made gown could cost three to four times as much as attempting the same dress at home or hiring a less expensive dressmaker. A cheaper ready-made garment "is generally made up from the poorer grades of cloth," the writer said, adding: "In nine times out of ten, the cloth has not been shrunk when it should be. The narrow seams will fray out in a short time, the machine-made buttonholes will fray and get out of shape, the stitches sewed with cheap cottons or weak silks will break and leave gaping holes, the dress will get out of shape for lack of the stay and strengtheners, and in a short time the wearer presents *a most slovenly and careless appearance, which marks her among her fellows as one who buys her gowns ready made.*"[36] The same article emphasized how the situation was different for men: "The contrast between the shops which furnish ready-made clothes to men and women should here be noted. The man demands as the first essential that his clothes be strongly and neatly made, and he usually gets the full worth of his money." In 1895, *Harper's Bazar* advised women that "the ready-made suits in the shops, sold all the year round, often include great bargains; but they must be very carefully chosen, and a little more money expended in having a gown made to order is, as a rule, much more satisfactory."[37]

The association of ready-made clothing with sweatshop labor further discouraged middle-class women, who supplied much of the energy for Progressive-era workplace reforms. Magazine writers urged women "not to countenance the selling of flesh and blood under the guise of ready-made clothing" and asked: "Has no one suffered that you may buy cheaply?" The warnings could become impassioned: "Women who struggle to secure cheap goods at a bargain counter little dream of the white slaves in fetid, crowded rooms, who impregnate the garments with weariness, starvation, and tears."[38]

Magazine advertising at the time confirmed the predominance of custom-made thinking. Ads aimed at women who made their own clothes greatly outnumbered those for ready-made garments and filled the pages with enticements to buy fabric, sewing machines, needles, thread, pins, patterns, dressmaking manuals, laces, ribbon, braid and other trimmings, skirt binding, hooks and eyes, buttonhole cutters ("every lady ought to have one"), thimbles, dye, dress forms, dress stays, and dress shields. The fashion writer's assertion that "the needle remains the symbol of womanly efficiency" found support in many different ways in the articles and advertisements of the day (Figure 15).[39]

At the most overt level, ready-made clothing struggled to find any beachhead in women's clothing long after ready-made clothing had become the sartorial standard for men. If the distinctive qualities of an emerging culture of mass consumption were to take hold in women's clothing culture, they would have to do so in a way that accommodated the custom making of garments. In fact, that is exactly what happened. One can see the leading edge of modern consumer culture lurking amidst the advice on high fashion and sentimental fiction of *Godey's,* a magazine devoted to handcrafted fashions since its founding in 1830. In late 1895 the magazine ran an article titled "The Poetry of Progress." Its opening passages spoke of evolution and attempted to make a connection between women's suffrage and fashionable dress. On its second page, readers learned the author's main point and definition of "progress": the development of Fibre Chamois interlining for dresses. Fibre Chamois was a substance manufactured out of vegetable fiber or wood pulp that could be used between the fabric and lining of a garment to stiffen it into its approved shape—a product that was quite useful when skirts flared to a six- or eight-yard circumference and sleeves ballooned to the size of basketballs. The *Godey's* article quoted "one of the leading ladies' tailors on Fifth Avenue" who "never uses anything but Fibre Chamois." And the writer warned: "If you do not see the trade-mark 'Fibre Chamois' staring you in the face, refuse to buy, for it is not the genuine article."[40]

This article was a puff piece, that is, an advertisement written and displayed in the guise of editorial content. Some of the first advertising manuals ever written included whole chapters discussing the merits of this stratagem.[41] Although such overt editorial hucksterism was relatively rare in the larger magazines, Fibre Chamois pulled off similar coups in *Harper's Bazar, Queen of Fashion* (the forerunner of *McCall's),* and *Lippincott's.* The company also received more coverage in *Godey's* early the next year.[42] The puff pieces serve as a reminder that the world of custom-made clothing and that of mass marketing were entangled in ways not immediately obvious. The Fibre Chamois example demonstrates that brand names and trademarks were not absent from the world of women's dress in the 1890s, they simply occupied a stratum that could be integrated with the values of custom-made clothing. For instance,

"You 'don't keep the

"S. H. & M."

Bias Velveteen Skirt Bindings'

Why, I thought this was a first-class house!"

Samples and Booklet on "How to Bind the Dress Skirt," for 2c. stamp. Address

The S. H. & M. Co., P. O. Box 699, New York

"S. H. & M." Dress Stays are the Best

Figure 15. Advertisements for women's fashions were much more likely to feature sewing aids than complete garments. They may have instructed consumers about modern retailing practices, such as the meaning and value of brand names, but they did so in the context of custom-made clothing. S. H. & M. advertisement, *Ladies' Home Journal* (March 1895): 31. Reproduced courtesy of the Winterthur Library: Printed Book and Periodical Collection.

Fibre Chamois advertisements used headlines such as "fashionable dress-makers everywhere use it" (Figure 16) and text such as "with such aids home-dressmaking becomes a pleasure." The company claimed that the renowned modiste Redfern had recommended the material.[43]

Although middle-class women's clothing rhetoric and consumption overtly resisted the ethos of mass consumption at almost every turn, this sneak attack by the Fibre Chamois company shows that the age of adver-tising was having its effect on women's clothing in more subtle ways. A look beneath the surface shows that the major attributes of the culture of mass consumption—scale of production, mass marketed symbolic sys-tems, and impersonal selling relationships—worked their way into the women's clothing trade as surely as they did the men's. Unlike the men's industry, however, for women's clothing this transition occurred only in ways that could still accommodate the overwhelming emphasis on cus-tom production.

To observe the impact of large-scale production on the women's cloth-ing market, consider two pages from Brown, Durrell and Company's cat-alogs of 1895. This wholesaler offered only a few ready-made garments, which it advertised as "equal to homemade" (Figure 17). Brown, Durrell seemed a business clearly oriented toward the world of custom clothing. However, the company's customers also could purchase at least a dozen trademarked brands of hooks and eyes: Nicholl's Patent, Eagle Talon Improved, Appleton's Patent Invisible, Golden Spring, Duplex Spring, Oscar A. Delong, Prym's Continuous, Feder-Haken, Boston, Camel Brand, Francis, and DeLong (Figure 18).[44] Not only were these items mass produced for a national market, the plenitude of choices illustrated the era's "avalanche of goods" and most advanced methods of merchan-dising. The hooks and eyes represented an early and exemplary instance of a style of product differentiation in which advertisers use small design gimmicks and brand-name awareness to create distinct product images for goods that are basically very similar. In its time, DeLong's advertis-ing tag line ("See that hump?") was as famous and as much a part of popular culture as Kodak's contemporaneous sales pitch, "You press the button; we do the rest." Students of advertising usually associate such sales tactics with late twentieth-century marketing campaigns for prod-ucts such as soft drinks or cigarettes. However, this strategy was in full bloom one hundred years earlier in a sector of the economy especially resistant to large-scale production and standardization.[45]

The influence of mass media on women's fashion began with publi-cations such as *Godey's* and the *Ladies' Home Journal*. The promotion of individuality and customized fashion habits by these magazines was some-thing of a contradiction in terms because their "exclusive" designs passed into the hands of hundreds of thousands of readers simultaneously.

Figure 16. Fibre Chamois offered a newly developed material for stiffening clothes and backed it with a quarter-million dollar advertising campaign in the mid-1890s. This advertisement emphasizes the importance of its brand name and vows to protect its patent rights, but mingles this with a custom-clothing appeal: "Fashionable Dressmakers everywhere use it." Fibre Chamois advertisement, *Ladies' Home Journal* (March 1895): 35. Reproduced courtesy of the Winterthur Library: Printed Book and Periodical Collection.

Figure 17. This 1895 advertisement offers a ready-made woman's wrapper, claiming its workmanship is "equal to home made" and stressing that it is "made to fit." Brown, Durrell & Company, *Trade Monthly* (April 1895): 41. Reproduced courtesy of the Winterthur Library: Printed Book and Periodical Collection.

CLASPS, ETC. — Continued.

1 dozen in box.

Wizard Cuff Holder	. . . . . $0.92 per dozen pairs.	
"I. X. L." "	. . . . . 1.00 " "	
Perfection "	. . . . . .55 " "	
New Slide "	. . . . . 1.00 " "	
Wizard Scarf Retainer	. . . . .50 " "	

HOOKS AND EYES.

Put up in 1 gross boxes. 1 great gross in package.

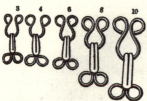

Common Black.

Nos.	2	3	4	6	8	10
Price, per great gross,	42c.	45c.	50c.	54c.	65c.	80c.

Common Silvered.

Nos.	2	3	4	6	8	10
Price, per great gross,	81c.	90c.	$1.00	$1.20	$1.56	$2.25

Bent Point.

	Nos.	3	4	6	8	10
Price, per great gross, black,		50c.	60c.	68c.	90c.	$1.00
" " silvered,		$1.20	$1.45	$1.80	$2.35	$2.45

Nicholl's Patent. ½ gross cards. ¼ great gross in box. Black and silvered.

Nos.	1	2	3	4	5
Price, per great gross,	$3.00	$3.25	$3.50	$3.75	$4.50

Eagle Talon Improved. 1 gross in box. Japanned and silvered. Nos. 3 and 4. $3.00 per great gross.

Appleton's Patent Invisible. Black and silvered.

Nos.	3	4
Price, per great gross,	$3.00	$3.50

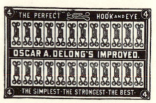

GOLDEN SPRING.   DUPLEX SPRING.

Per great gross.

Golden Spring. Black and silvered. Nos. 3 and 4 . $4.50
Duplex Spring. Black and silvered. Nos. 3 and 4 . 4.50

Oscar A. DeLong's Perfect. Black and white. Nos. 3 and 4 . . . . 4.70

PRYM'S CONTINUOUS.   BOSTON. Per great gross.

Prym's Continuous. Black and white $5.50
Feder-Haken. Black and white 1.75
Boston. Black and white. No. 4 . . . . 5.75

Camel Brand Short Bill. Nos. 2, 3, and 4 . . . 4.50

DELONG.   FRANCIS.

DeLong.	No. 2. Black, white, and drab	4.95
"	No. 3 and 4. Black, white, and drab . .	5.94
"	No. 5. Black, white, and drab	6.93
Francis.	No. 3	5.50
"	No. 5	6.50

Figure 18. Hooks and eyes, a basic sewing supply, might be expected to be as generic as a straight pin, but they were available in a wide variety of brand-name variations, each using a small design twist to create a unique product identity. In fact, straight pins were sold by brand name as well. Brown, Durrell & Company, *The Trade Monthly* (February 1895): 47. Reproduced courtesy of the Winterthur Library: Printed Book and Periodical Collection.

Women learned of new styles not in a one-on-one conversation (although advertisers and editors both worked to simulate that effect) but in the much more impersonal and mass-produced context of advertising and promotion. The *Ladies' Home Journal* boasted that its economic strength was mass appeal. In an 1895 promotional ad, it claimed that 3.5 million people read the *Journal* and therefore if only one in one hundred remembered the message of an ad the advertiser would still net 35,000 customers.[46] In addition, the *Ladies' Home Journal* was perhaps the most self-conscious and forward-looking publication of its time with respect to advertising. It maintained careful rules for both content and appearance of ads, often upgrading artwork submitted by merchants and editing ad copy as carefully as its editorial matter. Furthermore, the *Journal* advertised itself aggressively, spending as much as $1,000 a day on its own publicity in the mid-1890s.[47]

Long-distance selling relationships—another hallmark of a culture of mass consumption—became common in the women's fashion business through the dozens of mail-order companies established by the 1890s. Some of them had thousands of employees, hundreds of thousands of customers, and millions of dollars in annual sales. Big-city retailers began to sell in volume across a broad expanse of territory to customers who would never have any face-to-face contact with the company or each other. Mass merchandising created a sort of imagined marketplace. Although its members would never meet each other or the people they bought from, common reference points provided by goods and advertisements created an perception of mutual interests.[48]

Mail-order businesses that sold women's fashions were crucial in forging a relationship between customer and merchant that involved nonlocal markets and standardized transactions. The catalog merchants taught customers much about ordering by number, one-price policies, and long-distance marketing. The public's understanding of such activities could not be taken for granted. For example, rather than write down the product number, customers instead often tore apart the catalog and sent in the picture of the item they wanted. This approach not only was more inefficient for clerks attempting to fill the order, it made the mutilated catalog less useful as a reference for possible future orders. As a result, from the late 1880s through the early 1900s, catalogs frequently attempted to educate consumers in the protocols of mass consumption by including such instructions as: "Don't spoil your catalogue. Don't cut out the illustrations. Just write us the style numbers of the garments you wish. *Keep your catalogue.*"[49]

Mail-order houses attempted to compensate for the anonymity of their customer relationships by simulating a personal touch in their sales pitches. They frequently assured their customers that shopping by mail was no different than if you met face to face with the merchant: "There is nothing in our vast establishment that you cannot have precisely as if you stood before our counters, and at the same price."[50] A jumble of custom-made and ready-made values is apparent in the 1903 catalog issued by W. H. Frear and Company of Troy, New York. On the one hand, it included ready-made jackets, skirts, shirtwaists, and wrappers, but on the other hand, it stipulated that "if we don't happen to have the correct length in stock it will take about three days to have them made." While it offered extensive fabric selections, promising to deliver "odd, artistic, exclusive, beautiful" designs for the home dressmaker, the catalog pages included advertisements for the brand-name, mass production products such as R. & H. Simon ribbons, Hemingway's silk thread, Kleinert's dress shields, and the ubiquitous DeLong's hooks and eyes.[51]

Advertisers operated in a similar gray area between old and new models of consumption. Diamond Dyes published an ad in 1895 with the text: "To dye or not to dye, that is the question: whether it is better to wear that faded, shabby dress and endure the scornful looks of all your well-dressed neighbors, or to purchase a package of Diamond Dyes and restore its freshness in another color—making a new dress for ten cents" (Figure 19).[52] Once again we see the early use of certain advertising tactics—the emphasis on a brand name and a sales pitch based upon sociopsychological appeals rather than utilitarian claims—that historians generally associate with later phases of mass merchandising. However, this ad does not attempt to challenge the prevailing values of thrift, reuse, personal handiwork, or custom clothing. Purveyors of female garments created ads attempting to promote standardized goods in a customized context, using headlines such as "Your dressmaker told us" or text such as: "Fashionable modistes the country over are studying how to make the new Princess dress skirts hang properly. We have solved the problem."[53]

In short, the women's clothing industry was not immune to the onset of a culture of mass production. Yet it did not respond as the men's industry did with a shift to ready-made garments, but rather by incorporating productive and distributive advances into a context that continued to emphasize custom work. This happened because for women, custom clothing and fashionable attire embodied a set of cultural values singularly appropriate to the gender politics at the time.

To the fashion-conscious woman, the modish profile of the 1890s required huge puffed sleeves (which had not been seen since the 1830s), bell-shaped skirts (rather than the bustles that characterized the 1870s and 1880s), and mostly symmetrical and uncomplicated surfaces (contrasting to the heavy draping, many layers, and impulse toward asymmetry of the previous mode). The "hourglass" look peaked in the middle

To Dye

Or Not to Dye

that is the question : whether it is better to wear that faded, shabby dress and endure the scornful looks of all your well-dressed neighbors, or to purchase a package of **Diamond Dyes** and restore its freshness in another color—**making a new dress for ten cents.**

Diamond Dyes are made for home use. Absolutely reliable. Any color.

Sold everywhere. 10 cents a package. ☞ Direction Book and 40 samples of colored cloth, free.

WELLS, RICHARDSON & Co., Burlington, Vt.

Figure 19. Diamond Dyes attempted to capitalize on the common practice of remodeling old garments in this ad. It shows mass-marketing techniques (including a selling strategy based on peer pressure and social scrutiny) in the world of custom-made clothing. Diamond Dyes advertisement, *Ladies' Home Journal* (March 1895): 35. Reproduced courtesy of the Winterthur Library: Printed Book and Periodical Collection.

of the decade and then slowly began a transition to the "reverse-S" profile that typified the early twentieth century. As women's fashion cycled through this myriad of design details, there was no strong aesthetic or economic necessity for styles to evolve in a manner that rejected ready-mades or maintained an extreme polarity with men's clothing, yet both occurred. In an era when factory production and standardization were increasingly the order of the day, women's clothing styles, in word and practice, venerated custom production and individual fit. The resulting difference with men's clothes was in many respects starker in the 1890s than in any other period of American history (Figure 20).[54]

As the nineteenth century drew to a close, more and more middle-class women pursued higher education, entered the job market, and agitated for reform causes. In the domestic sphere women found that new technologies, products, and what the *Ladies' Home Journal* called "scientific plans of housekeeping" (shortly to spawn the home economics movement) were altering the standards of homemaking.[55] Middle-class women of the 1890s did not unequivocally embrace new values or roles any more than their male counterparts did. However, they did address the conflicts between past and present and those between self and society on different terms. As the closely fitted and stylized shapes of the 1890s might suggest, women's clothing discourse displayed much more concern with individual identity and expressiveness as opposed to men's concern with mastery and strength. Indeed, a government report in 1916 argued that the slow industrialization of women's clothing could be traced to a characteristic female attitude that "insists that no two gowns shall be alike" and to women's strong "desire for an adaptation of the fashion, style, and material of a garment to the particular form and personal characteristics of the individual woman."[56] In the context of the late nineteenth century, this emphasis on self-expression may have reflected an ongoing if indirect rebellion against the strictures of Victorian gender roles. At the same time, the elaborate styles and resistance to ready-made goods suggested a commitment to Victorian principles. Such a conservative undertone is not surprising, for middle-class women faced the same uncertainties of industrialization, urbanization, and immigration as their husbands and likewise sought to preserve a certain status and security that they had enjoyed in the past. In addition, female networks of support and affection flourished in Victorian America within the context of a female sphere. No less than men, middle-class women at the end of the century confronted a tension between old and new that was difficult to resolve.

The manner in which women worked out these issues via dress can be seen in the importance, and many meanings, attached to the concept of a good fit. The *Ladies' Home Journal* once summed up its fashion advice

Figure 20. This "promenade costume" from 1895 represents the peak of the hourglass shape for women's fashions in the 1890s. The enormous sleeves, tiny waists, and many folds and curves of the fashionable female silhouette established a stark contrast to the rectilinear male form projected by the sack suit (see Figures 4, 6). Annie de Montaigu, "Fashion, Fact, and Fancy," *Godey's Magazine* (December 1895): 665. Reproduced courtesy of the Winterthur Library: Printed Book and Periodical Collection.

with the words: "It is nothing unless it fits"; and an 1896 etiquette book put it this way: "When we say 'fitting' we have found the key to perfect dressing."[57] This concept has psychological as well as physical aspects; clothing must not only fit but must "be fitting." Getting a good physical fit would be a difficult technical problem as long as styles remained form-fitting and sculpturally rendered. Finding a good metaphorical fit was no less difficult—and no less important—during a time when female gender roles changed as much as men's did. The continuous attention paid to the issue of fit explains much about how clothing oriented middle-class women to changing social circumstances in the late nineteenth century.

From one perspective, the issue of fit clearly addressed the need for individual self-expression. In the *Woman's Home Companion,* Mary Katharine Howard explained that no one could hope to attain a good fit in ready-made clothing for the simple reason that "every figure to be fitted is a special law unto itself, and no method ever invented will fit any figure without alterations." She may have spoken literally, but the issue of fit encoded deeper meanings. Like Edward Bok of the *Ladies' Home Journal,* many advice writers of the day characterized dress as an "indication of our inner characters" and stressed that clothing must fit not only the body of the wearer but also her personality. Charlotte Perkins Gilman wrote in 1896 that "you can not wear lies on your outside and not feel it in your soul." One etiquette book published that same year asserted that "a woman's dress should be so much the expression of herself that, seeing it, we think not of the gown, but of the woman who is its soul." A sense of individual fit and fittingness permeated the women's clothing industry and put severe constraints on the acceptability of ready-made clothing. The same etiquette book suggested that a woman should "suit all accessories to her own personality" and urged the reader to "study your own individuality and assert it in your dress." Advice like this went so far as to tell women who were unable to make their own clothing how to customize a ready-made garment by adding trim or replacing buttons after it was purchased. As the *Ladies' Home Journal* said, "It is a laudable desire not to look exactly like one's neighbor."[58]

While the emphasis on fit sanctioned individual expression, the notion of "fittingness" also implied that clothing be appropriate to the circumstances, reflecting collective ties and group identity not only as women but, in this case, as middle-class women. In other words, clothing not only had to fit, but had to "fit in." Etiquette writers placed great emphasis on having dress appropriate for the social occasion, and again, this language reflected deeper meanings, invoking an acceptance and advocacy of special spheres for women and for the middle class. On the first point, Mary Katharine Howard wrote simply, "Mannish effects are to be avoided." On the second, she asserted, "The well-dressed woman . . . is she who is always consistently dressed with regard to time, place, occasion, age and the size of her husband's or father's income."[59] Fashion and class distinctions frequently overlapped in advice literature. Women should "adapt their dress to their circumstances and occupation," said one etiquette writer, somewhat tactfully, while another was much more blunt: "Never dress above your station; it is a grievous mistake, and leads to great evils, besides being proof of an utter want of taste."[60]

Clothing habits thus had some strongly conservative connotations. Of course, many middle-class reformers' attitudes—toward work, sexuality, and the importance of the family, for example—remained largely Victorian, seeking not a change in values (or in class distinctions) but a different role for women in maintaining them. The reluctance to abandon custom dress and its highly elaborated fashion system very nicely embodied this. Scholars have noted how the medical literature of this era ascribed to the female body the attributes of the preindustrial, preurban social body. It was hierarchical, and it had many constituent parts all working in harmony; it was a small-scale, closed system distinctly incompatible with the new, sprawling industrialized marketplace. These attributes could also be applied to the female fashion sense of the time.[61]

A poor fit, in short, was no mere surface flaw. It struck at the core of one's identity, as the etiquette books indicated: "A well-ordered dress helps put one at leisure with one's self. The ease of it, the sense of fitness it induces, prepare the mind for the right attitude and courtesy to others." Just as important, dress was vital for orienting oneself in the confusing, changing, increasingly impersonal modern world: "Our first impressions of those we casually meet are more often formed on the fit of their clothes and the manner of wearing them than on anything they do or say. Indeed, very little beyond the dress is remarked or remembered after a passing encounter with strangers."[62] One trade journal devoted to custom clothing ridiculed a dress reformer's plea that women ignore fashion to pursue economy and comfort in dress. The journal argued that if women ever followed the recommendation to adopt "a plain, sober uniform" for themselves, they would have to start wearing name badges or husbands would no longer be able to tell their cooks from their wives.[63] The goal of fashionable dress was frequently expressed in terms of the "eternal fitness of things," "the everlasting fitness of things," and the "highest fitness of things." The phrases promised order and coherence in a changing world. For members of the middle class, this meant a secure place in a gendered, class-conscious social structure.[64]

Women's clothing styles thus embodied the differing discourses of individualism and womanhood—in fact, managed to embed a discourse of individualism within a discourse of femininity, thus neatly summarizing the broader tendencies of the day's gender politics.[65] During the 1890s, the fashionable silhouette for women achieved some of its most stylized and curvilinear forms, clearly signifying femininity in terms of its extreme difference from the streamlined and blockish male image of the day. At the same time, individual suitability and self-expression remained a keynote of fashion advice. A *Ladies' Home Journal* columnist advised a would-be dressmaker in 1900: "Study the individuality of your customers, and design each costume to suit the individual." For women, it remained a custom-made world, as the magazine indicated when it warned that ready-made clothing could only be purchased "at the sacrifice of ability, individuality, and conscience."[66]

Just as clothing styles could enact both individualism and collective femaleness, the very activity of sewing offered those women who enjoyed it a sense of individual self-expression and satisfaction in their craft, while it also provided a link to a broader "female" identity. Sewing provided a setting (and rationale) for women to gather in groups and socialize. The increasing reliance by men on ready-made clothing cemented the sewing circle as an exclusively women's congress, as men no longer needed to visit such a gathering to try on a half-finished garment and would no longer have even a figurative presence through the making of their clothing. Ready-made clothing for women would eliminate this opportunity for female companionship.[67]

Although the cultural appropriateness of women's custom-made clothes was compelling, the success of fashion depended on aesthetic and business factors as well. The visual flow of women's fashion is apparent if one compares a chronological selection of fashion plates for the late nineteenth century, observing how various fashion details swell into prominence and then recede to secondary importance through small, mostly incremental, changes over the years. Sleeves ballooned and contracted, skirts blossomed and deflated, ornamentation multiplied and dwindled. Everything gained significance—expressing individualism or conformity, traditionalism and modernity—in comparison to what came before.

Business considerations also influenced women's dress in the 1890s. Custom dressmaking dominated women's clothing production in part because of the strength and attraction of the "female economy" sustained by the dressmaking trade. Dressmaking comprised women customers, proprietors, and workers, offering each advantages that were not available in male-oriented sectors of the economy. For proprietors and many workers, it meant "highly skilled work, creative labor, relatively high wages, and the very real possibility of opening an establishment of one's own some day." For customers, the trade offered individually tailored products and an intimate consumer-producer relationship in which they held considerable power. A shift to factory production would eliminate these sources of female assertion and self-satisfaction.[68]

Dressmaking, with 99 percent female practitioners, was a job category that women dominated almost completely. It was also one of the highest paid among women's employments. The move to large-scale production was for the most part a gendered transformation in which both dressmakers and their customers lost considerable prestige and power. This was true for women who worked in the made-to-measure departments of the new mass retailers, and it was even more the case for the women who made women's clothes in the factories that began to emerge. It was also important for customers, who were no longer able to dictate and personalize the details of their wardrobes. Hence women on every level of the system of custom clothing had a special incentive to resist large-scale production.[69]

Indeed, makers of made-to-measure women's clothing were even less likely than men's merchant tailors to use the tools of mass merchandising to defend themselves against ready-made goods. No phenomenon comparable to tailor-to-the-trade emerged on the women's side, and trade journals addressing the women's clothing trade went even further than the men's journals to situate business practices in the context of one-on-one, face-to-face transactions that reflected personal involvement, individual expression, and gender identity. Besides fashion trends, the most frequent topic of these publications involved interpersonal relationships with customers. Even the monthly column of fashion tips in the *American Dressmaker* was recast in the form of an imaginary dialogue between dressmaker and patron, running each month under the headline, "What to Say to Customers When They Ask." The journal speculated that one reason modistes were too lenient in extending credit to their customers was that, unlike businessmen, they were caught up in personal relations with their customers: "With us there is the element of personality, of sentiment, of flattery, to which we are subjected, coming in contact as we do with our customers and being privileged to use our own discretion in matters financial."[70]

The relationship sought by dressmakers extended beyond that of craftperson to customer or professional to client. Dressmakers wanted to deal with the women who paid them not only face to face but also as equals. More than one article railed against the snobbery of dress clientele:

Why is it that customers can ask any favor of a dressmaker, expect her to be interested in all private affairs and make her listen to tiresome tales of a hum-drum narrow life, and more than that, to reduce prices and not put more trimming on a dress than she can possibly afford to and then when she meets her in public almost ignore her? Dressmakers to-day are not what they were twenty years ago.

Now the trade is taken up by women of culture and in birth and education they could often put their customers in the background.[71]

Another article claimed that "dressmaking is an art and ranks very high in the commercial world, and the successful modiste compares very favorably in every way with the merchant's or banker's wife or with the society lady."[72] Of course, this snobbery worked to the advantage of customers who were trying to maintain an air of class-based distinction, and consequently both sides lost a weapon in the negotiation of class boundaries when the sales process no longer relied on this type of relationship.

Individual expressiveness was a vital part of dressmakers' perspective on their work. The trade journals stressed that dressmakers should study fashion plates but not copy them: "We have so many times urged our readers to avoid following the models too closely, but asked you to originate and change so that you have a gown of your own design." This would avoid the horror of having made a "customer look like every other woman who toddles out on a Monday morning." In this spirit, the *American Dressmaker* called attention to a news article from Washington, D.C., which reportedly ran under "great black headlines" reading: "Three Wore Gowns Alike! Society Women Who thought They Had 'Original Creations' Much Chagrined." The women in the story, who had purchased their garments in three different cities, were not victims of ready-made standardization but of dressmakers who mimicked their Paris model too closely. Thus "progress" assumed a different meaning in the women's industry than in the men's. When dressmaking trade journals boasted about the progress of their trade, they did not refer to increasing size, efficiency, or accessibility of their operations. Instead, they stressed that their business had become increasingly artistic.[73]

At the same time that the custom journals stressed individuality, they understood their obligation to group identities, that is, to womanliness and social class. One article heatedly disputed the claim that tailor-made suits were "mannish," and another implicitly suggested fashionable dress as a means of class distinction: "It is certainly most unnecessary to make your clothes exact reproductions of garments that are generally worn by the mobs."[74]

Not surprisingly, mass marketing techniques had little appeal for dressmakers. Although the custom-dressmaking journals did sometimes discuss business methods, including record-keeping and supervision of assistants, they never mentioned advertising. In the *American Dressmaker*, the only references through the early 1900s to the value of advertisements came, ironically enough, when the journal urged its readers to patronize its own advertisers: "Everything of interest to the modern and progressive modiste may be found in our advertising departments. This part of our journal is as important to our readers as the editorial and fashion portion."[75] In the editor's mind, evidently, this fact had no bearing on the business practices of the journal's readers. By the 1910s, the journal had shifted gears and had begun to recommend regular newspaper advertising for dressmakers, but even then many tradeswomen ignored the advice.[76] The whole system of custom production and consumption was embedded in a set of personal relationships and meanings for women that did not permit a smooth and rapid transition to a mass-market mentality.

One can glimpse the range of opinions evoked by the subject of fashion during the late nineteenth century in articles titled "Fashion's Slaves" and "Fashionable Dress Justified," "The Tyranny of Fashion" and "The Beneficent Influence of Dress." The breadth of interest in the meaning of clothes is underscored by the fact that the first two articles appeared in publications whose main concern was politics, while the latter two appeared in a leading mass-market fashion journal. Opinions on dress often ran to extremes. One writer opposed to fashion claimed that "women actually died of pleating." Another writer, who favored stylish dress, claimed that fashion consciousness represented the love "of all that is most beautiful and worthy of admiration." The intense emotions evinced in general commentary on fashion as well as in more specific debates over dress reform are not surprising given the close fit between the clothing system and key cultural categories within a middle-class ideology that was flexing under the weight of changing economic and social circumstances.[77]

It is testimony to fashion's ability to generate multiple meanings that both pro- and anti-fashion commentators ranged from ardent social conservatives to committed feminists. The *Ladies' Home Journal*, for example, frequently editorialized on behalf of a rigid view of separate spheres. "The woman is truest in her own sphere," the magazine stated in 1893, "reigning over her kingdom of home and children with a grace and sweetness, compared to which a public life is the hollowest of mockeries." The magazine's writers urged women to follow fashion carefully, as part of their "duty" to this sphere: "A dowdy will never have any good influence. Women in this country are the gentle power behind the throne, and knowing this they must remember that a queen would not retain her throne long if she did not surround herself with all the pomp and majesty possible."[78]

Support of a separate spheres ideology was no guarantee, however, that one would admire stylish clothing. Well-known author and physician John Harvey Kellogg offered the medical opinion that general housework was the best exercise for women and once wrote: "That the brain of the average woman differs in quality from the average man, is a fact too patent to require argument for its support. Each class of minds has its sphere, and is in its sphere superior. Men are undoubtedly best for their sphere in life, and women for theirs." At the same time, Kellogg was a fierce opponent of fashion consciousness, expressing in 1888 the hope that women reformers would persevere in trying "to rescue their sisters from the most thralling slavery of modern times,—fashionable dress." Kellogg argued that a taste for fashion led inevitably to a whole range of depravities, including nymphomania.[79]

Feminist ambivalence with regard to clothing can be traced in the pages of the *Woman's Journal,* a publication identified with the American Woman Suffrage Association. In the late 1880s, it printed some of Charlotte Perkins Gilman's first antifashion pronouncements, yet it also published a rebuttal that claimed "fashion is not the tyrant we make her out. She only wants to be better understood." Through the mid-1890s, the journal featured both "Dress Reform Notes," a summary of news about "rational dress," and "Fashion Notes," which summarized coming style trends, including the suggestion that readers consult *Harper's Bazar* for further information. In 1895, it dutifully reported a session of the National Women's Council in which "the women dress reformers had their innings," but it also published a series of articles on home dressmaking clearly meant to help women stay in fashion. The *Woman's Journal* regularly featured advertisements from Springer Brothers, the "fashionable cloak house" that promised "gowns of the latest fashion and finest material."[80]

A similar mixture of views emerges in more recent historical and analytical studies. Most second- and third-wave feminists have regarded fashion as an enemy to their cause, and it has been the subject of passionate attacks from Simone de Beauvoir to Susan Faludi.[81] Other feminist writers, especially since the early 1980s, have staked out positions much more sympathetic to fashion. They have been influenced by scholarly debates over resistance through popular culture, dissatisfaction with the theoretical concept of the male "gaze," and a perceived need to reclaim female sexuality from what they saw as a "prudish" feminist denial of the body. One scholar concluded recently that "fashion and feminism are still uneasily circling each other" with no final resolution in sight.[82]

The dress code's prismatic ability to refract different views may render any reconciliation of these views unlikely. Clothing's richness as a form of cultural expression lies in its dense overlap of meanings, which makes its study all the more revealing and important. The clothing habits of the 1890s show that women negotiated the onset of mass production very differently than men. Men found in ready-made suits and their advertised image a garment that depicted a new ideal body type and gave tangible evidence of their continued mastery over the business world, and over social and cultural change in general, while maintaining older standards of prestige and character. Women's clothing practices, particularly with regard to dresses, confronted and incorporated certain aspects of mass consumption—making use of mass-marketed sewing components, for instance—but only in ways that permitted a continued emphasis on the custom-made garments that so well embodied the conflicting values, the rebellious and repressive possibilities, the collective identity and individual expression that middle-class women attempted to integrate into their lives. For middle-class women at the turn of the century, the question of "what to wear and how to make it" usually begot an answer similar to one expressed in a 1904 novel by Gene Stratton-Porter: "Mothers . . . don't buy little, rough, ready-made things," said a character in the book. "They sit and stitch, and stitch. . . . There isn't much knowing about your mother that those little clothes won't tell."[83]

Chapter 3

Dress, Darwinism, and Sex Differentiation

"Will Women Ever Dress Like Men?"

After a burst of productivity that produced the manuscript for *Women and Economics* and a short lecture trip through New England, Charlotte Perkins Gilman—then still Charlotte Perkins Stetson—returned home at the end of January 1898 to resume her favorite pastimes. She wrote in her autobiography: "Back in New York on the twenty-ninth, and settle down comfortably to sewing, writing and seeing people."[1]

Gilman's passion for writing is well-known—she published more than two thousand works during her lifetime—and her activities as a lecturer and editor in the 1890s put her in contact with a wide network of people. Her decision to include sewing among her preferred activities seems odd for one of the most visible strategists in a "grand domestic revolution" that sought to overthrow women's separate sphere.[2] But Gilman loved to sew, and her insights into fashion's cultural work were among the most perceptive of the day. She also embodied the ambiguities that surrounded women's clothing styles because she specifically favored the adoption of ready-made clothing by women as a way of breaking down gender barriers, but she could never shake her fondness for the expressive satisfaction of making custom clothes.

Elsewhere in New York during the last few days of January 1898, Henry Theophilus Finck crisscrossed Manhattan to fulfill his duties as *New York Evening Post* music critic. He attended a presentation of *La Belle Hélène* at the Irving Place Theatre, a performance of *The Barber of Seville* at the Metropolitan Opera House, an orchestral concert by the Philharmonic Society at Carnegie Hall, and a program of "interesting novelties by native composers" at the Aschenbroedel Society hall on 86th Street.[3] Finck's newspaper commentary on these events gave no indication he had strong opinions on the subject of dress, but indeed he did. Among the earliest works in his prodigious and varied published output was an 1887 book in which he expounded at length on the relationship between fashion and civilization. Finck characterized women as less evolved than men because of their adherence to styles he considered aesthetically displeasing, while men, in contrast, were more culturally advanced and consequently less self-consciously fashionable. This line of reasoning led him to relatively early advocacy of the men's sack suit as worthy of wider adoption.[4]

The wide interests and broad-ranging writing careers of Gilman and Finck converged just after the turn of the century when each contributed several articles on the meaning of clothes to the same weekly periodical, in which they elaborated on ideas they had sketched in writings since the late 1880s. These articles reveal how both set their sails according to the prevailing intellectual conditions, integrating their fashion theories within the philosophy of social Darwinism that framed much intellectual and popular thought for the middle class. Their writings also reveal the importance of both Darwinism and clothing to the maintenance of gender roles. Finck and Gilman differed sharply in their characterization of women, but clothing habits and Darwinian theory were key props in both writers' arguments. Ultimately, as Charlotte Perkins Gilman wrote, clothing transformed the body into "a sort of ideograph" with which the history of turn-of-the century gender roles could be written.[5]

Although many factors helped push men's and women's clothing along different developmental paths, the ideological pressure for sexual differentiation provided the crucial impetus for the divergent development of the two branches of the industry. Business and aesthetic factors made their contributions, and the development of the clothing trade cannot be explained without reference to them. The fundamental pressure, however, came from gender ideology, which weighed particularly heavily on the clothing trades because of the importance of dress in maintaining gender roles and in turn because the conjoined concepts of gender and dress fit so nicely with the current Darwinian ideas of "progress" and "civilization." At the turn of the century, the celebration of these values underwrote an exceptionally powerful pressure for sexual differentiation. Psychologist G. Stanley Hall, relying on his own brand of evolutionary theory, wrote: "Differentiation ought to be pushed to the very uttermost and everything should be welcomed that makes men more manly and women more womanly; while, on the other hand, all that makes for identity is degenerative." On no topic did this prescription find more advocates than it did on the subject of men's and women's dress.[6]

According to the popular press of the 1890s, if most men wore ready-made clothing while the large majority of women continued to wear made-to-measure garments, this was only as it should be. The *Woman's Home Companion* reported that "nearly every lady desires to be able to make dresses." Such magazines published articles on mending and cleaning men's garments and even one entitled "How to Fold a Man's

Coat" but gave no advice on making men's clothing.[7] As Ethel Spencer recalled, in the 1890s her mother didn't even try to sew male attire. Although continually "up to her ears in sewing" for her daughters, when it came to her two sons she hired out the work "until Mark and Charles were old enough to wear woolen suits . . . [which] could be bought at department stores long before attractive dresses were available for girls."[8]

Historians seeking to explain the discrepancy between men's and women's industries frequently cite the dictates of fashion as the chief obstacle in the creation of a women's ready-made industry. They have argued that the rate of change and the elaborateness of styles caused women's clothing manufacture to remain mostly custom-made at the end of the nineteenth century.[9] The thesis that fashion was the decisive factor in the industry's development has received rather sophisticated support from some economists, who have shown that traditional supply-side analysis cannot explain this disparity, for men's and women's sectors of the clothing industry developed differently despite access to the same sort of management, labor, marketing, and distribution techniques.[10] Moreover, similar technological innovations had markedly different effects on men's and women's clothing. The sewing machine streamlined men's factory production at the same time it made women's clothing more elaborate and more customized. In fact, dressmakers used machine stitching as a form of ornamentation rather than as a production shortcut. The *Ladies' Home Journal* advised readers in 1899 that "there is no form of decoration more popular than rows of machine stitching."[11]

The historical development of marketplace demand provides only slightly more of a clue to the business split. The first markets for ready-made clothing tended to occur where large groups of men had moved beyond the easy reach of tailors and of women and thus needed new sources of clothing. These groups included soldiers during the Mexican-American War, prospectors during the California gold rush, troops during the Civil War, and railroad workers during the postbellum railroad boom.[12] In each case the existence of such a potential market encouraged the development of manufacturing techniques and capacity. These developments provided considerable impetus to the men's industry, but it is a large leap from the rough and ready clothes worn by railroad gangs in the 1870s to the respectable business suit worn in the 1890s by middle-class men who were *not* out of the reach of tailors and women who sewed. If middle-class women resisted the conversion to ready-made during this period, why didn't their male counterparts?

Ultimately, however, fashion's dictates offer at best a partial explanation of this disparity because there is no intrinsic reason that elaborate or rapidly changing fashions should be restricted to women's dress. In the eighteenth century "a pink silk suit, gold and silver embroidery, flowered and plain velvet, lace, jewelry and powder was regarded as perfectly masculine." As late as the 1840s, fashion-conscious men and women both sought a similar "hour glass shape." For both men and women, this meant carefully cut and padded clothes along with other aids—including corsets—designed to produce a fashionable silhouette. After a brief interlude in which simplicity was the mode for both sexes, women's dress moved toward the "ludicrous fussiness that characterized fashion from 1866 through the 1890s."[13] Men's clothing also became simpler and less ornate in the 1840s, but unlike women's fashion it did not revert to a mode of expressive opulence. Rather, it followed starker styles that lacked all flamboyance. J. C. Flugel famously characterized this divergence as "The Great Masculine Renunciation," although the term is problematic because men did not renounce "fashion" but rather adopted new clothing standards that were particularly distinguished by sharp separation from female norms. Nonetheless, a striking shift in cultural forms had occurred. In the mid-eighteenth century, both men and women wore vivid colors, rich fabrics, and elaborate ornamentation. By the mid-nineteenth century, these fashion details were restricted to women.[14]

Why was the women's half of the industry shunted down a track bypassing the factory while the men's industry steamed straight toward large-scale production? The decisive factor was that the bourgeois concept of separate spheres strongly favored a separation of the two trades, a separation that was especially important because of clothing's importance in maintaining gender roles. A separate spheres ideology predominated among the American middle class during the last two-thirds of the nineteenth century, and the emphasis on sexual differentiation became even more pronounced and hotly contested in the 1890s as the Victorian worldview came under siege. Although some aspects of "strenuous life" masculinity dated from earlier decades, the cult of differentiation reached its zenith in the later stages of the century when being a man first and foremost came to mean being *not* womanly. Earlier in the nineteenth century, manliness might have been defined in contrast to childishness, as a phase in a man's life cycle, but by the 1890s manliness was defined in strict opposition to femininity, as a normative gender ideal. For men who were committed to this ideal, such as Theodore Roosevelt, "any breach whatsoever in the wall of sexual difference would bring the end of male identity and national disaster."[15] This differentiation achieved a perfect cultural fit in linking masculinity, the men's sphere, the business world, and ready-made clothes, and then opposing this cluster of cultural categories to femininity, the women's sphere, home life, and custom-made clothes. The cultural priority on sex difference influenced the clothing business in a way that the possibilities of new technology or the potential of the mass marketplace could not quickly overcome.

Earlier I discussed the manner in which men's ready-made and women's custom-made clothing were well suited to embodying transitions in male and female gender roles at the end of the nineteenth century. The split between them was further reinforced because the turn-of-the-century belief in sexual differentiation was so strong that it was widely accepted as a law of nature implicit in Darwin's theory of evolution. In the midst of rampant economic and social flux—the changing nature of work, the changing demographics of the nation, the changing dynamics of the political system, the changing material world and visual culture—both men and women of the middle class found a means of stabilizing their interests and validating their values in a Darwinian rationale that stipulated Anglo-Saxon culture as the most highly developed form of humanity and stressed the essential difference of men and women as an essential part of that development.

Commentators on fashion often made the connections between these issues quite explicit. "Dress is one of the beneficent results of civilization," *Godey's Magazine* reported in an 1893 article that linked fashion, evolution, sexual differentiation, and individual character in a manner wholly characteristic of the age. According to the writer, "the evolution of costume" exactly paralleled "the gradual encroachments of civilization upon the strongholds of barbarism." Clothes provided a subtle expression of personal worth and means of individual expression, especially for women: "Nothing is so true an index to a woman's character as her clothes. They are part and parcel of her nature, as inseparable from her personality as her eyes or her hair. She stamps everything she wears with the impress of her own individuality." This association of personal identity and personal attire prompted the writer to lend emphatic support to separate spheres in men's and women's clothing.[16]

Indeed, maximum sexual differentiation in dress reflected the broad intellectual and cultural currents of the day. Under the influence of Darwinian thought, experts in the natural and social sciences developed the opinion that the more highly evolved the society, the more highly differentiated the sexes.[17] An article in *Popular Science Monthly* stated, "Plainly does it appear that differentiation is the way to perfection." According to this author, the women's rights movement "runs counter to Nature" and threatened to drag America back to the status of "the barbarian and the semi-civilized nation" through the propagation of "abnormal 'mannish' women." Herbert Spencer, Darwin's great popularizer, reflected with satisfaction on the gains women had made as humanity proceeded "up from the lowest savagery" and remarked, "If women comprehended all that is contained in the domestic sphere, they would ask no other." In the 1890s, scientist and professor Joseph LeConte summarized the scientific consensus: "The tendency of evolution is to make men more & more manly & women more & more womanly."[18]

Henry T. Finck and Charlotte Perkins Gilman both explicated the relationship of this Darwinian rationale to clothing, although they were hardly the first to see a link between Darwin and Dame Fashion. In fact, Charles Darwin's son George Howard Darwin wrote a widely reprinted article in 1872 that argued: "The development of dress presents a strong analogy to that of organisms, as explained by the modern theories of evolution." Yet George Darwin spent little time on sexual differentiation; his main concern was to use the history of dress to demonstrate the validity of natural selection. By the time Finck and Gilman took up the debate at the turn of the century, natural selection no longer seemed the most compelling aspect of Darwin's work, and the meaning and importance of sexual differentiation had assumed a new priority.[19]

Both Finck and Gilman were strong advocates of Darwinian thinking, which included assumptions about the hierarchy of races and the importance of ensuring the advance of white civilization.[20] While both believed in fundamental differences between the sexes, they differed sharply on many points. Finck believed women were innately irrational and given to frivolity. In his opinion, nothing good could come of the women's rights movement, though his reading of evolution meant that nothing much was likely to come of it anyway. Gilman believed women ought to be emancipated from domestic roles and restrictive "feminine" pursuits in order to fulfill the evolutionary potential of the race.

Finck, a Harvard graduate who spent forty-two years as a music critic and general editorial writer for the *New York Evening Post*, wrote more than twenty books. No simple reactionary or simpleminded thinker, he studied philosophy and psychology in Europe between his years at Harvard and those at the *Post*, counted intellectual luminaries such as William Dean Howells and John Fiske among his friends, and traveled widely throughout the world. Forward-looking tendencies toward scientific progressivism were evident in his thinking. For instance, his many periodical publications included an article urging federal regulation and truth-in-labeling laws to remedy the problem of food adulteration. (Gilman also wrote about this topic.)[21] The tenets of social Darwinism influenced Finck to the point that publishers billed him as the "originator of the theory that romantic love is a modern sentiment unknown to savages and the ancient civilized nations," a hypothesis he first advanced in his 1887 book *Romantic Love and Personal Beauty* and defended in an 1899 sequel called *Primitive Love and Other Stories*.[22]

Finck described his views on women's rights in a series of articles that appeared in *The Independent* in the first years of the twentieth century.[23]

One of them, in which Finck quoted Herbert Spencer, was called "Are Womanly Women Doomed?" In another, based on the notion that the woman's sphere was "one of the latest products of civilization," Finck announced: "In civilized communities . . . sewing is considered unmanly because it does not call into activity any of the distinctive capacities of strong manhood, but rather involves the feminine qualities of neatness, taste, good eyes and patience."[24]

Finck laid out his theories of clothing and civilization at greater length in an article called "Will Women Ever Dress Like Men?" He noted that "among animals—particularly birds—and the lower races of mankind" it was common for the male of the species to be more brightly colored. At the "higher stage of civilization" that now obtained in America, however, it had become apparent to men "that they were intended to be the useful sex" and therefore they no longer concerned themselves with idle display or impractical ornamentation. At this stage of evolution, "a man conspicuously given to finery is . . . a rare exception, apt to be regarded by most other men as effeminate." In contrast, women (evidently less evolved) adopted beautiful dress the same way animals—particularly birds—and the lower races did: "Beautiful dress is woman's natural element, to which she took as a duck takes to water." The result, quite literally, was that women would never wear the pants in the family. All efforts to introduce "the bifurcated garment" as part of woman's wardrobe had failed, according to Finck, because "the people feel instinctively that an attempt was being made to upset a law of social evolution." Masculinity and trousers were so strongly linked in the natural order that, according to Finck, "whether this or that kind of work is suitable for woman, can in most cases be decided by asking: 'Can it be done successfully in skirts?'"[25]

As discussed in Chapter 1, men sought to negotiate volatile economic and social changes by remaking their own ideals to suit a ready-made world. In doing so, they also sought to stabilize at least one set of social relationships by insisting on fundamental differences between men and women.[26] The slow development of the women's clothing industry in comparison to the men's trade reflected the emphasis on essentializing the difference between men and women, an emphasis Finck reinforced when he averred that differences in dress (and gender) were part of the "law of social evolution."

No one had a clearer understanding of clothing's symbolic role in gender issues than Charlotte Perkins Gilman, who as early as 1890 gave public lectures arguing that "the clothes of women will not change until the habits of women change."[27] During the years that Gilman articulated her sweeping critique and re-visioning of American gender relations, she addressed the issue of clothing many times, including in several articles that appeared in *The Independent*. She once explained that she took cloth-ing so seriously because it was "a medium of expression" that could convey "a whole gamut of emotions from personal vanity to class con-sciousness." Women needed to make progress in this area, Gilman said, because "the wide unnatural gulf between men and women . . . is no-where better shown than in dress."[28]

Yet Gilman's clear understanding of how changes in clothing pro-duction and style could break down gender roles did not diminish her satisfaction in making her own clothes. Her attitude reveals the degree to which custom clothing could support female self-expression while simultaneously representing female oppression. In her memoirs, Gilman commented how in 1899 she had made a particular dress "to suit myself" and was so fond of it she was still recycling parts of it decades later. She expressed pleasure at sewing for her daughter and referred to her Wilcox and Gibbs sewing machine as "a constant friend."[29]

Like Finck, Gilman grounded her beliefs in Darwinian principles, but she pushed conventional wisdom toward wholly unconventional con-clusions. For example, she accepted the Spencerian idea that advanced evolution meant increased individual specialization and collective inte-gration (an argument frequently used to equate industrial America with high civilization). To Gilman, however, this theory logically suggested the professionalization of housekeeping tasks, a shift of domestic duties from the realm of generic homemaking into the hands of trained spe-cialists. Such specialization would mean an effective end to the domes-tic sphere, a conclusion directly opposite to Spencer's own. Gilman did not deny that a difference existed between men and women, but she argued that women as individuals must be allowed to seek their individ-ual destinies if the race as a whole was to advance.[30]

When it came to dress, Gilman effectively showed that clothing styles could not be explained with reference to habitat, utility, aesthetics, or comfort. She argued that fashion's raison d'être was "symbolism pure and simple" and that the crucial aspect in this symbolism was sex dif-ferentiation. As Gilman wrote: "This dress of hers may or may not be healthful, may or may not be beautiful, may or may not be useful, may or may not be economical, but it must be 'feminine' above all!"[31] Typi-cally, she sought to use the logic of sexual stereotyping against itself. Women were told that their natural role and proper approach was to be modest, she pointed out, and yet they were required to wear a kind of "dress whose main feature is announcement and display." Women were told that reproduction and motherhood were their defining character-istics, but they were required to wear clothes that could impede their movements, injure their health, and "provide a constant detriment to the upbuilding of the race."[32]

When Gilman collected her thoughts on "The Dress of Woman" for a year-long series of magazine articles, she urged a switch to ready-made clothes as a pivotal step for the advancement of women. Tied up in "all the time-devouring struggles with the dressmaker," a woman finds "she must spend more on dress than a man—more in time, thought, labor or money—sometimes in all. She is required to dress in a certain kind of manner on pain of more kinds of loss than threaten him." Ready-to-wear clothing could solve this problem by standardizing clothes and making them cheaper. Widely accessible, standardized clothing would limit the ability of clothing to maintain rigid gender distinctions and would mean people could be judged on personal qualities rather than appearance. Gilman also argued that if mass production allowed fewer workers to clothe the same number of people, it would free the labor of the others for more ennobling and fulfilling work. This redistribution of human labor would allow civilization and evolution to proceed.[33]

Although Gilman's projections for the future of ready-made clothing may have been unrealistically utopian, she recognized that the cultural force of gender politics had put the brakes on the development of the women's ready-made industry. When she reported that "on the level plains of our great West a common measure of a mile is 'as far as you can tell a man from a woman,'" Gilman indicated that, literally and metaphorically, Americans at this time took the measure of themselves by how well they could differentiate men from women. One key to this difference was clothing.[34]

Gilman's evocative notion that clothing transformed the body into "a sort of ideograph" reflected her awareness of the extent to which the body, and with it gender difference, is socially constructed. She wrote far in advance of later scholars who claimed that "there can be no natural way of considering the body that does not involve at the same time a social dimension" and who argued that in fact the body itself is the product of social processes.[35] Gilman also acknowledged the importance of clothing to bodily ideals and hence to gender definitions. In her words, clothing turned the body into "a conventionalized symbol of a living form" and above all, women "must so dress as to cry aloud to all beholders, 'I am a female—and don't forget it!'" As Gilman knew, clothing not only evokes but enacts gender; fashion not only communicates but constitutes gender identity.[36]

Institutions that served to mold the body into conventionalized male or female forms had enormous cultural significance because, although the relationships between body, identity, and power may not be absolutely fixed, a continuing presumption of American society had been that a person with a man's body had a man's identity and was entitled to a man's power.[37] In the late Victorian era, the prevailing medical consensus clearly reflected this attitude. Physicians believed the body was a closed energy system dominated in the male by the brain and in the female by the reproductive organs. Hence Victorian Americans doubted the suitability of higher education for women. Similarly, a man who stimulated his reproductive organs at the expense of his mind also risked physiological disaster. Thus Victorian proscriptions against masturbation were a basic element in the male role model of self-control. In defending this system of values, people sought not only protection against disruption in the spheres of men and women, but also reassurance against the whole realm of social and economic changes that were loosening the world from its moorings.[38]

The scientific validation of sexual differentiation represented a turning away from Enlightenment philosophy that through the late eighteenth century emphasized the commonalities shared by all people. This philosophy "gradually gave way in the nineteenth century to a stress on differentiation and hierarchy. Environmentalism lost favor; categories hardened and were made permanent." This intellectual shift occurred precisely as a similar split occurred in men's and women's fashions. By the late nineteenth century, a new medical subspecialty of sexology began to further subdivide sexuality by establishing categories designated as "deviant behavior." In essence, the sexologists sought to control social disorder by projecting it onto gender and establishing what was normal and what was deviant. Richard Krafft-Ebing, whose major work on the subject first appeared in Germany in 1888, took the next step and identified deviant female sexuality with "a strong preference for male garments." Dress became analogous to gender in Krafft-Ebing's analysis.[39]

The connection between dress, body, and gender functioned in a very direct way because clothing created the publicly seen body. Indeed, in the 1890s, the clothing prescribed for women often directly disciplined their bodies: collars wired in place, sleeves puffed to suitable dimensions, bodices boned to a precise shape, skirts carefully stiffened and flared. The Empress Skirt Company of Frankfort, Indiana, produced an underskirt with a wire framework embedded in the fabric to hold it in place. The company's advertisements showed a diagram of the wire circling the skirt and claimed that the "light, highly tempered, spiral steel wire which never rusts compels the gown covering an Empress Skirt to maintain the shape and contour so much desired by every woman appreciating grace and comfort."[40]

Etiquette books and magazine articles presumed that one goal of clothes was to structure an ideal body. Certain sleeves would "give flesh to the slender arm, and conceal it in one that is too plump." A certain bodice has "ribbons crossing it in such a way that the waist is made to appear smaller, and the bust and hips broader." Letters from readers sought advice for the "short-waisted" and "overly plump." They were advised that in making a dress one should be "endeavoring to add to the side of the very slender and take away from the appearance of the too solid flesh of the stout woman."[41] One dressmaker recalled a woman who specified that her waist measure was 24 inches, although it took all the strength of two dressmakers' assistants to pull the corset laces tight enough for the woman, "gasping for breath and perspiring rivers," to assume that dimension. In the end, her dress "fitted like a glove, but the poor lady's face was the color of blood and she could hardly speak." The situation was hardly unique. "All the fat women insist we shall make them look slim," the dressmaker said.[42]

Despite occasional claims to the contrary, these bodily prescriptions had nothing to do with "natural" or average body size. One magazine writer reminded her readers: "Few of us are constructed on the lines of the ideal figure, so that much of the beauty of our forms depends upon a good-fitting corset." In her 1890s etiquette guide, Maud Cooke argued, quite contrary to the law of averages, that "there are proportionately more women that are too short, than too tall." Furthermore, the ideal changed regularly. "In the fashion world there is a new figure for every season," the *Chicago Dry Goods Reporter* noted, adding, "through the use of various improvers, in the form of bustles, pads and extenders of all sorts, the figure is changed at will" (Figures 21, 22).[43]

Advertisers did not miss their opportunity to promote brand-name body fabrication. "Beauty of figure is largely under a woman's own control. With the braided wire bustles and bust forms any defects of form are remedied," ran one appeal. "W. B. Corsets are cut in such a manner that they give a graceful appearance to almost any kind of figure, reducing remarkably the apparent size of the waist without undue pressure," said another. "We guarantee a figure as shown in the illustration by wearing The Sahlin Perfect Model Distender," said a third. "Thousands of the best tailors and dressmakers welcome the latest invention, and testify as to its superiority over any kind of interlinings, *producing a natural figure* without padding" (Figures 23, 24). Another ad offered a nostrum called Aquamiel, which was touted as a "magical bust developer" that "never fails to round out thin people into graceful proportions."[44]

A woman had to do more than mold her figure with the proper clothes. She also had to adjust her movements and gestures to match. "The best of tailors may fit you perfectly, and yet by your mode of walking or sitting the good effect may be entirely lost," said one writer. Another acknowledged that wearing a wrap does not sound difficult "and yet to keep your arms in a position that does not pull the wrap out of place really becomes an art." Yet another lamented that "it is really pitiful to see how badly the majority of women walk" and suggested they imagine a "string tied about the breast bone" pulling them forward so that "the chest will rise, the body will incline a little forward, and at each step the weight of the body will poise on the balls of the feet." Proper movement tied directly to gender distinctions, as etiquette-book author Florence Howe Hall made clear: "A mincing gait is extremely disagreeable in a man, and will always make him appear effeminate. In the same way women should avoid a long striding walk, which makes them look ungraceful and masculine."[45]

Figures 21, 22. In the late 1890s, a wide assortment of bustles and pads were available to help women construct the approved body shape. (*Top*) Warren Featherbone Company offers "shirt waist forms," "bust form extenders," and bustles. (*Bottom*) Thos. P. Taylor has a selection of more than a dozen bustles and "extenders." Warren Featherbone Company advertisement, *Chicago Dry Goods Reporter* (April 23, 1989): 14; Thos. P. Taylor advertisement, *Chicago Dry Goods Reporter* (November 25, 1899): 26.

SLENDER WOMEN

We guarantee a figure as shown in illustration by wearing

The Sahlin Perfect Model Distender

Thousands of the best tailors and dressmakers welcome the latest invention, and testify as to its superiority over any kind of interlinings, producing a natural figure without padding.

It gives to tailor-made and other tight-fitting garments the beautiful curves and graceful lines so much desired by every woman. The illustration is a faithful reproduction of the Distender as worn.

No. 150. Best Grade, $1.00
No. 160. Medium Grade, .50

Ask your dealer. If he does not keep them, order direct, giving length of waist and bust measure. Add 8 cents extra for postage. If not entirely satisfactory, return, and your money will be refunded. Write for free catalogue.

PATENTED July 26, 1898.

SAHLIN NOVELTY COMPANY, 195 Market St., Chicago

Eight million women

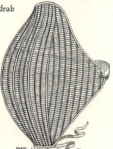

On every genuine "Sahlin Waist Front Distender" (the only one that produces the correct shape) You will find this trade mark.

have been told during the past week through our advertising in the Sunday papers and women's magazines about the various merits of the

Sahlin Waist Front Distender

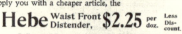

If only one in every hundred of these women asked their dealers for the "Sahlin" as they are instructed to do, it would result in several calls for each dry goods retailer in America. Why not supply this demand with the original? It is the one and only article that will produce the shape desired by every lady that makes any pretense to be stylish, and the only distender advertised to the consumer so as to make them an active, easy seller in the corset, notion or shirt waist stock. They are made in white, drab and black. All sizes. Price, $4.50 and $7.50 per dozen, less discount. We can also supply you with a cheaper article, the

The Sahlin Waist Front Distender.
Pat. May 3, 1898.
Can be adjusted to low or high bust.

Hebe Waist Front Distender, **$2.25** per doz. Less Discount.

Sells quickly at a quarter. Made in the four popular sizes. White only.

We again call the attention of the trade to the patents covering our distenders, and to the fact that no concerns are entitled to manufacture similar articles except those licensed under our patents. Unless the articles bear our trade mark or are stamped "Licensed Pat. May 3, '98," they are infringements and merchants should refuse to handle them for their own protection. We will gladly send samples for inspection, or if you prefer, **ORDER DIRECT FROM YOUR JOBBER,** but insist on the distender bearing our trade mark.

I wear the Sahlin Waist Front Distender.

Sahlin Novelty Co., 195 & 197 Market St., CHICAGO. 640 Broadway, NEW YORK.

PAT. MAY 3, 1898.
HEBE.

Figures 23, 24. The Sahlin Perfect Model Distender promised "a natural figure" providing "the beautiful curves and graceful lines so much desired by every woman." The claims made on behalf of this widely advertised item were supposedly seen by 8 million women a week based on the circulation of the newspapers and magazines in which the company promoted its product. Sahlin Novelty Company advertisement, *Ladies' Home Journal* (October 1899): 40, reproduced courtesy of the Winterthur Library: Printed Book and Periodical Collection; Sahlin Novelty Company advertisement, *Chicago Dry Goods Reporter* (June 18, 1898): 18.

If gender is, as Judith Butler has argued, "the repeated stylization of the body," merely the sum of "acts, gestures, enactments" replayed over and over according to the dictates of social discourse, then there is a sense in which the wearing of appropriate attire did not display or symbolize gender but constituted it.[46] Dress was the practice of gender, not merely the depiction of it; dress was one of the places where gender was created. Many nineteenth-century writers understood this, at least implicitly. As one etiquette writer summarized: "The old proverb, 'Handsome is as handsome does,' which we have heard so much in our childhood, has a far deeper and subtler meaning than either children or parents give it." Dress was so inextricably linked with gender roles that an 1898 article divided the world into "the petticoat sex" and "the trousered sex." Certain items of attire were considered innately feminine. Mary Katharine Howard warned her *Woman's Home Companion* readers: "Unless a bow of some sort is worn under the chin, a woman is sadly out of fashion—and it might be added, lacks femininity." Conversely, she also stipulated that "mannish effects are to be avoided" (Figure 25). In 1894, *Godey's* complained that the fashionable woman of the day was borrowing too much from men's clothing styles:

Why does she do this? Does she want to be a man? Many of the tailor-made costumes so popular to-day are neat and natty enough, but why should not men don the costumes of women, if the women are to appropriate so much of the male attire? One can hardly imagine anything so ridiculous as a man clad in a bonnet and gown; yet only a few years ago we should all have stood aghast, had we seen one of our modern tailor-made girls out for a promenade, with her derby, her cutaway coat, shirt-front, and bulldog.[47]

The situation was summed up in a contribution to an 1894 publication called *The Woman's Book*, a two-volume reference work that promoted itself as "dealing practically with the modern conditions of home-life, self-support, education, opportunities, and every-day problems." In this book, a writer argued that body-shaping devices were integral to women's clothing: "Belts, stomachers, girdles have always prevailed in feminine attire. They have a meaning, just as long skirts have a meaning."[48] Skirts and corsets did indeed continue to have meaning, specifically, as the book's title suggested, in the constitution of gender.

The body-dress-gender link also achieved expression in a more figurative sense—at the level of representation—because clothing styles and fashion underwrote the entire concept of the normal body. Visual and pictorial conventions historically have established what was considered "natural" for both the human body and for human attire. Late nineteenth-century images of bodily form were normalized in material form by fashion styles and in representational form by widely circulated illustrations of them.[49]

Advertisers struck some interesting pictorial compromises in trying to cope with simultaneous developments in visual media, advertising, and fashion. For a period around the turn of the century, fashion advertisements and illustrations often used a drawing of the latest style topped by a photographic cutout of a woman's head (Figure 26). The predominance of this technique can be dated fairly accurately to mid-decade. In its 1895–1896 catalog, Chas. A. Stevens & Bros., a large mail-order cloak company, published only engraved illustrations. In its 1896-97 catalog, the illustrations all had photographic heads and engraved bodies.[50] The timing was similar for a variety of other advertisers.

This technique had some fashion-plate precedents. Earlier engravers sometimes used a generic drawing of head, shoulders, and arms as a "hook" upon which they could hang clothing in different fashion plates,

Figure 25. The caption on this *Life* cartoon read: "Isn't Heaven in there?" "Yes, but this is the ladies' entrance." The link between gender and clothing provided fodder for many satirical drawings in the late nineteenth century. Note, however, that while the cartoonist apparently thought the woman's clothing represented masculinity to the point of caricature, the cut and fit of her outfit are far from truly "unisex." *Life* (January 9, 1896): 25. Reproduced from the collections of the Library of Congress.

Figure 26. In the late 1890s, it became increasingly common to see fashion illustrations and advertisements featuring a drawn garment topped by a photographed head. The technique allowed for rigid control over the appearance of clothing and body while taking advantage of the verisimilitude of photography and the recent technological advances that made photo reproduction easier. "Leading Ideas of Spring," *Chicago Dry Goods Reporter* (March 26, 1898): 39.

perhaps preferring to expend time and energy on the more crucial part of the drawing, or perhaps not having developed the techniques needed to render faces with the same skill that they learned to depict garment drapery and decoration.[51] The appearance of the photo-illustration represented a new twist, however. Photographs, made available to mass circulation publications for the first time through the recently perfected halftone reproduction process, were popular with advertisers. As one ad journal put it, a public made suspicious by "unscrupulous advertising methods" found photos convincing because "a photograph presents the article in a form absolutely true to life."[52] Yet clothing advertisers used photography only for the heads of their fashion illustrations rather than entire bodies, probably because advertisers had not yet developed the sophistication to deliver the ideal body image photographically. Today's fashion images are the product of lighting, processing, and retouching

Figure 27. Mail-order catalogs from 1896 onward increasingly used cutout photographs of heads atop the highly stylized fashions of the day. Jordan, Marsh & Company, *Our New 1897 Price List* (Boston, 1897): 13. Reproduced courtesy of the Winterthur Library: Printed Book and Periodical Collection.

subtleties—not to mention a pool of models seemingly bred to represent the favored body type—that were unavailable to nineteenth-century photographers. The halftone heads atop the thin-waisted bodies of the late 1890s or the reverse-S posture of the early 1900s suggest that advertisers were eager to capture the convenience, modernity, and realism of photographic images but were constrained by the need to depict the conventionalized female body (Figures 27, 28).

By the 1910s, many clothing advertisers had switched back to drawings, perhaps because the novelty of photographs had waned and because photography still had not been widely adapted either to fashion in particular or to advertising in general. In the 1920s, however, fashion, photography, and advertising began a cross-pollination that eventually established fashion photography as a distinct genre and delivered some of the prototypical advertising images of the later twentieth century.[53]

SILK WAISTS.
(Shown by the Economist Waist Co., 134 Spring St., New York)

Figure 28. By the turn of the century, the shape of women's fashions had changed, but illustrators continued to find the engraved body-photographed head technique to be a useful representational strategy. "Silk Waists for Spring," *Chicago Dry Goods Reporter* (February 23, 1901): 21.

Moving beyond the garments and pictorial representations of them to a more broadly metaphorical level, one finds that published ruminations on bodily form and fashion sense often suggested clothing could fairly be interpreted to stand for the entire person. Isabel Mallon, one of the most prolific and popular writers in the 1890s *Ladies' Home Journal,* wrote: "I wish I could make all women understand how unconsciously they express themselves in what they wear, and how, if they cultivate the finer part of them, it will show itself in their gowns."[54] Mary Katharine Howard told her *Woman's Home Companion* readers: "Every woman should study herself, and select with care everything she wears with a view to having it becoming." The garment and the wearer almost merge in such injunctions. Many writers celebrated fashionable dress with the word "becoming" or praised a particular garment for its "becomingness." A *Ladies' Home Journal* writer once used the word four times in a single paragraph, and another used it or a variant five times in a one-page article on "Gowns for Unusual Figures." Florence Howe Hall summarized the main issues succinctly: "The two chief points which a woman should always bear in mind in regard to dress are—first, is it appropriate; second, is it becoming?"[55] This terminology, as when one says to a person, "that dress becomes you," has suggestive ontological implications concerning the relationship of fashion, fashion talk, and the self. Although we may not intend it, with such statements one very literally asserts that the dress has come to "be" the individual, a position that many of the writers on fashion of the late nineteenth century would have cheerfully accepted.

Another frequently used and revealing term concerns the "effect" of a garment. Often the term has limited resonance, as in reference to "close-fitting effects," "a smart effect," or to the sought-after "jacket effect," "basque effect," or "bustle effect." Sometimes the usage is more telling: "The whole effect of the blouse jaquette, when properly made, is to give a very feminine figure." Such active terminology underlines the notion that these garments were designed for much more than simply to keep their wearers warm.[56]

Although clothing styles—as circulated in garment, image, and text—exerted pervasive pressure that reinforced female stereotypes, women's clothing was more than simply a tool of oppression. A woman could assert individuality and presence in the world through her dress, and more specifically through the custom making of the dress. Gilman, who supported herself as a writer and certainly knew about both self-expression and self-assertion, referred to sewing as her chance to "compose in cloth." In the *Woman's Home Companion* column "What to Wear and How to Make It," fashion writer Dinah Sturgis argued that the well-dressed woman had managed "to make her clothes subservient and her personality dominant." Clothing allowed women to assert competence ("I can make a dress *sure,*" wrote diarist Emily French in the midst of her desperate struggles to hold home and family together) as well as self-possession. Men's ineptitude and unobservant behavior regarding fashion provided cover to mock and criticize them, as magazine writers occasionally did.[57] Moreover, the standards of dress could be used as a more overt challenge to the status quo when women chose to flout them or test their limits. Clearly making a link between dress, self-assertion, and social protest, Edward Bok, the *Ladies' Home Journal* editor, longed for the days when women "did not don hideous garments that unsexed them, nor did they climb into trees and address howling mobs of Anarchists." This remark demonstrates that the dress code was important, widely understood, and had its rebellious as well as its repressive aspects when constituting gender roles.[58]

This project of fabricating a bodily image through clothes was not solely the concern of women, as advice manuals make clear. Etiquette writers, on the whole a conservative lot, sought to maintain a world of rank and privilege through a relentless categorization of people and things into their "proper" places.[59] That drive for categorization (which mirrored the prevailing scientific emphasis on classification and differentiation) included clear distinctions between the sexes. Usually the manuals listed advice for men and women separately and sequentially, not together, and they stressed that dress was important for men as well as women: "Not only are men judged by the coats they wear, but by the hats, the shoes, the shirts, the ties, the jewelry, and indeed, aside from the countenance, there is no other means available for us for reading the characters of the vast majority of those who we meet in the various walks of life." It was important for men to understand the differences in what was required of them from what was required of women: "Don't—we address here the male reader—wear anything that is pretty."[60]

The switch to ready-made clothing and the business suit has sometimes made middle-class men seem "inexpressive," "anonymous," and "undemonstrative" to historians, but these clothing styles did not really exempt men from the discourse of fashion, they merely changed the terms under which they participated.[61] Edward Bok included men in his admonitions on dress and more than once took up the cause of the sack suit against evening dress. "The streets of our large cities are not filled with men in frock coats and silk hats going to afternoon teas or receptions. . . . And where one sees such men, one generally does not see the men who hold the respect and confidence of the community. The latter are at their places of business, dressed as is most suitable for the purposes of business." Bok claimed that occasion-specific rules about evening dress were outmoded and rarely followed. He urged men to ignore etiquette books and warned them not to be too interested in "fashion": "A young man should not allow himself to forget that what are known as the fashionably-attired young men are seldom the successful ones." In discussing "the fop, or one of our modern 'dudes,'" Bok simply said, "[his] ignorance is so dense that I shall not try to enter into the spirit of [his] belongings."

It is worth repeating that although Bok urged men to disdain "fashionable" attire he did not suggest they should be inattentive to their clothes. Quite the contrary, he believed that clothing could show "innate refinement" on the one hand or "weakness of character" on the other. As he said: "Many a business man judges a young man's character by his dress. And it is a truer indication than many believe or dream of a young man's birth, his training, his tastes, his tendencies, his thoughts, his inner character—all are depicted in his dress with unerring accuracy."[62]

Henry Finck, in accordance with his theory that fashion and barbarism were linked, argued in 1887 that "the several styles of dress worn by men are fashionable in proportion to their ugliness." To him, that meant the dress coat was the least desirable garment, the frock coat next, the cutaway next. Only the sack coat, he said, "follows the natural outlines of the body" and therefore it was a great pity that the sack suit was not yet acceptable in all social occasions.[63] In these remarks Finck mistakenly asserted that men's body type existed independent of dress. Gilman was far more perceptive, as evidenced in her comment: "It is masculine to have a broad chest and square shoulders—typically masculine. If the customer chanced to lack these distinctions . . . the tailor sees to it that his garments should symbolize his sex beyond dispute."[64] Indeed, the massive shoulders, padded chests, and rectilinear shape of turn-of-the-century men's fashions, far from following any "natural" outline, represented a project of bodily construction all its own. The discussion of these matters was less overt than for women, but it occasionally leaked through in advertising promises such as: "The square-cut shoulders and built-up front will give dignity to the figure" or "all of our coats this season have the broad shoulder effect and are made with the felt shoulder pad and haircloth front, making a garment which will retain its original shape." One catalog promised to deliver a double-breasted sack suit that "emphasizes the shapely figure and conceals the unshapely one" by providing "athletic shoulders" and a "broad chest" (Figure 29).[65]

Filtering the experience of the past through the prism of separate spheres is risky business, and applying the concept to historical circumstances has become "notoriously problematic," according to one fashion historian.[66] Scholars have worried that this binary model inevitably

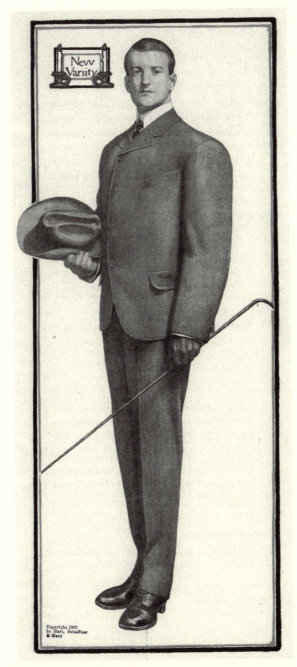

Figure 29. Sack suit styles for men were designed to create a powerful, muscular-looking upper torso through padding in the shoulders and stiff linings in the coat front. Hart, Schaffner & Marx, *Hand-Book of Styles* (Chicago, 1902). Reproduced from the Warshaw Collection, Archives Center, National Museum of History, Smithsonian Institution.

produces a reductionist interpretation, focuses too much on the white middle class, ignores or downplays interdependence between gender roles and other categories of analysis, and diverts scholars from the workings of the larger social system. They also warn that the separate spheres concept implies static relations of power and resistance and arbitrarily normalizes heterosexuality. Finally, they argue that the separate spheres never had much basis in the everyday lived experience of American women, that it is a mere trope or metaphor that historians seized upon after the fact to try to make sense of the past and has nothing much to do with the "real" past at all.[67]

These caveats are well founded, and any consideration of dress and gender must take them into account. Indeed, the link between fashion sense and the logic of social Darwinism suggests how dress and gender are parts of a larger cultural matrix. The emphasis on sex differentiation was not an isolated phenomenon but was a dimension and perhaps even a rationale for the class-based, race-based worldview of the American middle class. Furthermore, these relationships are not stable and unchanging. The backdrop and probably the impetus for the commentary of Gilman and Finck was precisely one of social and economic change, and the whole point is to understand how sexual difference was used to comprehend, deflect, or master change. Nor does the connection between dress, Darwinism, and differentiation imply a simplistic rigidity about gender roles, a single masculinity or a one-size-fits-all female gender role. Gilman's approach to the subject of fashion sought ways to use its powerful imagery to subvert the dominant regime.

At the same time, separate spheres for men and women appear in clothing habits as neither a historian's delusion nor a nineteenth-century abstraction. The evidence points strongly to separate spheres as a continuing concern for men and women at the turn of the century. When such a concept is enacted in the everyday presentation of the self, when it is meant to be apparent at a glance, when the weight of the economy and an emerging mass media reinforce it continually—this concept is manifesting social structure and power relations in a very real way. Clothing, as Gilman pointed out, saw to it that a woman "must not only be, but symbolize, femininity." The continuing importance of gender distinction in clothing practices is particularly suggestive because during the past 100 years, distinctions of class and region have lost ground as clothing markers, while gender differentiation has proved extremely resilient.[68] If, as one feminist scholar has written, "the representation of gender is its construction," then clothing habits were gender's building blocks, one of the basic constituents of everyday lived experience.[69]

After the English writer Samuel Butler died in 1902, editors found this unpublished fragment in his notebooks:

A little boy and a little girl were looking at a picture of Adam and Eve.
"Which is Adam and which is Eve?" said one.
"I do not know," said the other, "but I could tell if they had their clothes on."[70]

Given the tight cultural links between clothing, body politics, and gender roles, it only makes sense that men's and women's garment production followed different paths, and in particular that women's clothing remained in a custom-made world despite general business or economic tendencies to the contrary. This generation placed enormous importance on sexual differentiation, ascribing it not only to nature but also to the continuing evolutionary improvement of nature's original plan. Dress naturalized the relationship between the sexes as a fact of everyday life. Gilman's observation that clothing habits could be attributed to "symbolism pure and simple" hit close to the heart of the matter, and her suggestions on how clothes could exemplify as well as symbolize completed the picture. The uneven development of the clothing industry during the late nineteenth century reflects the foundational nature of a belief that clothes make the man—and the woman.

Chapter 4

Clothing and Citizenship
"Real American Machine-Made Garments"

Have we worked out our democracy in regard to clothes farther than in regard to anything else?

—*Jane Addams, "The Subtle Problems of Charity," 1899*

What did dress have to do with democracy? At the turn of the century, Americans often saw a relationship between national identity and clothing. In newspapers, magazines, and store windows, advertisers tried to sell everything from men's suits to women's corsets by associating them with events such as the election of President McKinley, George Washington's birthday, and the Declaration of Independence.[1] William Browning, the New York clothier who in 1895 chronicled the industry's rise to respectability, boasted: "If it be true, as I think it is, that the condition of a people is indicated by its clothing, America's place in the scale of civilized lands is a high one."[2] The relationship between clothing and citizenship became particularly visible during the 1890s with respect to two issues. First, as American nationalistic fervor reached new heights during the Spanish-American War in 1898, so did its linkage with dress. Second, questions of citizenship and national identity intermingled with the emphasis many European immigrants placed upon acquiring new clothes as a means of "becoming American." Wartime patriotism and immigrant adaptation provided a means not only for sharpening the definition of Americanism, but also for creating a context in which middle-class Americans sought to strengthen gender ideology and maintain their class identity. An examination of this issue will demonstrate how fashion mediated questions of gender, class, and nationalism simultaneously, offering a glimpse at the connections between these different aspects of personal identity as their compatibilities and conflicts manifested themselves in the routines of everyday life.

Linking dress and ideas such as citizenship or national identity requires thinking of these concepts as relational and fundamentally symbolic. In other words, citizenship is best thought of as existing in the relationships between and among people rather than as a status or attribute within an individual. Such relationships must be articulated and to a certain extent sustained by everyday symbolism because a nation, as an abstract entity, has no palpable existence outside of the symbols that refer to it and the actions that mobilize them.[3] Clothing, operating at the literal boundary between self and society and possessed of enormous symbolic potential, was well suited to represent issues of late nineteenth-century citizenship.

In the United States, this symbolic nationalism was especially important. Because the nation was founded upon a break from the past and an influx of new residents, its symbols had to be invented and accessible.[4] The attempt to fashion patriotic symbols became especially urgent in the late nineteenth century as the country became more integrated economically while it simultaneously diversified culturally. The emblematic importance of the American flag as an icon of "Americanness" emerged during this period, and the clothing styles disseminated by the new mass media contributed in ways that, being less direct, may have been all the more effective. Americans pieced together their own senses of national identity and made their own claims to "proper" citizenship in no small part through their manipulation of the material goods at their disposal.[5]

In the years around the turn of the century, at least three distinct approaches to American nationalism bid for public favor. A populist nationalism relied upon an ideological commitment to civic republicanism and a producerist commonwealth. In general it was hostile to the idea of big capital and worked locally and cooperatively, though its tendency to idealize the moral community or public virtue could have exclusionary and conformist aspects. A progressive nationalism, in contrast, accepted the growth in size and power of capitalist business interests but also sought to inflate the size and power of the government to counterbalance it. Americanism in this model involved civic relations that were less localized and more heavily structured by scientific expertise and scientific management. Finally, a multicultural nationalism suggested that a pluralistic and federated version of nationalism would and should emerge from a coexistence rather than a merger of America's many parts.[6]

The populist agenda suffered a stunning defeat in the presidential election of 1896, and the multicultural definition of nationalism, although it had articulate advocates in the 1910s and 1920s, did not receive very much public debate or acceptance until the last half of the twentieth century.[7] As the clothing evidence indicates, the triumphant form of nationalism in this era was a progressive version of national identity that attempted to bind people into a relatively uniform, scientifically produced, economically up-to-date, imagined community.[8] Examining efforts to dress "like an American," one understands the degree to which the immediate American future would be broadly nationalized, increasingly standardized, and tightly intertwined with big business and mass markets.

As the Spanish crisis loomed in February 1898, the *Chicago Dry Goods Reporter* editorialized against "the tendency among the more irresponsible jingo dailies to shout for war." The magazine feared the impact war might have on business. "Jingoism is one of the most inveterate enemies of peace and of trade in this country," it warned. A week after this editorial appeared, the same journal published a column describing how to make an effective window display based on the sinking of the battleship *Maine*. The column began: "The window dresser who is ever alert for novelty will not allow the disaster to the battleship Maine to pass without getting an idea out of it for a window display."[9]

This quick reversal suggests how nicely the Spanish-American War rode along the cultural currents swirling through the United States at the end of the century. The war provided an opportunity for further demonstration of a Darwinian concept of racial hierarchy and another opportunity for practicing a "strenuous life" version of masculinity. In addition, the war offered a means for further expansion of U.S. business interests that had grown concerned over productive capacity outstripping the needs of domestic markets. Politicians also cultivated expansionism as a partisan issue capable of reinvigorating emotional attachment in the electorate, using the issue as a tool to compensate for party sympathies and practices that had weakened as a result of the economic and demographic changes in the country. The impulse of "progressivism"— a righteous engagement in social activism on behalf of middle-class American standards—found a foreign outlet in the fight over Cuba. So did a renewed spirit of manifest destiny: the belief that the United States was fated to bring ever more territory under its enlightened rule.[10]

These trends collectively marked ascendant elements in American culture, but the war also provided a chance to revitalize a vision of America's past. Incorporation, industrialization, and the influx of immigrants had threatened the perceived harmony of interests and unambiguous moral plane upon which the dominant culture of Victorian America preferred to operate. In addition, although the United States had become more closely knit in its economic, communications, and transportation systems, it remained divided by sectional differences, and as an extraordinary wave of immigrants from eastern and southern Europe poured into the country, American society grew ever more demographically diverse.[11] This diversity further threatened the Victorian view of a settled world order, and it posed a new challenge to the whole concept of

"Americanness," which likewise had rested comfortably on a substratum of Anglo middle-class cultural values. The upsurge of nationalism in the late 1890s at least temporarily reestablished a sense of consensual values that had become increasingly difficult to maintain in a decade that had witnessed bloody labor conflict, a serious economic depression, and a bitterly divisive presidential election.[12] Economically, politically, ideologically, and emotionally, the Spanish-American War made sense to a great many Americans.

Clothing merchants constantly pushed the link between war news and store news in 1898. Sometimes they made only passing reference in an advertising illustration, although on other occasions they pursued the analogy quite vigorously. New York's Wanamaker store ran an advertisement with an illustration showing a fashionably dressed woman standing at attention and delivering a smart salute, although the text made no reference to the current military conflict (Figure 30). The Indianapolis Saks store ran an advertisement with the headline "We stand by our colors" without any follow-up in the text except a generic testimony to the reliability of its goods. Some references were more specific, if no less strained, as in headlines such as "Manila has fallen and so have our prices" or "We would like to C-U-B-A purchaser of a pair of our stylish fitting shoes."[13]

Other advertisers devoted their entire space to war themes. A New York tailor ran an ad with copy that boasted: "Into the enemy's ranks goes the hot shot from our guns. . . . The suits that we make to order for $15.00 are the amunition with which we are reducing the ranks of the higher priced tailors." The accompanying illustration showed a row of cannons launching cannonballs labeled "$15" (Figure 31). An Indianapolis shoe store commissioned an illustration appropriate to the following text, which was published under the headline "Uncle Sam . . . Crushing a Tarantula" (Figure 32):

> One foot is placed upon the Don—
> (The other foot's in Washington)—
> Both feet are dressed in honest leather
> To stand all kinds of wear and weather.
> In short, our Uncle Sam has got
> Shoes just like those sold by Marott.[14]

An effort to stay in step with the news was evident. Readers could find on one page of a Chicago newspaper a story headlined "President's Call for 75,000 More Volunteers," while on the opposite page of the same edition they would see an advertisement that read: "Uncle Sam means business and wants 75,000 more fighters. The style and quality of Foreman's Challenge Shoes prove that we mean business and we are doing it

Further News of
Dresses and Jackets

THERE are various grades and kinds of tailor-made Dresses, but we carry only one kind—the very best we can find. That doesn't mean the highest priced sorts only. "Best," although superlative, admits of comparison. There's the best $10 suit, as well as the best at $100. We have tried to get both, as well as all the intermediate bests. We hate trash, and next to trash come "second-bests." You'll find neither here, look as hard as you will.

As to prices, of course good goods cost more than inferior kinds, but not much more, and when you are face to face with such reductions as these, they cost absolutely less.

Here is news of honest and liberal reductions on the very best of garments,—fresh made and correct in every way.

At $8—Value $14
At $10—Values $12 to $18
At $25—Values $30 to $37

At $12.75—Value $18.50
At $22.00—Values $30 to $35
At $30.00—Values $40 to $42

JACKETS

A manufacturer eager to close his most expensive line, unloaded his remaining lot here at a positive bargain. They're now at a uniform price—one-half or one-third actual value.

At $10—Of kersey, Venetian or covert cloths, in black, navy blue, green, tan and other fashionable shades; box front or fly-front; lined throughout with fancy taffetas. All the newest touches of styles to these garments. They were $20, $25 and $30.

Here Are Dress Goods Reductions

It is closing-out time in many lines of Spring and Summer fabrics, and this is the evidence thereof:

Fancy Mixed Cheviots that were 37½c. are 25c.
Figured Vigoreaux that were 50c. are now 30c.

Figure 30. New York's Wanamaker store illustrated the tendency of advertisers to try to find some link to war fever of 1898 with this image of a stylishly dressed woman striking a military pose. There is no text in the ad (about one-third of which is shown here) making any reference to the war or the significance of this illustration. Wanamaker advertisement, *New York Times* (May 18, 1898): 4.

INTO THE ENEMY'S RANKS

goes the hot shot from our guns. The battle is as good as won, and victory is ours. The suits that we make to order for

$15.00

are the amunition with which we are reducing the ranks of the higher priced tailors. Money back if dissatisfied.

W.C. Loftus & Co.

Broadway, cor. Prince (11th floor).

1,191 B'way, near 29th. | 125th and Lexington Ave.
Sun building, near Bridge. | 25 Whitehall St.

Figure 31. W. C. Loftus attempted to reduce the ranks of the men's suit competition with cannonballs labeled "$15." Many advertisers, both large and small, filled their ads with this kind of wordplay and visual pun during the war. W. C. Loftus advertisement, *New York Tribune* (June 2, 1898): 4.

Figure 32. This Indianapolis merchant used specially made illustrations and rhyming text to link his merchandise to the war effort. The subhuman characterization of the enemy evokes a prevalent style of Darwinian thought that asserted that Anglo-Saxon Americans represented a higher stage of evolution than any other people. Geo. J. Marott advertisement, *Indianapolis News* (May 4, 1898): 10.

too." In early June, naval officer Richmond Hobson undertook a daring mission in the harbor of Santiago de Cuba, attempting to trap the Spanish fleet by slipping past enemy cannons and scuttling a small ship in the harbor entrance. Within days the Hub, a Chicago department store, ran an advertisement with a custom-made illustration and text reading: "It was Hobson's choice to risk his life in the fiery mouth of Santiago. . . . For eleven years The Hub—through choice—has braved the storms of competition." Later that month Gen. William Shafter, field commander of the United States ground forces during the war, sent his troops ashore in Cuba. The Hub responded immediately with a drawing illustrating that event in an ad that opened: "Shafter holds the key to the gates of Cuban liberty and The Hub holds the key to the clothing trade of Chicago" (Figure 33).[15]

Figure 33. The Hub, a Chicago department store, ran a weekly advertisement with an illustration depicting a battle scene accompanied by a headline and introduction tied closely to that week's war news. The advertising manager for this store once told an interviewer that he always tried to base his advertisements on current events: "The public eye, you know, is always focused upon some particular thought or event. It is my aim to always be within that focus and the nearer the center the better." See *Profitable Advertising* (December 1896): 8. The Hub advertisement, *Chicago Tribune* (June 26, 1898): 15.

To a certain degree, advertisers employed war motifs just as they had used the Klondike gold rush, the latest theatrical sensation, the election of 1896, or any other current event as grist for the ad copywriters' mill. In part, the merchandising strategies were a testament to mass-market capitalism's capacity to take virtually any human activity or aspiration and turn it into a sales opportunity. In addition, as war fever and the sensationalizing tactics of yellow journalism produced increasingly dramatic display for news articles, advertisers believed they needed to raise the volume of their own appeals to avoid getting drowned out.[16] Yet the frequency with which advertisers made these associations and the apparent ease with which consumers accepted them suggests something more than retail opportunism was at stake. This is not to suggest that the merchants were not opportunistic or that they were necessarily conscious of any greater purpose than building sales. But just as aesthetic and economic factors may illuminate how a particular fashion style takes form without satisfactorily explaining why it achieves acceptance (let alone what it means), so trends in advertising connote more than mere sales pitches. Advertising, like clothing, helps define basic categories of social knowledge and terms of public discourse, and these definitions become common points of reference that circulate beyond the purely commercial realm. In response to criticism over flag desecration in advertisements, *Printers' Ink*, an advertising trade journal, responded: "The flag has never been more widely used for advertising purposes than it is to-day; yet never has it evoked more enthusiasm and patriotic ardor."[17] However self-serving, this statement appears to be essentially true; advertisers perpetuate and legitimate values even as they attempt to appropriate them.

While advertisers in many fields adopted war motifs, the relationship was especially powerful for clothiers and dry goods merchants. Americans did not, in any great numbers, begin to furnish their houses with Army cots or alter their diets to simulate military rations. They did, however, adorn themselves with emblems of patriotism and adapt military motifs to a variety of garment designs. Thus clothing ads evoked not only a nationalistic discourse of advertising but one of fashion as well. As a result, the merger of merchandising strategies and nationalistic zeal seemed to know no bounds among clothing and dry goods merchants of this time. A single 1898 issue of the *Dry Goods Economist*, a trade journal, contained eighty-two advertisements with war themes. War relics—captured flags, battle swords, and so forth—became hot commodities for use in window displays. The traffic in such items became so lively that trade publications warned merchants about counterfeiters.[18]

The effort went beyond advertisements and window displays to store decorations and special promotions—even to the type of merchandise sold. One writer suggested that a successful "fall fashion opening" could be arranged around an "Army camp" theme. Customers invited to the store (which would be awash in red-white-and-blue bunting) would imbibe some facsimile of hardtack as refreshments and receive military-style buttons as souvenirs. The writer added: "And if you could get several of the soldier boys lately returned home to act as ushers, in uniform, of course, it would make a big hit." Large department stores enticed shoppers with a version of the currently popular tableau vivant, in which mannequins or actors depicted war celebrities in various poses ("here are Sampson, Schley, Dewey, *et als*, with the sailor and the soldier, and the President and his more important secretaries of the cabinet"). As successful battle reports began to come in, wholesalers rushed into the marketplace with patriotic souvenirs—lapel pins, buttons, buckles, badges, toys, puzzles, and knickknacks. Dry goods and clothing merchants were advised to add these items to their product lines or simply to purchase a quantity and give them away as promotional items. One St. Louis department store advertised "Dewey souvenir bargains in every department, in every aisle, on every counter." The *Dry Goods Economist* observed that "the whole market seems to be rampant with patriotism" and later asked, in its "Wide-Awake Retailing" column: "Are you reaping the harvest that the wave of patriotism is bringing to every live dry goods man?"[19]

Consumers seemed mostly willing to mix consumption strategies and war fervor—at least very little resistance appears in the trade and popular press. The *New York Tribune* reported one woman's negative opinion: "'Do I think it shows true respect to our flag to see it made up into gowns, fashioned into shirt waists, turned into petticoats and utilized for stockings? . . . Most assuredly I do not.'" Whereupon a host of readers responded with comments such as: "I do not think we can ever see that flag too often. No matter where it appears, it is an evidence of patriotism," and "I cannot think it possible for women to show real disregard for the significance of the flag, or that any irreverence can be meant by the most excessive display of the colors, and even in an apparently exaggerated way of personal adornment."[20]

Americans bought red-white-and-blue ribbons, neckwear, fans, hatbands, parasols, vest chains, and walking canes—even garters and petticoats. They purchased suspenders with portraits of Dewey or images of the battleship *Maine* woven into the design; they wore belt buckles ornamented with eagles, swords, and flags. They bought veils with "all styles of red, white and blue chenille dots and borders"; tricolor shirtwaists and straw hats; and handkerchiefs in red, white, and blue; handkerchiefs with Dewey's portrait; and handkerchiefs with depictions of the American and Cuban flags. They wore badges and emblems shaped like military decorations; they favored faux military buttons on belts, shirtwaist sets (cufflinks and studs), and hat pins; they used lace pins topped with tiny knapsacks and flags—"and so on down the list of nearly everything worn or used by the American people."[21]

The patriotic fervor also affected fashion cut and detail. Garments began to appear "trimmed *à la militaire*," and an advertisement in the *Ladies' Home Journal* declared that military-style capes were "a necessary article in the wardrobe of patriotic American women"; fashion columnists recommended adding a military collar (a standing collar decorated with flat gold braid and brass stars) to bring the previous year's outerwear up-to-date. Cavalry caps were popular as casual headwear for both women and children. Bunting, the worsted material used to make flags, gained favor as dress material. Popular colors listed in fashion descriptions included army gray, army blue, and army red, as well as navy blue, artillery red, cadet gray, battle gray, and later "Sampson blue" and "rough rider brown." In the meantime, yellow became distinctly unfashionable because of its association with the Spanish flag. The "Spanish flounce," a popular design treatment early in the year, was reborn as the "Dewey flounce." Fashion writers also promoted "Dewey vests," "Dewey hats," and "Roosevelt cloth."[22]

Clothing transported the ideology of American nationalism into a wide spectrum of everyday activities. Even schoolchildren made the connection. Ethel Spencer, who grew up near Pittsburgh and would have been eight or nine years old when these events happened, recalled the era in her memoirs:

The Spanish dress too had a long, but dishonorable career. It was made for me while the Spanish war was in progress—a red and yellow gingham, the colors of Spain. How my patriotic soul hated that dress! My schoolmates teased me every time I wore it, called me Spanish, implied I was a traitor; but I had to wear it anyway. And when I thankfully outgrew it, it passed to Mary and then to Elizabeth carrying with it a heavy load of built-in hatred. I don't think my little sisters had the faintest idea why it was hateful, but they loyally hated it anyway.[23]

Masquerade balls, an especially popular pastime from the 1880s to just after the turn of the century, allowed people to entertain themselves with clothing's capacity for projecting identity. During 1898 the *Delineator* commented that at such occasions "Columbias, Liberties, Brother Jonathans and Uncle Sams are sure to be seen in bewildering variety, charmingly patriotic, often gracefully dignified." The magazine then proceeded to offer for sale sewing patterns for yet another Miss Liberty and yet another Uncle Sam, although their designs promised to do justice to both patriotic feeling and fashion sense: "The suit represented is the one always given to Uncle Sam, although cut upon more graceful lines and showing perfect adjustment."[24]

A proposed boycott of Paris clothing, a protest aimed at France's sympathy with Spain, received widespread publicity. On one occasion, the *New York Journal* published a compendium of dispatches from Philadelphia, St. Louis, Cincinnati, Boston, Charleston, and Savannah indicating the boycott was spreading across the country. Indeed, the *Indianapolis News* published an editorial cartoon supporting the cause, as well as articles under headlines such as "Patriotic Women. They will Not Buy Anything that is Manufactured in France." One headline in the *Chicago Tribune* exclaimed, "Cause for Boycott"; another article urged that "the leading society women all over the country join . . . in inducing their friends to buy only home-made styles or those which come from London." Harriet Pullman, widow of railcar tycoon George Pullman and a leader of the boycott movement, announced: "A true American woman will make any sacrifice for her country's dignity, and is willing to wear homespun if necessary."[25]

Because the war was so short, we don't know how substantial or significant this effort would have become. By the time the fall and winter styles arrived on the market and the nation's fashion resolve might have been truly tested, the fighting was over. Nonetheless, these displays of military fervor by women draw our attention to the historical relationship between concepts of citizenship, militarism, and masculinity. This connection has its roots in theories of democratic citizenship that focus on a public, civic sphere in which independent individuals forge a common good. This concept of citizenship has weighed heavily against women, who historically have been ideologically situated within a private, domestic sphere in economically dependent roles. Under such conditions, women's identities as citizens were both legally and socially submerged into their husbands' identities, or at least filtered through their family role.[26]

American ideals of citizenship have always been highly gendered and have often included the notion that the full privileges of citizenship were reserved for those who accepted the full obligations of citizenship, including specifically the duty to take up arms in defense of the nation. The outbreak of war typically strengthened these cultural assumptions by underlining the importance of military service to the national ideal and by initiating cultural processes that staked out the boundaries between masculinity and femininity with increasing sharpness. War in the United States has tended to divide the world into battle front/home front, warrior/protected, men/women. In addition, the rhetoric and rituals of war have often been drenched in masculinist assumptions.[27]

I have already described the manner in which sexual differentiation achieved renewed ideological emphasis at the end of the nineteenth century, and the Spanish-American War occurred at an opportune time to enhance this tendency. Indeed, historians have noted that "this particular war with Spain was especially characterized by a rhetoric and iconography of sexual melodrama." Kristin Hoganson in particular has argued that the Spanish-American War functioned in part as an attempt to reestablish political action as an essentially male activity. This attempt occurred precisely in response to the pressure on existing gender roles exerted by women reformers at this time. Opponents of women's suffrage made the argument that women, who did not bear arms and defend the country in combat, should not be granted the same voting rights as the male population, which did. A writer for the *Ladies' Home Journal* summarized this distinction and suggested its connection to clothing practices when she wrote, "the needle remains the symbol of womanly efficiency as the sword does of soldierly achievement."[28]

The adoption of so many military motifs in women's clothing, what one fashion writer called "a craze for all things military," seems at first glance to be a symbolic effort to assert female legitimacy in this realm. Indeed, women at this time argued that their own contributions to the war effort ought to merit equal consideration with men's contribution in any discussion of citizenship rights, as Harriet Pullman implied in describing the boycott effort: "American women now have as good an opportunity to prove their patriotism as the men who shoulder muskets and go to the front." Yet on second glance, Pullman's assertion of female patriotism actually restricts female involvement, establishing a clear boundary between home front (women) and battle front (men). Fashion characteristically attempted to mediate this ambivalence, both giving voice and placing restraints on female assertiveness, finding symbolic ways to reconcile conflicting cultural claims. In broader terms, it mobilized women's support for the war effort but attempted to do so in a manner that did not transgress prevailing gender ideology. Thus fashion commentators acknowledged and celebrated the trend toward nationalistic display but also frequently urged women to keep their patriotic aspirations within the bounds of feminine modesty and submissiveness. At times their qualifying statements were quite gentle: "The American woman's dress may bear the stamp of patriotism in elegance and proclaim her pride of country effectively and unobtrusively, with no sacrifice of modesty and good taste." At other times their comments were more disapproving: "Shirts of red, white and blue striped percale are being worn by patriotic women, whose feelings are all right, if their taste is a little wanting." At their most pointed, they frankly tried to rein in the tendency toward masculinization, praising a certain style of cape for "imparting a delightful touch of femininity, especially when in contrast with the more mannish military wraps and jackets affected by the tailor-made girl." We see in such statements how dress attempts to create a coherent personal front for multiple claims on individual identity, in this case that of "woman" and that of "American."[29]

Commentary and advertising for men's clothes hardly ever betrayed such ambivalence. Patriotic-themed advertisements for women's clothing rarely pictured women in military poses, yet such imagery was casually tossed into men's clothing ads, which were filled with illustrations of men charging with bayonets, firing cannons, or simply rolling up their sleeves to display the bulked-up physical form of the new masculine body ideal. The association between men's clothing, male power, and military service appears everywhere in ads, but often in a very offhand manner, suggesting that such an equation refers to a "taken for granted" social reality, but one that nevertheless merits timely reinforcement (see Figure 31; Figure 34). Rare advertising illustrations showing a woman in a soldierly stance, such as the Wanamaker ad mentioned earlier (see Figure 30) perfectly capture the ambivalence on the female side. The woman in the advertisement snaps off a military salute, but shoulders a fashion accessory, not a weapon; she is also awaiting orders, not charging into battle. The ad demonstrates the manner in which multifaceted and potentially contradictory impulses could be encapsulated in a single fashionable image.

The men's industry sought to cast the development of the ready-made industry as quintessentially American, a move that would further serve to exclude women.[30] "Ready-made clothing is the legitimate outcome of a want peculiar to the character and conditions of the American people, and it, in turn, has exerted no little influence in affecting the relations of American society," said the *Clothing Gazette*. "The idea of ready-made clothing may not be indigenous to America; but as a factory system it has not developed in any of the old countries." Clothing ads and trade journal articles touted the quality of their goods as a distinctly American accomplishment. "To-day Americans lead the World in everything. We lead Americans as far as Clothing is concerned," ran one advertisement. "It is a fact that in no country of the world are the whole people so well dressed as in the United States," said a trade journal. In addition, trade publications urged clothing merchants to promote their products as "made by American labor, sold by American skill, approved by a patriotic public." The journals assured successful business owners that "the history of a great nation and the history of a great business house [are] parallel."[31]

The ready-made product fit nicely with the tenets of progressive nationalism. One mail-order house liked to refer to its "army of specialists" and "scientific workmen" in order to contrast its goods with those of "the custom tailor who hasn't changed his ways since he hung out his shingle." The modern garment, according to this company's catalog,

Prepared!

A complete line of FULL=
DRESS SHIRTS (compris=
ing NEW and CORRECT
Styles).

A LARGE line of STIFF
BOSOM FANCY SHIRTS
for Autumn wear (all
of them EXCLUSIVE
patterns SPECIALLY
DESIGNED for us).

Patterns which have
CHIC and SNAP, but not
"loud"!

Patterns which are GEN=
TEEL, but not "tame"!

Don't place your order
until you have seen
THE CORRECT STYLES;
always brought out
and introduced by the

MANHATTAN SHIRT CO.

760 BROADWAY = = NEW YORK

Figure 34. The sailor uniform and saber set a militaristic tone and superimpose
it on the new muscle-bound body ideal for American males in this 1898
advertisement. No direct mention of the war is necessary to make the
connection between masculinity, male attire, and the United States' current
show of military force against Spain. Although the overall tone of the ad is
overwhelmingly aggressive, the text still situates its message in the context of
bourgeois respectability: "genteel, but not 'tame.'" Manhattan Shirt Company
advertisement, *Clothier and Furnisher* (May 1898): 1. Reproduced from the
collections of the Library of Congress.

was an example of "the evolution of clothes." Moreover, clothing sales talks and ad pitches used nationalism to resolve a contradiction between clothiers' boasts of essential modernism ("progress has made us what we are") and their claims on historic American virtues ("that style and character in dress that is essential to the self-respect of a free, democratic people"). The Hub showed this process at work when it claimed: "History rings with victories for the gallant Stars and Stripes. And Chicago's trade history is replete with victories for The Hub."[32]

Nationalists and businessmen could also use such advertisements and statements to mask certain dissonances between the market and the nation. The mixed messages of the *Chicago Dry Goods Reporter* on the subject of military intervention, deriding war fever while urging merchants to take advantage of it, reveal some of the underlying tensions. While some business leaders hoped to dampen America's foreign adventurism because they feared it would disrupt trade, others encouraged it because their search for profits had outgrown national boundaries. In neither case did the needs of the marketplace necessarily match those of the nation, but in the twin discourses of advertising and fashion, the market and the nation could be made to seem perfectly congruent, as when the New York tailor advertised: "The American Admiral of '98 guided his fleet carefully and successfully. It is our aim to pursue the same course, with the assurance of entire satisfaction, or your money back."[33] A forced congruity of national and commercial interests is also represented in the response of the ad journal *Fame* after department store pioneer John Wanamaker offered to form a regiment of volunteers and lead it into battle himself. *Fame* published a light-hearted article suggesting Wanamaker make up his corps entirely of advertising writers: "Imagine a dry-goods cohort dashing upon the enemy while the standard bearer boldly unfolded the inspiring words, 'Great Slaughter Sale of Foreign Goods!' or 'Sweeping Sacrifice of Imported Novelties.' Picture to yourselves, if you can, the horror of the Spaniards if they noticed on a department store regiment flag the ominous words, 'Bargains in Bullets. We'll give you two for one all the time.'"[34]

When the sinking of the United States battleship *Maine* in Havana harbor provided a new focus and rallying cry for prowar agitation, one Boston clothing store labeled all the price cards in its front window with the slogan: "Remember the Maine, boys, and the price of this suit."[35] Americans managed to do both during the surge of nationalism in 1898, and some of their stylistic innovations lingered after the war. Just as certain men dramatized their version of "strenuous life" masculinity during the war and continued to act on this philosophy in daily life during the years immediately succeeding it, so men's fashion styles for the next several years continued to offer suits designated by names such as a "military sack suit" or with features such as "army shoulders." Although less noticeable, war fever also echoed in later women's fashion, as when a tailoring journal commented some years after the war on the popularity of certain "military effects" in female fashion, describing them as "decorative details of feminine warpaint." The spirit of war lingered not only in clothing styles but also in advertisements for them. In January 1900, a clothier boasted in an ad: "The imperialistic trend of America's future promises a vast colonial trade. All American-made clothes are better than any foreign clothing. Snellenburg clothing has been for 30 years the best manufacturer in this country—therefore the best in the world. . . . Our newest booklet 'Snellenburg Clothes in Other Climates' is a little edition de luxe with text in Spanish and English."[36] Linking the "imperialistic trend of America's future" with American ready-made clothing illustrates advertising opportunism, and it also indicates how the ongoing clothing discourse framed the key issues of the day.

Advertisers were not the only group that understood these connections or tried to use them to their own advantage. The country's rapidly increasing population of southern and eastern European immigrants also tried to link American militarism and American clothes to citizenship, in this case asserting their own claims on national identity. Between 1880 and 1910, more than 17 million immigrants poured into the United States, which had a population of about 92 million at the end of that period.[37] Those who intended to stay pursued many of the more formally recognized attributes of citizenship, such as English language skills or an understanding of constitutional rights and the American political system. Even more quickly and avidly, however, European immigrants pursued Americanization of their dress.[38] Acquiring American dress was easier than, say, learning English, and many immigrants understood the significance of dress, based on the religious or cultural importance clothing had in their European cultures. They may have had trouble understanding people who spoke to them in English, but they had no trouble comprehending communications that came via clothing. Additionally, material culture offered an important source of education to people thrust into a social context in which traditional knowledge and traditional role models no longer served effectively to orient them. Consumption (including dress) provided a means by which newcomers angled for position not only within wider society but within the immigrant community, which lost many traditional forces of cohesion and structure during its transplantation to the United States.[39]

The title character of Abraham Cahan's novel *The Rise of David Levinsky* is a Russian immigrant who has been in the United States only ten minutes when he observes: "The great thing was that these people were better dressed than the inhabitants of my town. The poorest-looking man wore a hat (instead of a cap), a stiff collar and a necktie, and the poorest woman wore a hat or a bonnet."[40] A nonfiction Russian immigrant later recalled her own arrival in strikingly similar terms: "I wanted to be an American very much. I saw people who looked better and dressed better and I wanted to be like that kind."[41]

Contemporary observers and later scholars often treat dress as a superficial part of cultural assimilation.[42] However, precisely because dress seems rather frivolous it becomes the perfect site for serious assertions, able to cloak a rhetorical function behind its utilitarian facade. The dominant social group is typically uninterested in such a marginalized mode of expression or unable to deny its symbolic resources to other groups. When Margaret Byington surveyed immigrant habits in Homestead, Pennsylvania, during the early 1900s, she commented on the "quickness with which they adopt *our* style of clothing." This observation amused, startled, and dismayed her in varying degrees, but only for a passing moment. Byington seemed to ascribe no serious importance to this matter, although she did note that for the immigrant it "evidently gave the wearer a proud sense of being dressed like other Americans."[43]

Assertions of equality and membership—of being "like other Americans"—were very much at issue at the end of the nineteenth century. The influx of "new immigrants" engendered an increasingly adverse reaction among the native-born. Groups such as the American Protective Association, founded in 1887, and the Immigration Restriction League, founded in 1894, gained strength and a public voice. In 1889, the U.S. Supreme Court for the first time upheld a broadly exclusionary immigration law (directed at the Chinese). In 1891, the federal government asserted its ultimate authority over immigration control, and the next year it established the screening operation for new arrivals at Ellis Island. The Darwinist theories of racial hierarchy and social evolution so popular at this time provided another rationale for restrictionists, who argued that diluting the American population with inferior classes of people tampered with natural progress of the United States.[44]

This debate sometimes filtered on to the pages of fashion journals. The *Designer*, a monthly periodical devoted mainly to publicizing Standard Fashion Company dress patterns, complained bitterly in 1898 that the United States had "come to be regarded as Europe's general dumping-ground" and that the new class of immigrants "lowers the standard of our citizenship, thus affecting our national status in the eyes of other countries." Ironically, the increased national chauvinism wielded by Americans at the end of the century provided a weapon that their foes could use as well. By stressing national pride and made-in-America campaigns ("be patriotic and you will be patronized," urged a columnist in the *Dry Goods Economist;* "American made for American maids," proclaimed a corset company), nativists insisted on an equation between goods and national identity that the immigrants could seize upon for their own purposes (Figure 35).[45] Once the link between American garments and American citizenship became common currency, immigrants could employ it to make their own claims of American identity.

Many European immigrants placed great emphasis on acquiring new clothes as a means of "becoming American." After interviewing more than one thousand working-class women early in the twentieth century, Louise Odencrantz noted that "immigrant women usually . . . bring large quantities of clothing with them from Italy, representing sometimes their accumulations for a dowry." Odencrantz continued: "But they have scarcely landed at Ellis Island before they begin to discard these Italian costumes for American clothing." Indeed, if the newly arrived did not discard their European clothing on their own, very often their already settled relatives would do it for them.[46] Sometimes immigrants did not even wait until they landed. The disparaging comment of an experienced New Yorker prompted at least one immigrant to throw her carefully packed clothing overboard during her voyage to America because she believed "it was better to come empty-handed than to arrive improperly dressed and be labeled a greenhorn." Others did not even wait until they left Europe. A North Dakotan wrote back to relatives who were preparing to join him: "Don't take any clothing, because when you get here we will not let you wear those clothes. Take only two dresses and a few things to change on the way."[47] Dress provided a medium for an ongoing if sometimes indirect discussion of national identity. Mary Antin experienced this after she came to the United States from Russia in 1894. When she recalled her arrival some years later, she vividly described the moment when she and her siblings "exchanged our hateful homemade European costumes . . . for real American machine-made garments, and issued forth glorified in each other's eyes."[48]

Notably, immigrants did not respond equally to all aspects of Americanization. For example, they were much less willing to give up ethnic foodways than ethnic clothing.[49] The differences may have been partly psychological, based on the stage of life in which an individual was socialized to various aspects of identity.[50] Other reasons may have been practical, because sewing was an important job skill to women, for whom the garment industry represented a major employment option, and many employers sought "American-looking" and well-dressed workers.[51] However, the most important reason is that clothing much more than food involves the public presentation of the self. Clothing is the interface between the individual and the social world, and if citizenship involves participation or membership in civic or community enterprise, then clothing can help mediate that relationship in a way that food can not.

Figure 35. The Gage-Downs Corset Company ran a series of advertisements late in the 1890s with the tagline: "American Made for American Maids." Statements such as this were an effort to draw lines of exclusion for the foreign-born. Using fashion, consumer goods, and advertising in this manner, however, made these symbols available to immigrants or other subcultures to put to their own uses. Gage-Downs Company advertisement, *Chicago Dry Goods Reporter* (November 25, 1899): 40.

As the examples provided by Abraham Cahan (for the mid-1880s) and Mary Antin (for the mid-1890s) indicate, the immigrant impulse to adopt American clothing was well established by the time social scientists began to study it in the early twentieth century. The impact of the immigrants' transformation stayed with them for years, as oral histories illustrate:

> My first day in America I went with my aunt to buy some American clothes. She bought me a shirtwaist, you know, a blouse and a skirt, a blue print with red buttons and a hat, such a hat I had never seen. I took my old brown dress and shawl and threw them away! I know it sounds foolish, we being so poor, but I didn't care. I had enough of the old country. When I looked in the mirror, I couldn't get over it. I said, boy, Sophie, look at you now. Just like an American.[52]

The vividness of this recollection and the rich, ritualistic quality of the experience (literally throwing her past on the trash heap and beginning again "like an American") speaks to the power of clothing as a signifier.

Attempting to align national identity and gender identity through appropriate dress was an overt strategy of many of the Americanization efforts launched by middle-class reformers in the early twentieth century. These Americanizers wanted to remake the immigrants' home life, not merely their political beliefs. They attempted to reinforce gender ideals about women as homemakers, wives, and mothers by making such roles synonymous with the "American Way of Life." In other words, the movement hoped that "the stereotypical notions of the woman's proper sphere would become articles of patriotic faith." This not only was a way of imposing cultural standards on new residents but of maintaining them for the native-born.[53]

An attempt to get immigrant mothers to adopt "American style" was central to these efforts. Eventually, at least one agency established a sort of clothing store to serve newcomers as they stepped off the boat at Ellis Island. A worker remarked that one woman gladly accepted a new hat when she was told that covering her head with a shawl "would mark her as a newcomer at first sight."[54] Immigrant mothers learned that such roles involved not only wearing the proper clothes for an American woman but also making them. "Instruction in sewing and needlework was pervasive throughout the social settlement movement," according to one researcher, who noted that the lessons continued to focus on hand-sewing well into the ready-made era of the twentieth century, when such skill no longer offered practical training either for wage work or homemaking. This training did, however, reinforce the notion that sewing was an essential feminine art that should remain, in Edward Bok's words, "among woman's highest arts and truest accomplishments." Thus the powerful association between female American gender roles and custom-made clothing took on added significance. One magazine article described these "domestic education" efforts in the immigrant communities of Buffalo, New York, like this: "In the matter of clothing the women were equally ignorant and equally teachable. The mothers were sincere in protesting that they would be glad to make cheap, simple garments *for themselves and their children* if they only knew how. In these cases they were supplied with a pattern and enough material for one garment and given one or more lessons in cutting, fitting and fashioning it."[55]

Note that the lessons pointedly omit any reference to making men's clothing. For immigrant women, the effort to "look American" and to make American clothing involved adopting both a national identity and a gender identity. The immigrants' previous experience of gender expectations might vary significantly from the American standards. Russian Jews, for example, "had long validated the role of married women as breadwinners," but that didn't fit the middle-class American gender concepts. Thus Jewish immigrants who aspired to bourgeois notions of respectability learned to limit the wife's role to domestic duties. Of course, many immigrants could not live solely on the husband's wages, and so sought solutions that allowed women to contribute income but didn't require them to leave the home, such as doing piecework or taking in boarders. In this way, immigrant families attempted to address their economic needs within the framework of dominant gender stereotypes.[56]

Fashion both symbolized and constituted these roles as *American* and American *woman*. In Abraham Cahan's 1896 story "Yekl," a Russian Jew called Jake comes to America in advance of his wife and child and aggressively pursues his own Americanization. His first glimpse of his wife, Gitl, three years later is soured by her "un-American" dress: "His heart had sunk at the sight of his wife's uncouth and un-American appearance. She was slovenly dressed in a brown jacket and a skirt of grotesque cut, and her hair was concealed under a voluminous wig of pitch-black hue." Gitl's unwillingness to adopt an American appearance taints her relationship with Jake as the couple struggles to reconcile their personal sense of self with a new self-image not only as Americans, but as an American man and an American woman. By the end of the story, Gitl has negotiated a bittersweet accommodation of American values, and Cahan conveys the transformation with a point-by-point comparison of her appearance. Gitl now goes about her business without a wig, wearing a "broad-brimmed winter hat of a brown color and in a jacket of black beaver. The rustic, 'greenhornlike' expression was completely gone from her face."[57] Similar plotlines appeared in productions of the Yiddish theater, a form of cultural expression that served Jewish immigrants as a bridge and a guide to an American way of life. In *Without a Home,* a woman immigrant's refusal to follow her husband in adopting an American style of living produces tension that eventually drives her mad. However, in *The Nextdoor Neighbors,* a comedy, the same kind of conflict has a happy ending when the husband sees the wife in a fashionable dress and new hairdo and patches up their differences.[58]

Resistance to American standards of dress could cause conflict not only between husband and wife but between parents and children or between an individual and the local ethnic community. Generational relationships manifested themselves in dress as immigrant family members struck different balances between traditional and new values. More than one daughter attempted to "Americanize" her mother by providing her with new clothes; more than one mother watched with tolerant or proud eye as her daughter assumed an American appearance. Yet clothing could also emphasize and even constitute a stark difference between children who embraced the allure of American appearance and parents who sought a sense of stability and continuity in old-world styles. After studying the immigrant community in the 1910s, Sophonisba Breckinridge wrote: "There is probably no question on which the ideas of the child and those of the parent are so likely to conflict as on the question of clothes, especially clothes for the girl."[59]

Social workers also had mixed feelings about the desirability of fashion consciousness among the new arrivals. Viola Paradise, representing the Immigrants Protective League of Chicago, wrote that "almost immediately upon the girl's arrival her relatives buy for her American clothes." Paradise considered this a "false standard" and the "dark side" of Americanization. She believed it would lead to negative results ranging from "vulgarity of dress" to immoral acts. On the other hand, Jane Addams's 1899 essay rejected this attitude. "The charity visitor may regret that the Italian peasant woman has laid aside her picturesque kerchief, and substituted a cheap street hat," Addams wrote, "but it is easy to recognize the first attempt toward democratic expression."[60] Historians have joined this debate too. Some argue that American fashion "mesmerized" the immigrants and "subverted" their values. Others assert that immigrants adopted the ways and means of consumption and fashion quite willingly and quite skillfully, making good use of them as tools of assimilation and advancement in their new homeland.[61]

As always, the function of fashion was fundamentally ambivalent. Its symbols frequently supported the dominant culture, but because its associations were indirect and its mode of expression ambiguous, clothing also could challenge established norms. Adoption of American dress by the immigrant was not just an act of conformity, it was a claim of membership in American society. Such an assertion exerts pressure, however slight, on the concept of citizenship itself, suggesting that native-born elites must expand their concept of "real Americans" to include the immigrant newcomers. Indeed, the pressure exerted by such sartorial assertions of membership may not have been so slight. Social commentators from entrenched groups were quite as likely to react with dismay rather than encouragement when confronted by the fashion aspirations of the immigrants.

Such conflicts reflected still another category of personal identity that dress helped symbolize and constitute: class. Dismay over immigrant clothing mirrored both nativist and class biases that characterized Anglo middle America. Etiquette books aimed at this audience frequently expressed concern over the clothing habits of the lower classes, worrying that "too much attention is paid to dress by those who have neither the excuse of ample means nor of social claims." Such immigrant activities undercut dress as a marker of social distinction for the middle class because "Mrs. Hauton, in New York, is very apt to see [her servants] Bridget and Dinah emerging from the rear in a close copy of her last Paris suit, at the moment she walks out of the front door clad in the original."[62]

The immigrant press responded: "I think Sarah way down on the East Side has as much right to the daintiness of dress as Ida on Madison Avenue," an indication that donning this dress was a form of cultural agency for the otherwise disempowered.[63] Working-class fashionableness upset some social workers and etiquette writers, who complained about "the four-dollar-a-week shop-girl displaying her last penny on her back . . . quite unmindful of the disapproving frowns of her wealthy sisters, who will soon have to adopt a Puritan simplicity in order to be distinguished from the plebeians."[64]

The etiquette writers' insistence on minute categorizations and distinctions of dress and behavior represented a species of social control. Indeed, it is difficult to read the endless list of social occasions and dress requirements in the advice manuals without sensing an effort to put everything (and everyone) in its place. "In our own country we have no recognized aristocracy, no absolutely superior class, and we have reason to be devoutly thankful therefor," began one etiquette writer reassuringly, only to add: "But our democratic form of society is attended with some evils, and one of these is the boundless self-assertion with which many people strive to eke out what else were very insufficient claims to social pre-eminence." Clothing provided a metaphor and a physical marker for desired class distinctions: "A cheap copy of a handsome dress is apt to be a wretched affair. . . . As a rule, what is appropriate in a silk dress is not suitable for a calico, and *vice versa*."[65]

These statements express the anxieties of the middle class during an era when working-class unrest and the influx of immigrants—coupled with the rapid transformations of economic, social, and cultural life—

placed middle-class prestige and power in jeopardy. Etiquette book authors echoed these anxieties, criticizing, for example, "the girl of all-work [who] leaves the house by the back door, dressed in such close imitation of her mistress that it puzzles a stranger to place her." Another writer complained that the "sewing girl, the shop girl, the chambermaid, and even the cook, must have their elegantly trimmed silk dresses and velvet cloaks for Sunday and holiday wear, and the injury done by this state of thing to the morals and manners of the poorer classes is incalculable." Clearly, in a world where impression-management and appearance played a crucial role in middle-class respectability, the fashion aspirations of the working class were not to be taken lightly.[66] Clothing provided a means of exerting control over personal space in a time of flux and turmoil, of expressing one's attitude toward others and asserting one's place within society, of establishing both physical and metaphorical boundaries against perceived threats. For the late nineteenth-century middle class, that also meant protecting a claim to American identity and control of American resources. For immigrant newcomers, however, it provided a means to claim that identity as their own.

The nationalistic fervor of the 1890s held different connotations for the immigrant than for the native-born middle-class American, yet both tapped into the same symbolic systems of fashion and advertising to make their claims on citizenship. The clothing discourse—and by extension the discourse on nationalism—was open for interpretation by everyone. The *Yiddishes Tageblatt*, the largest and most influential Yiddish-language paper in the country, boisterously supported the war effort in 1898 and proclaimed the patriotism of the Jewish immigrant.[67] The paper's appeal to its readers' fighting spirit was based partly on a proclaimed Americanism and partly on an asserted hostility toward Spain that dated from the Inquisition and expulsion of Jews in the fifteenth century. Thus, the editorial position of the paper managed to merge American patriotism with ethnic loyalties. The differences between ethnic and native-born nationalism should not be minimized, but the overlap between the two approaches to national identity is striking as well, and employed both clothing and advertising to assert their nationalistic commitments in everyday life.[68] One clothing store owner ran advertisements in the *Tageblatt* in which the only English words were his name, address, and the slogan: "Remember the Maine!" (Figure 36). In general, clothing merchants took the lead in adapting American advertising techniques to this paper, clearly outdistancing merchants and advertisers in other fields. The *Yiddishes Tageblatt* also reported that Jewish women throughout the country pursued fashionable attire ("all women are slaves to fashion and the Jewish girls are also subjects of her majesty"). The paper ran fashion tips that could have come from the *Ladies' Home Journal* and stressed the

Figure 36. This clothing advertisement from the immigrant press combines distinctly American nationalism with distinctly ethnic traditions. The advertisement's use of the *Maine* slogan in English puts it in direct relationship with similar ads in the mass circulation dailies and again illustrates the pervasive effects of war fever, but its Yiddish text points to a specifically Jewish immigrant form of national identity. M. Yachnin advertisement, *Yiddishes Tageblatt* (July 27, 1898): 4.

way its readers fit the national clothing discourse: *"Our* American women are undoubtedly the best dressed people in the world," it reported, counseling its readers to dress in styles that "are all appropriate to their own particular time and place." The immigrant sense of assuming their place and the nativist sense of putting things in their appropriate place were using the same words—and, more to the point, the same clothes—to jockey for cultural status.[69]

One could sketch out models of immigrant acculturation that competed for supremacy in roughly the same manner as I described competing notions of nationalism. A melting pot ideal envisioned an automatic and continuous blending of cultures, as immigrants evolved into Americans as a result of their experience and efforts in the United States. A second concept, Anglo-conformity, was a coercive form of the melting pot that allowed no room for contributions by the immigrants' own cultures, and in its ultimate form allowed scarcely any room for naturalized citizens at all. Anglo-conformity was another manifestation of Darwinian social thought, stressing the evolutionary superiority of the Anglo-Saxon people and claiming priority for their norms. A third model, cultural pluralism, argued for the continued existence of multiple ethnic traditions in a polyglot Americanness.[70] During the 1890s, the melting pot may have represented the consensus view, but Anglo-conformity was the rising ideal, as is apparent in the *Designer* columnist's comment: "Every week in the year the immigration companies bring across the ocean crowds of more or less ignorant peasant women, many of whom have never, during the whole course of their lives, set foot in a decently appointed habitation, and, by consequence, have absolutely no conception of what civilized life really is. If these women are neither German, Scandinavian nor British, the chances are that they are lazy and shiftless as well as ignorant."[71]

Anglo-conformity became the reigning model during the two decades after the Spanish-American War as cultural norms for immigrants evolved from a relatively benign, voluntaristic mode to enforced Americanization. During World War I, the dominance of Anglo-conformity extended to an attempt by the federal government to regulate the styles and choices in civilian clothing. The regulations (nominally issued in the name of wartime efficiency and rationing) stressed conformity and restricted any hint of exoticism by attempting to limit stylistic variation, to restrict unnecessary adornments, and to require standard colors and fabrics.[72]

The construction of a sense of American nationality in the nineteenth century simultaneously sharpened the notion of immigrant ethnicity in the United States, for in order to define their own "Americanness" more clearly, Americans began to define more insistently what was non-American. They began seeing ethnicity in others when they had not done so before.[73] This emphasis on fixing the meaning of American-ism helps explain the calls for specifically American fashions and a specifically American clothing industry that appeared in trade journals, popular periodicals, and advice manuals of the late nineteenth century. Writers argued for such causes on the grounds of American superiority, American independence, and American uniqueness. "Now let us join hands, all lovers of liberty, in earnest cooperation to free American women from the dominion of foreign fashion," said one typical plea.[74]

Calls for American freedom in matters of dress are as old as the nation. Nonetheless, the campaign did pick up new urgency, and gained more acceptance as accomplished fact rather than cultural ideal, at the end of the nineteenth century. The clamor steadily increased through the 1910s, when the *New York Post* called for a "new war of independence" to free women from Parisian fashion. Just as fashion's relationship to gender evoked extreme opinions, the relationship of fashion to national identity aroused strong emotions. The reason is the same in both cases: because clothing embodied important ideals, it became the focus of sharp debate.[75]

For Benjamin Flower, editor of the journal *Arena* and an ardent proponent of women's rights in fashion and elsewhere, attitudes toward dress, gender, and Darwinism blended easily with attitudes on dress and nationalism. In his article "Fashion's Slaves," Flower argued for the emancipation of women from fashion in the interests of cultural hierarchy and advancement: "Teach the girls to be American," he wrote, "to be independent; to scorn to copy fashions, manners, or habits that come from decaying civilizations."[76]

To partisans of American dress, clothes not only reflected America's civic ideals but also constituted them, just as they constituted gender roles. The alleged democracy of clothing in the United States "exerted no little influence in affecting the relations of American society," according to the *Clothing Gazette*, which claimed "the clothing trade has leveled social distinction to a large degree." The writer asserted that on a typical Sunday outing the bystander would "be able to discover no remarkable difference between the well-dressed millionaire, and the clerk and the mechanic in his Sunday clothes." Boasts of American superiority drew on the same Darwinian belief in national evolution that helped underwrite military conflict abroad and sexual differentiation at home. One tailoring journal advised: "To be correctly dressed in accordance with the latest styles should be the ambition of every American citizen who wishes to lead in the march of civilization and to stamp upon the era . . . a footprint of progress. . . . Correct dressing and beautifully fitting and made garments is one of the best evidences of the onward march of civilization."[77]

If one considers the way dress simultaneously organizes different categories of social knowledge—citizenship, gender, and class, for instance—one begins to understand how such relationships relate to each another and why it is so difficult to disentangle them. Fashion's drive toward the new—its way of producing meaning by creating a stylistic difference from what came before—is a way of continually reinventing "otherness." This production of difference can mobilize a variety of cultural ambivalences. I have already discussed male/female, middle class/lower class, American/foreign, and we could add a host of others: old/young, heterosexual/homosexual, conservative/radical, urban/rural, and so on. All these categories intersect in individual lives, and fashion is one way to view their intersection.

Throughout the 1890s, the attributes of the fashion system were particularly appropriate to the discussion of national identity. In describing American Jews, the *Yiddishes Tageblatt* said: "On the average the American Jewesses are beginning to closely resemble other women in their appearance. Only a person accustomed to observe can recognize that they are of Jewish lineage." The writer then made the connection: "Her patriotism is innate and imperishable, and for *her country* she would sacrifice her gold and her jewels as readily as the ancient Jews did for her religion."[78] As the *Tageblatt* comment further indicates, clothing also framed citizenship in terms of the social presentation of the self and placed high emphasis on visual interaction. These matters came into focus for Abraham Cahan's protagonist David Levinsky during his first full day in the United States. As the new immigrant undergoes the ritual of reclothing, the importance, self-consciousness, and flexibility of the dress code as a means of articulating national identity becomes apparent. At the end of the shopping spree, his patron stands Levinsky in front of a mirror and exclaims: "Quite an American, isn't he?"[79]

Chapter 5

Ad Experts and Clothiers
"The Truth About Good Goods"

As John Wanamaker recalled it, on the day in 1861 when his men's clothing store opened, he sold $24.67 worth of goods. "Of the $24.67," he said, "I put 67¢ in the cash drawer to make change for the next day and took the $24 to the *Public Ledger* where I paid for an advertisement for the new store."[1]

Wanamaker's commitment to advertising was characteristic for him but unusual for its time. Many merchants considered advertising a sign of weakness and an unnecessary expense. Thirty years later Wanamaker's philosophy remained the same, although his business had progressed from a men's clothing shop to a department store and his advertising budget had grown to an estimated $400,000 per year. Meanwhile, the temper of the times had caught up with him, and the trade press of the 1890s insisted that advertising was crucial to business success. Between 1870 and 1900, the amount of advertising done annually in the United States climbed from $50 million to $542 million.[2] The men's clothing business, which was enjoying similar growth during this period, found a willing and compatible partner in advertising. In 1890 the *Clothing Gazette* launched a series of articles called "Essays on Advertising" by confidently proclaiming that "advertising is to-day one of the great forces of business. It is the foundation stone upon which rests most of the great retail clothing houses of the day." Throughout the 1890s the magazine featured articles and departments headlined "The Science of Advertising," "A Talk on Advertising," "A Little Chat on Advertising," "Good Advertising," "Clever Advertising," "Effective Advertising," and "Top-Notch Advertising."[3]

Both ad writers and clothiers revered Wanamaker's example (an early advertising manual stated "it is in the Wanamaker store that the true art of advertising was discovered"), and many other clothing merchants and manufacturers also became aggressive advertisers.[4] The practice had a certain logic to it, because large-scale clothing manufacture required wide markets and broad communications to support its increased volume of production. Advertising also provided clothiers with a means of articulating the combination of old and new values represented by ready-made clothing.[5]

Advertising added yet another layer of meaning and interpretive necessity to the dress code at the same time that it made the forms of fashion available to an unprecedented range of people. At the end of the nineteenth century, fashion, advertising, and image-making forged a strategic alliance so strong that it eventually made them seem virtually interchangeable. The trade journals and clothing advertisements of the 1890s provide embryonic examples of the manner in which advertising and fashion became common currency for personal identity and social relations in twentieth-century America. As with clothing, however, advertising did not represent a simple, sharp break with older cultural traditions. Advertising's symbolic system provided another set of tools that could be used in the ongoing reformulation of middle-class norms, incorporating both older Victorian values and more modern proclivities.

Advertising's advocates laid claim to Victorian virtues—honesty, dignity, hard work, individualism—and attempted to reconfigure them in the context of a spreading business culture that emphasized hustle, change, expertise, and publicity. They even attempted to adapt older modes of face-to-face communication and personal salesmanship to mass-market merchandising. The philosophy of advertising most often propounded by the trade press in the late nineteenth century can be summed up in a pitch from the Curtis Publishing Company: "Good advertising is merely telling the truth about good goods." In reality, however, a much more complex process of self-promotion was taking place.[6] Advertising in the 1890s may not have produced the intricate and meticulously constructed commercial messages that came to characterize the industry in the twentieth century, but the scholarly view that key advertising strategies did not develop before the 1920s appears to be greatly overstated.[7] By the turn of the century, the techniques and themes that ever since have characterized advertising had already emerged, although often in a tentative, trial-and-error form.[8] The gears of the advertising and fashion systems began to mesh, able for the first time to conjoin mass-produced goods, mass-circulation publications, and vastly improved techniques for reproducing illustrations, creating the symbolic strategies that would pattern the daily discourse of modern consumer culture.

Advertisers of the day were not innocent of the deeper manipulative potential and subtler psychological dimension of their efforts, even though they did not often speak of them. A magazine such as *Ad Sense* could publish at the top of one page the blameless sentiment that "the ad should hold the mirror up to your goods" and at the top of the next promote the more insidious notion that "the up-to-date merchant of to-day endeavors to first create the want, then to satisfy it."[9] Another example of these contradictory viewpoints appeared in *Fame,* one of the most respected advertising journals.[10] In 1892 its editor stated that "advertising is teaching truth" and that the field was "being purified by the growing honesty of tone in the public print." Yet on the very same page, a regular contributor to the journal asserted that advertising was literally a form of hypnotic suggestion: "If people bought goods under the carefully observed dictates of reason, advertisements would be couched in the form of logical syllogism. But they don't. They buy because they have been hypnotised to a certain degree. The public stares at the advertiser's name until the nerves of sight are tired, and thus the mind is reduced to a state where the suggestion of the advertiser, 'Buy of me,' comes with the force of a command."[11] Nonetheless, the overwhelming predominance of advice in these journals recommended a sincere and courteous approach that would do justice to any Victorian gentleman. "In the long run it does not pay to deceive the public," said *Printers' Ink.* "If by chance it should temporarily pay, then it is pretty clear that the same capital and energy employed in frank and earnest appeal on the merits of goods alone will in most cases pay very much better."[12]

Charles Austin Bates, who got his start creating advertisements for a clothing store in Indianapolis and later ran the largest ad writing bureau in New York City, wrote in 1898 that "the advertisement that pays best is the plain, honest, forceful talk, written just as if the writer was talking to the reader face to face—a statement of facts." In an article published about the same time, Bates took his argument even further: "Advertising never creates a demand," he wrote, "it supplies one that already exists." Pressed as to whether advertising hadn't created a demand for many patent medicines of dubious efficacy, he stood by his position that advertising merely filled existing needs. "As a matter of fact," he wrote, "most people are sick. . . . There are very few people who cannot with advantage use a blood medicine or a tonic."[13] The emphasis on sincerity and the necessary correspondence between appearance and object struck a persistently Victorian note. More specifically, these assertions reflected an effort to throw off the Barnumesque associations that advertising had developed because of the snake-oil claims of the patent medicine hawkers, who were among the first and heaviest newspaper advertisers in the United States.[14] Ad journals urged merchants to avoid "pyrotechnic English" and shun "'flumdoodle' advertising" and to rely instead on "honest, earnest, heart-to-heart statements and . . . strong though dignified typographic display."[15]

In a similar vein, *Fame* frequently compared the rules of advertising to the rules of Victorian etiquette. "Great similarities exist between proper social manners and proper advertising" went the introduction to one article; another warned that deceptive advertising would be disliked for its "absence of good manners."[16] This assertion contained an ironic element of cultural truth, for in many ways the twentieth-century fixation on consumer goods, fads, and fashions provided a modern counterpart to the nineteenth-century codes of etiquette. The "possession-reading skills" of modern consumer culture, by which people are attuned to every socially significant detail of their purchases, have much in common with the Victorian era's elaborate etiquette rituals, in which the nuance of a turned corner on a calling card or the propriety of removing or assuming one's gloves served an important function of identification and communication. Advertisements became the etiquette guides of the new age, reflecting not so much a transformation of social relations as a new way to communicate them.[17] The ad writers seem to have sensed the parallels in these codes of behavior, insisting that the design of an ad "must be courteous in spirit" and frequently casting their advertising advice in terms of dignity, taste, refinement, and character.[18] In fact, just as etiquette writers insisted upon a correlation between good manners and good character ("the manners of a gentleman are the index of his soul") or between good dress and good character ("refinement of character is said never to be found with vulgarity of dress"), advertising writers claimed a similar correspondence between business practices and the character of the person who employed them: "In the advertising field the character of the man and the goods is inevitably related."[19]

In another attempt to fix the mores of advertising within the bounds of Victorian propriety, some advertising professionals adapted religious language to what they termed "the gospel of advertising."[20] *Fame*'s editor Artemas Ward particularly liked these allusions, saying at one point: "Next to religion, advertising calls for faith. It is casting bread upon the waters which will not return for many days." In another article he suggested that "in the great temple of advertising it would befit all to be humble."[21] Ward proudly rebutted readers who claimed he had misquoted the Bible: "If there is one thing in the doing of which *Fame* prides itself it is quoting Scripture correctly" and correspondingly chastised advertisers who made irreverent use of biblical matter in their ads: "*Fame* always has protested, and ever will, against the careless use of scripture text in advertising."[22]

In contrast to this appropriation of Victorian religiosity, the ad journals' emphasis on expertise and science expressed newer values of the era. As part of their drive toward credibility, advertisers sought to establish their calling as worthy of the status and respect of a "profession," a distinctly modern form of group self-identification. In doing so they demonstrated that they had caught a bug that had infected everyone from morticians to private detectives during the latter nineteenth and early twentieth centuries.[23] The advertisers' aspirations are apparent in descriptions of ad writers as "advertising attorneys," "doctors of public-ity," and "publicity professors."[24] Claude Hopkins, an ad man still labor-ing in relative obscurity who later emerged as "the premier copywriter of his era," wrote an article in 1896 that compared advertising work not only to that of doctors and lawyers but to "civil engineering, chemistry, accounting, authorship, business—anything that requires special edu-cation combined with innate ability."[25] Equating their work to that of engineers or accountants allowed advertising advisers to look beyond Victorian gentility to a more modern self-image as highly specialized men of science and business. The repudiation of their snake-oil past and aspiration to a professional future are nicely encapsulated in this advice from "A. N. Observer" in *Profitable Advertising:* "It doesn't pay to *experi-ment* with this or that quack device when one is in need of a physician. There is no economy in it. Neither does it pay to squander time and money in the vain attempt to produce good results in the advertising world when one possesses such shallow and superficial knowledge of ways and means as does the average amateur advertiser."[26]

The ad writers' quest for recognition included assertions that they deserved public recognition in the same manner that a magazine writer received a byline or a fine artist signed his or her work. Ad journals claimed that an ad writer's professional expertise and achievement merited individual recognition and acclaim. They argued that ads had become sought-after reading matter and should be recognized as such: "The time is not far distant when it will be announced that this or that noted advertisement writer will contribute a special advertisement to a forthcoming issue, for the same reason that publishers of magazines now announce that the next number will contain a story by Howells or a poem by James Whitcomb Riley."[27]

If the key identifying factors of a profession are claims to expertise, credentials, and autonomy, advertisers clearly aspired to professional status. Despite all the talk about advertising being merely "the public announcement of a fact," those in the advertising business stressed repeatedly that only a specialist could do the work properly. "You, who know all about clothing, cannot sit down at a desk and dash off a telling ad. It's not your line," said one writer. Rather the merchant needed to be "willing to hire [an advertising] man and give him carte blanche." The full push for credentials, including a major drive for the establishment of university programs to teach advertising, intensified immediately after the turn of the century.[28]

The entire concept of the "expert," unknown before the middle decades of the nineteenth century, was socially useful in a period when the old ways of knowing faced challenges on so many fronts. People came to rely on experts because they could not know everything for themselves in a fast-changing, urban-industrial world. They needed new cultural forms to supply knowledge previously available through personal experience and face-to-face encounters.[29] Advertisers were willing and able to offer their services as expert guides to the modern world of goods—and to affiliate themselves with the scientific and technical breakthroughs that defined progress in that time. A pioneer ad writer, Nathaniel Fowler, Jr., wrote in 1893: "During the last ten years, and particularly during the last five years, the quality of advertising has passed through a fiery revolution. The brilliant minds of the country are now giving attention to the preparation of advertising. Advertising has become a science."[30]

Just as advertising professionals worked out a self-image to match the times, clothing merchants sought an image for themselves based on a similar mixture of Victorian and modern attributes. The similarity was not coincidental, for the clothing industry trade press frequently urged clothiers to follow the advice of ad experts. A *Clothing Gazette* correspondent characteristically cited Wanamaker's example, making reference to the retail entrepreneur's famous ad writer J. E. Powers: "That man Powers has done good work for Wanamaker, and Wanamaker gave him $10,000 a year. Now John Wanamaker don't give $10,000 a year to a man unless he is worth it." The lesson for other clothing merchants, according to the writer, was that "the question, does advertising pay, seems to be answered very clearly in the affirmative." Elsewhere the *Clothing Gazette* argued that the only merchants who did not believe in advertising were "fossilized, moss-covered store-keepers who are still going round in the same old gum shoes they wore 'before the war.'" Clothing manufacturers and merchants, like advertising professionals, concocted a self-image that blended a desire for respect and prestige with a drive for up-to-date business tactics.[31] The clothiers' commitment to advertising, like their commitment to their product, reflected a specific configuration of transitional values.

Clothiers tried to fashion a reputation that incorporated tradition and innovation, heritage and progress, Victorian steadfastness and modern hustle. Looking to the past, the self-characterizations of the clothiers often reflected allegiance to Victorian principles of dignity, respect, refinement, and politeness. A trade journal characterized an unscrupulous business tactic as "extremely undignified," while wholesalers in the same publication promoted their goods as offering "comfort with dignity" and "refined, sensible styles."[32] Ad journals assured merchants that self-promotion would in no way compromise this standard: "The man who advertises stands before the public in full, legitimate and dignified prominence," said *Ad Sense*. Similarly, in the opening pages of perhaps the first book of advertising advice ever written, Nathaniel Fowler stated:

"An advertisement is a public and perfectly refined and legitimate invitation from the dealer to everybody."[33]

The clothing industry reinforced the advertising industry's own drive for respectability by attempting to invest its ads with Victorian sobriety and solidity. "There is nothing humorous about the selection of wearing apparel," warned one article. "Therefore the advertiser cannot call upon the cartoonist for inspiration. Neither can he wander into the realm of fancy. . . . His mode of procedure is limited to straightforward, honest representation of the merit of the goods." Phillip Conne, praised as the creator of "without a doubt . . . the best clothing ads in Chicago," told an interviewer: "A little humor [in an ad] is well enough, once in a while, but buying clothes is a serious business."[34] The *Clothing Gazette* asserted that "dignity is a component part of proper business progression," and it took every opportunity to distance the contemporary clothing industry from its undistinguished beginnings in seaport "slop shops." Just as those in the advertising business sought to distance themselves from the bombastic days of Barnum-style ads, so clothiers worked to overcome the dubious reputation of their industry's early days. Having begun in lower-class markets (and contributed the word "shoddy" to the language as a synonym for cheap goods), the industry's leaders were still struggling to constitute themselves as a respectable and progressive force in the community.[35] As advertisers, they needed to overcome the unsavory past reputations of both the advertising and clothing businesses. A Denver clothier commented:

It took years to uproot the many-price system, the "barker," and the various tricks of the trade which kept the retail clothing business so long in disrepute. . . . May we not take courage and anticipate that in another decade the extravagantly-worded advertisement, the abusive reflections on competing merchants (as they appear in many advertisements of to-day) will be tabooed, and the high-sounding cymbal and brass-drum exultations which shock all decent sentiments . . . shall disappear forever?[36]

This was one of many ways clothiers joined with advertising writers to pursue their common interests. The *Clothing Gazette* condemned "circus advertisements and bombastic spread-eagle announcements." Frank Chambers, ad director at Rogers, Peet & Company, a New York clothing store, and creator of some of the most admired ads of the 1890s, offered similar advice: "The theory that 'a sucker's born every minute and he's just as likely to come in here as anywhere else,' won't do for a permanent thing."[37]

The clothing industry pursued its grail of respectability throughout the 1890s, campaigning ceaselessly against fly-by-night merchants who traveled from town to town advertising bogus fire or liquidation sales, often selling poorly made goods at highly profitable prices. The *Clothing Gazette* called for legislative action to protect "legitimate dealers" from the "traveling clothing swindlers" and their "fake bankrupt sales" and reported on the progress of court cases involving them. This crusade had multiple motivations: Both established retailers and the large-scale manufacturers who sought their business saw itinerant retailers as a threat to their profits as well as their respectability. Such campaigns also could help convince local retailers (who sometimes resisted the idea of nationally marketed goods) that their best interests lay in a united front with distant manufacturers, thus integrating the local merchants into the mass market. The call for regulation also reflected a contemporary acceptance of some government oversight of industry in return for relief from the cutthroat competition that characterized many businesses of the late nineteenth century. Still, the tone of this self-described "crusade" against business fraud was so evangelistic it seems to denote deeper—and perhaps more personal—motivations.[38]

The clothing trade press also reached out for credibility through its frequent articles on the history of clothing and the dress of famous and successful people. Readers could learn everything from the story of trousers in ancient Syria to the clothing allowance of American Pilgrims, from the history of stockings back to the twelfth century to the cost of the Prince of Wales's wardrobe. The "dress of men of genius" was analyzed, as were the "Wall Street Beau Brummels." The *Clothing Gazette* assessed the fashion sense of world leaders from Marie François Sadi Carnot, president of France ("a striking example of good taste in dress in public men"), to Prime Minister William Gladstone of Great Britain ("no one has ever accused him of being over particular about his dress"). Some of the articles were fillers; others were illustrated feature stories. Their manifest irrelevance to the practical business advice in which the trade press specialized suggests that they fulfilled some other function for the magazine's readers. By associating the ready-made business with established sources of tradition and prestige, the clothing industry hoped to shake off its parvenu aura, establishing itself instead as the latest, most advanced incarnation of a glorious heritage.[39] Advertising provided a useful means of pursuing this end, for an advertisement was able to juxtapose in a single frame of reference both the innovativeness of ready-made clothing and the timelessness of historic ideals, thus creating a visual association that was meant to suggest an underlying connection between new goods and old values.

The clothier's self-image was not composed entirely of genteel, Victorian decorum. That quality coexisted with a contradictory spirit of aggressive modernism that glorified novelty, industrial efficiency, and "strenuous life" masculinity. The celebration of newness—an important component of a culture of mass consumption and an essential ingredient of the modern fashion system—was reiterated frequently in articles and advertisements. "Be on the lookout for new things," suggested one writer. "It is by helping the manufacturer make his new ideas go, that the retailer increases his little pile in the till," said another. In their ads, clothing wholesalers sought to attract the "progressive dealer" and "up-to date retailers."[40] An appreciation of the American industrial genius for system-building and expertise also echoed in the trade press, which praised the "well systematized" operation of a manufacturer and argued that "legitimate advertising is conducted on a systematic basis." In a booklet published just before the turn of the century, John Wanamaker touted his business methods under the title: *The Wanamaker System: Its Place in Applied Economics and Its Helpful Relation to the Social System in Intellectual, Moral and Material Ways.*[41] Advocacy of the "strenuous life" philosophy of the 1890s further underscored the merchant's modern ideals. The *Chicago Dry Goods Reporter* advised retailers: "Every move must be full of life and vigor, or you are likely to be disappointed in the result." A *Printers' Ink* article titled "The Wanamaker Style" stressed the importance of "making the ads just as full of selling force, snap, vim and electricity as possible." The *Clothing Gazette* praised Kaufmann Brothers of Pittsburgh as an "immense business which the firm has built up through the energy of the members and a liberal use of printer's ink."[42]

The "dress for success" advice favored by the clothiers also seemed to anticipate a modern emphasis on the cultivation of outer personality traits at the expense of inner character development. In the first of a series of articles called "Friendly Chats with Clerks," the store employee is counseled: "Appearances count for a great deal in this critical world of ours. . . . Wear a suit of a quiet dark shade. The plainer the better. Eschew loud-colored shirts and ties. There is nothing so becoming to the average man as a spotless white shirt and a tie of dark color." A clothing ad from E. C. Almy's in Boston states flatly: "The well-dressed man may be no better than his opposite, but he'll meet with more consideration every time. Therefore, if you're looking for success, dress well."[43]

Whether a sharp shift in emphasis from "character" to "personality" actually occurred in this period, as some historians have claimed, is somewhat doubtful, for similar business advice can be found at least as far back as Benjamin Franklin's autobiography. What was more certainly new was the promulgation of this principle through advertising.[44] Moreover, while a Victorian moralist might well look to a character defect to explain a business failing, the *Clothing Gazette* explicitly rejected this reasoning when discussing the ravages of the mid-1890s depression: "Because a man fails it by no means follows that he does not possess valuable faculties and accomplishments in his line." At the very least, clothiers believed that good character would count for little in business without good advertising. Clothing and advertising trade journals cited everything from the Christian gospels to the Boston Tea Party as noble and beneficial examples of publicity. Revealingly, ad writers borrowed from the better-established fashion codes to justify advertising's own rationale for publicity: "The individual who thinks he does not advertise is simply foolish," ran one article in *Fame*, which added: "The woman who moves serenely up and down Fifth Avenue in her Worth constructed gown plainly indicates in every feature that perfect happiness and satisfaction are hidden in its folds."[45]

A subtler form of this mingling of new and traditional appeared in the tendency of clothing wholesalers to advertise with drawings of their warehouse and factory buildings rather than pictures of their goods. These impressive edifices conveyed an image of solidity and reliability in a depression-wracked economy awash with failed businesses. Descriptions of buildings, businesses, and advertisements all used similar terms evoking Victorian decorum and respectability: a "solid, refined and imposing" building, "the solidity and success of your establishment," the "solid, straightforward, honest ring" of an ad.[46] At the same time, the buildings themselves represented the legacy of technological advance. The development of steel-frame construction and inventions such as the elevator, telephone, mimeograph, and typewriter made large commercial structures both physically and functionally feasible, and the *Clothing Gazette* noted approvingly: "The work of demolishing the old buildings is going on at a merry pace, and ere another buying season comes around many old landmarks will be replaced by towers of steel and stone." As builders sheathed steel-framed structures in traditional masonry facades and ornamentation, these buildings manifested a sentimental glossing over of contemporary pressures. Thus the new Brokaw Brothers building in New York earned praise as a "splendid commercial edifice" with a "facade of the mixed classic school" (the entrances were surrounded by columns and capitals). This building, which included two passenger elevators, represented "the practical being combined with the beautiful" to the businessmen of the day.[47]

Overall, the members of the clothing industry tried to construct an identity poised between the mid-Victorian and Progressive periods. While they valued "respectability, orderliness, control and discipline," they also celebrated their own energy, engaging in various forms of "booming" and "boosterism" and adopting the cause of the eternal new.[48] This sometimes uneasy mixture permeated the very design of the *Clothing Gazette*. The magazine, although self-consciously devoted to the practical, festooned its pages with ornamented letters and decorative motifs of the most filigreed style. This technique had long associations with a tradition of fine printing that seemed the antithesis of the mass production future that the trade press celebrated (Figure 37).[49] The page design demonstrates the manner in which men's clothiers wanted to promote their efforts as exemplifying progress, yet it also sought to maintain older values that promised continuity and legitimated their efforts.

The advertisements created by ad professionals and clothing merchants in the 1890s appear at first glance almost as straightforward as is implied by proclamations like "the truth about good goods." Clothing ads in the 1890s frequently consisted of a box of type devoted to product description and prices. They employed relatively few illustrations and many of those were stock drawings. Many merchants undoubtedly considered advertising a straightforward and uncomplicated bid for business.[50] Economic determinants—technological advances in communications, concentration of markets in cities, refinement of mass-production techniques—certainly had enormous impact on the form and content of advertisements. However, economic and technological circumstances no more explain advertising's cultural meaning than they do clothing's social significance. Advertising could allow merchants and manufacturers to work out an accommodation to modern values while still self-consciously espousing adherence to Victorian ideals. The emerging advertising discourse also offered consumers an opportunity to develop their own accommodations to changing times. Together, advertising and fashion created a double-hinged system of articulation, each providing multivalent yet prefabricated units of expression that were capable of dramatizing cultural contradictions or enveloping and neutralizing them. Fashion and advertising formed a kind of feedback loop, in which each drew upon and recirculated the other's key attributes, amplifying the cultural priorities of the day in the process. Trying out mixtures of old and new values in various combinations throughout this period, advertisements and dress became touchstones for the transition to the age of mass consumption.

Even at their most straightforward, advertisements in the 1890s tended intrinsically to promote and normalize certain aspects of modern consumer culture: the inevitability of change, the universality of price cosiderations, the naturalness of long-distance transactions, and the importance of visual images. The advice dispensed by advertising professionals reinforced these tendencies. For example, the *Clothing Gazette* quoted an advertising manager's advice that a clothing merchant should "never use the same 'ad.' twice, no matter how good it is in your opinion." If good advertising truly amounted to nothing more than "a sentence or two of general description on each article advertised and then prices," then frequent copy changes would be difficult to justify, but the advertising trade encouraged incessant change: "Even the same thing

MANLEY M. GILLAM.

AN INTERVIEW WITH THE GREAT DOCTOR
OF PUBLICITY.

AWAY up on the fifth floor of Hilton, Hughes & Co.'s mammoth building, screened off in a sunny corner and surrounded by newspaper files and a miniature printing office, I found Manley M. Gillam, for many years writer of the famous Wanamaker advertisements, and now advertising manager for Hilton, Hughes & Co., at a salary variously estimated at from $10,000 to $15,000 a year.

"The editor of GIBSON'S CLOTHING GAZETTE wishes me to interview you," I said by way of introduction. "Have you time to talk with me?"

"I guess so," said Mr. Gillam, with a smile. "Sit down. Now what is it the CLOTHING GAZETTE would like to know?"

I explained the case briefly.

"The question is," I said, "can clothiers, in your opinion, advertise with profit?"

"I think," replied Mr. Gillam, "that merchants in every line of business can advertise with profit if they have the right thing to advertise, and go about it in the right way."

"In other words," I said, "If a man is successful, he will succeed."

Mr. Gillam's eyes twinkled. "That's about it," he said.

It was evident that I would have to approach him on another tack. "Let us take a suppositious case," I said. "Here is a haberdasher with a business, say, of fifty to a hundred dollars a day. After deducting expenses, the

Figure 37. This interview in *Gibson's Clothing Gazette* featured Manley Gillam, an ad writer who made his reputation with Wanamaker's. The layout of the article seems "progressive" in its use of a halftone photograph and the title "The Great Doctor of Publicity." However, it positions the well-known ad man in a gilt frame that is almost swallowed by spreading vines of Victorian ornamentation. "An Interview with the Great Doctor of Publicity," *Gibson's Clothing Gazette* (August 1895): 69. Reproduced from the collections of the Library of Congress.

may be talked about in a different way, but the heading and body matter must be different from what they were yesterday or last week."[51] Advertisers encouraged people to welcome the new and then to deal with it through consumption. This attitude was good for business, of course, but also appropriate to an era when the pace of social and economic change seemed almost overwhelming, a period when, according to *Fame,* "the 'end of the century' has come to be a synonym for restless and frantic speed."[52] Advertising images and consumer goods offered people a chance to take possession of the symbols of change and so master it.

At the same time, these goods established a framework for everyday life that took capitalist social relations for granted, limiting the possibilities that an alternative to modern consumer culture could be envisioned, let alone adopted.[53] For instance, the relentless trumpeting of price in the ads (the numerals often appeared in especially big and bold type) registered in contemporary discussions of advertising as merely informative (Figures 38, 39, 40). The advertising journals insisted that one should always state the price of goods in an ad—"there is no advertising like the right kind of prices"—based on the argument that an ad must "educate its readers in the matter of qualities and values." One cannot overlook the practical need to emphasize low prices in the mid-1890s, as the country was attempting to fight its way out of a depression. However, this efflorescence of price consciousness also represented a new cultural understanding of consumption. In earlier times, a customer would "spend as much time haggling over the price as in selecting the suit." Placing a tag with a plainly marked and fixed price upon a product was a relatively recent innovation, and clothiers were among the leaders in this development during the last third of the nineteenth century. John Wanamaker, an early advocate of fixed prices, recalled the "primitive" days when "the purchase of a suit of clothes was often a subject of from half an hour's to a whole morning's discussion." As late as the 1890s, some clothiers were still converting to the one-price system, and unmarked prices and haggling remained the norm in some businesses well into the twentieth century.[54]

The one-price system helped establish money as a common denominator of value, a simple index of worth that could be applied to almost anything, and a mass medium that "seemed to operate according to an autonomous and lifeless code."[55] Some system such as this may have been a logical or even necessary outcome of an era when face-to-face communication and personal knowledge became less and less feasible, but it nonetheless represents a vastly different worldview from one that is based on barter relationships or a production theory of value.

The conversational tone of much advertising text, which often addressed the reader in the second person, was no accident. "It is best to write as you talk," said one of the *Clothing Gazette*'s columnists. Another column of advertising advice suggested, "Talk to the public in your advertisement as you would talk to an intelligent customer standing before your counter." *Printers' Ink* added, "When people see your name constantly in the paper *they begin to believe they know you* and it is but a short step from acquaintance to patronage." As the last comment suggests, the conversational approach masked the impersonality of emerging market relations and put them on a basis that was accessible to people who were more familiar with one-on-one salesmanship.[56] *Fame* regarded this "marvelous intrusiveness" as one of advertising's most striking attributes. The advertisement, according to the magazine, can "assume a confidential

Figures 38, 39, 40. Most early clothing advertisers embraced the frequently stated advice to stress prices in their ads, often placing them in bigger and bolder type than anything else. Implicit within this strategy, however, was a new kind of relationship between buyer and seller that replaced face-to-face haggling with standardized cash transactions. A whole realm of personal needs and aspirations could now be neatly subdivided by price. "The Art of Publicity," *Clothing Gazette* (August 1894): 59; "Examples of Advertising," *Gibson's Clothing Gazette* (November 1895): 23. Reproduced from the collections of the Library of Congress.

attitude which would be impertinent to an acquaintance. Our friends would never allude in our presence to a new hair dye, a new brand of soap, or, perhaps, a new corset, if they thought we were likely to adopt them; but the advertisement recommends them in terms of unabashed cordiality." Advertising's intimate tone again suggests a new pervasiveness and presumption of universal applicability for commercial values as well as an attempt to frame the distant, impersonal relationships of the mass marketplace in terms people could associate with their immediate experience.[57]

Joseph Beifeld & Company provides an example from the clothing trades. Beifeld began making cloaks, among the earliest ready-made garments for women, in the 1870s. By the 1890s, the company was attempting to deal with a large and geographically dispersed market. Although Beifeld was a wholesaler, it began in 1898 to advertise in popular magazines such as the *Ladies' Home Journal,* attempting to communicate directly to individual consumers whom the manufacturer had never before addressed except through the intermediary of local dealers. The company's advertising manager, Sol Kline, claimed the company made the decision because "a careful study of the subject revealed to us a good, moral effect as the result of extensive publicity."[58]

Beifeld's new advertising campaign of course stressed its prices, prominently placing them in bold print. The ads also adopted the tone of direct address ("You take no risk in selecting the guaranteed Beifeld cloak") and self-consciously sold fashionability and social status along with garments ("our artists, who make the fashions, design especially for well-dressed women"). Kline remarked that the ads generated response "from all parts of the country" and marveled that magazines such as the *Ladies' Home Journal* and the *Delineator* "seemed to reach every hamlet in the land." The Beifeld ads offered producer and consumer a means of relating to each other across the vast expanse of a national marketplace.[59]

In articulating their philosophy, advertising experts borrowed from ready-made fashion's discourse to explain themselves: "Some advertisers are successful with home-made ads and survive on chestnuts, but these same advertisers wouldn't wear home-made clothing," wrote *Printers' Ink.* Paradoxically, according to the magazine, "home-made ads do not usually *look as truthful* as the ads of experts." In a world where expertise, appearance, and modern production techniques forged a new definition of social fitness, ad man Nathaniel Fowler advised the merchant: "Not only should he advertise honestly, but the advertisement should have *the appearance* of that generous, openhearted truthfulness which carries with it conviction, and which makes a friend of the reader." Indeed, trade journals stressed the appearance of truth as something to be prized for its own sake. Writers praised ads that conveyed the "tone of truthfulness," the "ring of earnestness," and the "appearance of honesty."[60]

Advertising's use of illustrations gained considerable momentum in the 1890s, thanks in part to technical breakthroughs in printing and photographic equipment, but the move to illustrated ads did not come without resistance. One journal complained that advertisers had "gone picture mad" and argued: "Pictures are merely adjuncts to the ad. . . . When they dominate the ad they weaken it." An article titled "The Sin of Over-Illustration" advised a subordinate position for advertising illustrations, which were called "cuts" because the images were engraved, or "cut," onto metal plates. The article emphasized that "the cut should be considered as an assistant to the literary matter." This kind of attitude, grounded in concerns over the emotional directness, easy accessibility, and nontraditional authority of mass-produced pictorial images, warily acknowledged the extent and power of late nineteenth-century transformation in visual culture.[61] A concern over the rapid spread of illustration reflected the era's heightened visual awareness and intense interest in reading the "signs" of the social environment. Just as *Ladies' Home Journal* editor Edward Bok thought that "everything we wear . . . is an indication of our inner characters," the ad manager for a large clothier believed that "it is not too much to say that the character and tone of a business may be safely gauged by the character and tone of its advertising."[62]

Concerns about "over-illustration" did not slow the trend toward visual imagery, however, as more and more advertisers recognized the communicative effectiveness, reader appeal, and opportunity for distinctiveness that illustration offered. For ads aimed at connecting with a polyglot urban market or a diverse national audience, advertisers appreciated the fact that "a picture appeals to all classes, races and languages, irrespective of culture or intellect." As a result, the consensus grew that "the age of illustration has become an age of illustrated advertising" and "the advertising of the future will be illustrated. There can hardly be any question about that."[63]

However, advertisers still had to work out the exact terms of that visual future, as the illustrations in clothing ads reveal. The ad manager for Beifeld & Co. might claim, "I believe in pictures," but many illustrations in clothing advertisements in the 1890s were simply stock drawings showing people posed as stiffly as paper dolls. Often the illustrations only had a generic relationship to the products advertised (Figures 41, 42); sometimes they seemed irrelevant to both text and product (Figures 43, 44). In fact, for most of the nineteenth century, newspapers banned advertisements that included illustrations, large display type, or layouts more than one column wide. Throughout the 1890s, the ad journals

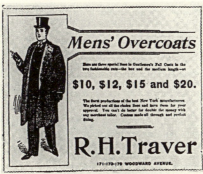

Figures 41, 42. The illustrations in these advertisements came straight from a catalog of mail-order advertising cuts. Thus their relationship to the goods (in one case manufactured by the store in Pittsburgh and in the other case "the finest productions of the best New York manufacturers") was indirect. It is not always easy even to tell which goods the figure was supposed to illustrate. This was preferred by some retailers, who did not necessarily want illustrations to function in a literal way. "Examples of Advertising," *Clothing Gazette* (October 1895): 2. Reproduced from the collections of the Library of Congress.

found it necessary to maintain a continual drumbeat of praise for newspapers that dropped restrictions on such advertising display and criticism against those that persisted. In 1892, *Printers' Ink* complained that "the idea that a paper looks better without display type or cuts is antediluvian," and in 1899 the *Advisor* was still lamenting: "Publishers must awaken to the fact that this is a progressive age. They ought to abolish their absurd rules as to broken column ads. and extras for displays."[64]

The stock illustrations' appeal is partly explained in practical terms: They were cheaper than custom art—one catalog offered a selection of several hundred such figures at $1 each (see Figure 4)—and recent advances in newspaper printing technology made them especially inexpensive to reproduce.[65] Yet the generic cut was admired in its own right as well. Although some writers criticized stock cuts and irrelevant illustrations in favor of the specific and pertinent, not everyone agreed.[66]

You have learned to your sorrow that a poor ill-fitting suit is easy to get.

A suit well put together—from cloth standing the necessary test for all-wool and fast-color is not so easy to find, unless you know just where to go. We are trying every day to tell you of three good places.

One of the successes of this season is that short English walking coat with flaps.

ROGERS PEET & Co

Prince and Broadway.
Warren and Broadway.
32d and Broadway.

For three degrees of weather we have three degrees of overcoats—light, medium and heavy.

Light, for the early autumn—good for next spring.

Medium, for the particular, careful-of-his-health man; who finds the light not heavy enough and the heavy too heavy.

Heavy, for the good, cold, bracing weather; when warmth and comfort are the considerations.

All the correct cloths, correctly fashioned in all the three kinds.

ROGERS PEET & Co

Prince and Broadway.
Warren and Broadway.
32d and Broadway.

Figures 43, 44. Even when customized drawings were used, some advertising illustrations were strikingly irrelevant to the text. Rogers, Peet & Company advertisements, which were widely praised during the 1890s, frequently fell into this category. Rogers, Peet & Company advertisements, *New York Tribune* (October 2, 1895): 10; (October 3, 1895): 12.

Reflecting on this period, *Printers' Ink* recalled the "widely held belief that 'any cut was better than no cut at all,'" and commented, "If nothing else was available—often in preference to anything else—the advertiser used an illustration that was wholly irrelevant to the text or the product." Indeed Manley Gillam, who followed J. E. Powers as the head of Wanamaker advertising, summarized his views on advertising illustration by saying: "Whether the advertiser uses a monkey and organ or the Angelus matters little so far as arresting the attention goes." *Fame* praised a totally irrelevant illustration in one of Rogers, Peet's acclaimed clothing ads as an "odd and original" cut that provided "just a bit of bright nonsense to attract the eye." And when the *Chicago Dry Goods Reporter* added stock cuts to the sample ads in each issue, it stressed that there was no necessary relationship between the illustration and the advertising pitch. "The sample ads are complete without the illustration," it assured readers, "as the wording says nothing about the cut."[67]

Clothing ad illustrations could trace a lineage back to women's fashion plates, which fashion magazines and specialty publications had used to convey style information since at least the 1830s. The mass-produced, generic quality of the stock images from later in the century makes their deeper meaning harder to grasp, but it is clear that they represented a glimmering recognition of the increasing importance and complexity of visual culture in the United States. Advertisers were taking the first halting steps toward the development of an iconography for consumer goods that would grow into a vast symbolic reference system for modern Americans.[68]

Advertising experts often related issues of appearance in advertising to those in dress, perhaps seeking a more completely formed visual culture onto which they could graft their own nascent visual identity. "Be careful in your dress, whether it be in your person or your advertisement," advised one advertising journal. Another article suggested that the novice advertiser model his approach to the marketplace after "the entrance of a man into society . . . a well dressed man bearing a respectable name."[69] These statements elucidate the manner in which the symbolic systems of advertising and fashion borrowed from each other. Although they functioned as separate communicative codes, they developed an increasingly symbiotic relationship. Thus to understand the symbolic meaning of a clothing ad, one must interpret it both in relation to advertising's mode of cultural address and with reference to the dress code. A typical Kaufmann's advertisement (see Figure 41) incorporates the advertising emphasis on price consciousness ("no need for any man . . . to pay more than $9.95), change ("the styles are the latest"), direct address to smooth long-distance selling relationships ("Don't care how particular you may be"), and visual communications (the use of a

variety of illustrations). The ad also draws on the clothing industry's concurrent interest in attaching custom-made values to ready-made goods
("place them alongside the most expensive custom work and they won't
suffer by comparison"), in national identity ("selected from the foremost
American mills"), and in the solidly built, assertive masculine body ideal
(the various illustrations). The two meaning systems mesh nicely and
open up a window onto a variety of underlying social issues and cultural
dynamics, but the systems are not identical, as is evident in the fact that
the history of advertising is replete with futile attempts to influence or
create fashion.[70]

In any event, the role of advertising's visual elements did not occur
naturally. Systems of representation had to be worked out and conventionalized. In 1898, *Ad Sense* published the story of a person who mistook
a calendar illustration for an advertisement and tried to order a spin-
ning wheel from an insurance company. The function of advertising
illustration was still up for grabs as late as 1914, as is demonstrated by
the small-town clothing merchant who told *Printers' Ink* that he would not
use advertising illustrations supplied by a manufacturer if they displayed
a trademark too prominently. "Don't try to get your money's worth by
sticking your name all over it," he said. Using such "electros" (a certain
type of cut) eroded his individuality and made him look cheap. "I will
not use electros . . . which advertise a manufacturer's product too obviously," the merchant announced. "I can't afford to have people think I
am cheap. Rather than give that impression I would send 50 or 75 cents
away to a stock cut house, whose catalogues I have, and get cuts of my
own."[71] One might argue that branded illustrations depicting specific
items would build name recognition for a line of goods and be much
more effective—and no more conformist—than stock cuts that were
mass-produced and sold by mail order. The clothier didn't see it that
way. For him, the manufacturer's illustrations and trademarks carried
connotations of cheapness and commonness. In the ads of the 1890s,
we can sense the logic of graphic communication being worked out by
trial and error. The conventions of advertising illustration were under
construction.

Although advertising presented itself as plain talk, it offered a still-
developing and ever-fluid system of meaning that tended to bend communications in directions that naturalized some attitudes and made others
literally unspeakable. Advertising's emphasis on staying up-to-date normalized change as part of daily life. Its reliance on the one-price system
embedded in daily transactions the idea that money was an index of worth
applicable to an unlimited range of disparate items. Advertisements
smoothed the transformation of social relations by putting them into
familiar cultural terms, adopting the language of face-to-face, personal

address to describe impersonal, long-distance interactions. The ads' increasing emphasis on visual images—and the mass production of these images—guided consumers toward a prevalent and emotionally powerful culture of appearance, one that raised new questions about the increasing standardization of daily life and offered a new means for people to orient themselves to the changing visual landscape. Advertising's marriage with mass media and the industry's insistence that "wise advertising is a continuous performance" created a widely available and widely understood new mode of social communication.[72] The tendencies of modern advertising merged profitably with fashion, which provided a constantly changing product and an emphasis on appearance that was perfect for advertising.

Intellectual and ideological trends such as sex differentiation and social Darwinism influenced advertising, and advertising in turn influenced those trends. In 1894, *Printers' Ink* offered the following opinion: "If the suffrage is ever granted to the weaker sex, a big bargain sale announcement in the papers on election day will be a blessed boon to any candidate who doesn't happen to be popular with the female workers." A few months later, the *Ladies' Home Journal* published an ad with an illustration of a stylishly dressed woman and the text: "I don't want to vote, but I would like to emancipate womankind from unnecessary work. If they'll use 'Redfern' Bias Corded Velvet . . . on their dresses, one binding will save the work and expense of putting on several other kinds" (Figure 45).[73] This advertisement attempted a harmonious, symbolic resolution of custom-made clothing, the traditional women's sphere, and the contentious issue of female suffrage. The ad used the image of a stylish, seemingly up-to-date young woman and copy written in a tone of direct address to try to naturalize this relationship between dress, gender, and citizenship.

Advertising's function in these matters was no accident. *Ladies' Home Journal* editor Edward Bok would reject ads whose portrayal of females failed to meet his standard of "womanliness."[74] Advertising trade journals reflected the contemporary urgency to depict sharp distinctions between the sexes. They characterized women as having a "shopping instinct" and a "keen scent for bargains," terminology that not only situated women in a domestic role but cast them as intuitive, emotional consumers rather than rational beings. As one trade journal said: "Women are the most persistent readers of advertising. The fact that they are more emotional, and consequently far more readily influenced than men, makes it considerably easier to appeal to them. They are, in addition, far less skeptical." Advertising trade journals reinforced sexual differentiation by asserting that a man's life in the productive sphere included little time for advertising ("work-a-day men have not the time

"I don't want to vote,

but I would like to emancipate womankind from unnecessary work. If they'll use

'Redfern' Bias Corded Velvet

a brand of the famous

"SH&M

FIRST QUALITY

Bias Velveteen Skirt Binding

on their dresses, one binding will save the work and expense of putting on several of other kinds."

Look for "S. H. & M." First Quality on the label of every bolt you buy.

"S. H. & M." Dress Stays are the Best

Figure 45. Advertising in the 1890s was not always so blatant as this in attempting to establish guidelines for "proper" gender-role behavior, but the advertisements and advertisers very early began to assign distinct attributes to men and women readers. Source: S. H. & M. advertisement, *Ladies' Home Journal* (January 1895): 22. Reproduced courtesy of the Winterthur Library: Printed Book and Periodical Collection.

to waste on long, flowery statements about bargains") while women had time to immerse themselves in ad copy ("once a woman is attracted to an advertisement she will read it all through, no matter how long it is or how fine the type is"). The key was gender difference: "Women are differently constituted; they delight in being allured into the purchase of a bargain."[75]

Clothing merchants, whose product contributed so greatly to the process of gender construction, incorporated these distinctions in their own approaches to advertising. The Rogers, Peet advertising manager declared: "Women have more time than men and read the advertising portion of the newspaper more carefully. You can point out a dozen bargains to them and they will carefully note each one. It is different with the men. They do not go shopping. If they want a ready-made suit of clothes they want to know where to go and get it." George Gardner, advertising manager for the Mabley and Carew department store in Baltimore, agreed: "In addressing men, be brief. . . . With women you may beat about the bush a little—if you're nice and interesting." His formula: "Colloquial simplicity for women; epigrammatic terseness for men."[76]

The developing language of advertising also complemented the fashion system in conveying a sense of Darwinian social progress and American national supremacy. Attitudes about gender roles and evolutionary hierarchy are implicit in Charles Bates's comment, "There isn't a woman in any *civilized* country on the globe that doesn't hanker after a bargain." Advertising trade journals emphasized the importance of up-to-date methods, often in terms that evoked the popular understanding of social Darwinism: "Possibly the law of evolution is at work with greater force in the advertising field than it is in any other. . . . The survival of the fittest must be conceded the rule of advertising." One writer in *Fame* specifically cited Herbert Spencer, the great advocate of social Darwinism, in discussing the "evolution of advertising" and making a case that the field was "emerging in the direction of something cleaner and better." This faith in progress offered particular consolations to middle-class Americans, who could ascribe their relatively privileged place in society to the laws of nature rather than haphazard or unjust accumulation of wealth and power. It helped them create a blend of cultural values that embraced the future while maintaining their traditional social status.[77]

Advertisers also supported America's blossoming nationalism and imperialistic tendencies. "It is impossible for me to deny, at the outset, that English clothing advertisements are exasperatingly behind the standard of those we are accustomed to see and marvel at in American newspapers," said one writer. Another claimed that during his travels it became apparent that Latin America was in "need of characteristic, snappy American advertising." He recalled "the extraordinary joy which came upon me one day . . . when crossing a lonely trail in Honduras I came upon the tin sign of a Chicago manufacturer." As he said: "Near by were the ruins of ancient cities, about was the thickness of the jungle, but American progress was in the sign."[78] These attitudes exemplified a sort of "ad man's burden" in which the advertiser would characterize himself as an apostle of culture who was willing to "consecrate his life to the work of spreading general enlightenment."[79] Militant American nationalism, like social Darwinism, reflected an aggressive, sometimes violent, social attitude that incorporated new gender and political ideals while preserving in native-born white elites their traditional sense of entitlement and superiority.

As we have already seen, the dress code fit comfortably with a sense of national pride and progress. The clothing trade press reinforced this by describing the era before ready-made clothing as "those primitive days" and praising successful retailers as "progressive, aggressive and better able to stand the consequences of the law of the survival of the fittest." John Wanamaker expressed it this way: "As animal life in its primary forms was uncouth and clumsy and the ascent to the modern creation was only by slowly stratified ages so commercial life has slowly risen through the strata of centuries to the higher atmosphere of civilization." The trade press boasted that the American clothing industry stood at the pinnacle of its own development ("there never was a time in the history of this country when a man could dress so well for so little money as he can to-day") and the world's ("it is a fact that in no country of the world are the whole people so well dressed as in the United States").[80]

Like fashion, the meaning of advertising was still adapting to parameters and possibilities linked to mass production and mass merchandising. Clothing manufacturers and retailers willingly joined their symbolic might with that of the developing discourse of advertising. As American society moved into an age of large-scale consumption, national markets, and mass communications, fashion and advertising drew on each other's strengths to become the sign systems that Americans increasingly relied upon to provide a bridge between past and future.

All these elements converged in the career of Joseph Schaffner, cofounder in 1887 of Hart, Schaffner & Marx clothing manufacturers. Schaffner got his first taste of business in a country store where barter transactions were still common. A proper Victorian in many ways, he loved to quote Matthew Arnold and Walter Pater to friends and acquaintances, and he was acutely aware as he entered the business that the clothing industry was, in the words of a company historian, "not highly respected." Schaffner aimed to make his company's clothes the essence of respectability. He summarized much contemporary thinking on the influence of clothes when he wrote:

The clothes a man wears are to some extent a true index of his character and tastes; but they're also an influence upon his character and tastes; they affect in an unconscious and more or less indirect way his standing in the community. This being true, it is easy to see that the clothing man has a duty to his fellow-citizens which ought not to be neglected or treated lightly; and a part of that duty is to maintain his own dignity in the business.[81]

In contrast to his insistence on Victorian respectability, Schaffner's diligent attention to advertising showed a side of his business practices that was decidedly more modern. Among clothing manufacturers, Hart, Schaffner & Marx was notable for its innovation and aggressiveness as an advertiser, and Schaffner took a personal hand in preparing ad copy and supervised the use of illustrations. He also encouraged the company's local dealers "constantly to do more as well as better advertising."[82]

Hart, Schaffner & Marx was characteristic of clothing manufacturers in its persistent efforts to imbue the ready-made suit with custom-made cachet, supplying at one stroke an appreciation of both the past and the future: "Instead of going to the tailor this Spring, suppose you try a Hart, Schaffner & Marx ready-tailored suit at half the tailor's price. You will find it will fit better, wear longer, keep its shape and be in better style and taste than anything the average tailor can make to your measure." The strategy worked. Barely thirty years after the firm was founded, the company had assets of nearly $25 million.[83]

After his death, Schaffner's colleagues remembered two things in particular about his early business success. First, they recalled his pioneering use of national advertising, which he "applied so effectively that it revolutionized the promotion side of the business." Second, they noted that he operated so respectably that he "gave to the clothing industry a dignity and standing which it did not before possess."[84] Advertising zealotry and Victorian propriety may seem like an odd couple, but clothiers of the late nineteenth century did not find them contradictory. They did not confront the new culture of mass consumption as a simple displacement of old values but rather as a more complicated reformulation of an entire set of cultural norms. Fashion and advertising provided ideal tools for the job.

"Fitness and Unfitness in Dress"

One definition of culture is the stories people tell themselves about themselves. Directly or indirectly, people continually narrate the facts of their culture to see if they still make sense, if they provide a basis for action in day-to-day life, if they render the material world intelligible.[1] Not all meanings will necessarily be held in common, but the symbols that express them must be widely available and understood for the meanings to exert broad influence. Culture depends on the symbolic systems at its command, and in the 1890s, fashion and advertising became more widely accessible than ever before, providing symbolic systems particularly well situated to explain the economic and social changes occurring at that time. These symbols make everyday life comprehensible by providing coded appearances that people can use to interpret and navigate the social world.

People told many kinds of stories about clothing in the 1890s. Some were self-consciously produced fictions that sought a broad audience. The March 1896 issue of *Good Housekeeping,* for example, included a short story titled "Fitness and Unfitness in Dress: Two Girls, Two Wardrobes, and a Lover." It is the story of two young cousins who have a chance to visit the city, each receiving an allowance to prepare herself for the trip. One cousin, Belle, is beautiful, but as the story says, "unfortunately her sense of fitness was not great." She spends most of her allowance on one dazzling outfit and of necessity filled out her wardrobe with cheaper goods. The other cousin, Aynah, is plain-looking but has excellent fashion sense. She shops not only for value and versatility but for things that express her individuality: "She was rather short and plump so she avoided the extreme mode in skirts, and while using the best of linings throughout did not stiffen hers to flare extravagantly. For the same reason, she avoided the voluminous double capes that are so becoming to a tall, slender woman." Aynah finds items that particularly matched her identity. The author of the story, Sharlot Hall, writes that Aynah "studied her dress in relation to herself till she found out what was peculiarly suited to her own odd little personality." When they reached the city, Belle too often looks "sadly bedraggled" or inappropriately attired, while Aynah is always "trim and neat." Consequently, before the trip is over Aynah wins the love of a man ("wealthy, quiet and devoted to art and literature") who was at first attracted to Belle's beauty. A year later Aynah and the man are married.[2]

The story specifies that the two women lived in a custom-made world (Aynah first selects appropriate fabric for her clothes and then has it made up according to her specifications) and the story links dress very clearly to the social presentation of the self, to the construction of a body and of an identity through clothing. The author devotes about 40 percent of the narrative to an item-by-item description of how Aynah selects her wardrobe. Belle's bad fashion sense betrays her as a foolish, superficial person. Moreover, to a great degree her bad fashion sense constitutes her foolishness and superficiality. Aynah's "odd little person-ality" meshes perfectly with her wise clothing selections, providing a socially acceptable way to assert an individualized presence in the world. As with much women's fiction of the Victorian period, however, the payoff for the heroine comes at the wedding altar, suggesting that the symbolic world of dress, while offering certain satisfactions and agency, constrained its participants into prescribed gender roles. Women had various but limited means of adjusting between the expressive and the repressive ends of the fashion system's spectrum.

Another story, this one from *Browning, King & Co.'s Illustrated Monthly*, appeared in January 1898 under the title "A Clothing Conversation." It begins: "They were two chums who had not seen each other for a week, and each was critically eying the other's attire." One of the men, Ledger, is wearing a brand new outfit and announced proudly, "I'm through with ready-made suits." His friend, Daybrook, elicits the information that Ledger's suit has been made-to-measure by the tailoring department of a local department store. Before the vignette runs its course, Ledger realizes he would have been better off with a high-quality, ready-made suit, one that was made under "the supervision of an expert." Daybrook predicts that his own ready-made suit "will still be shapely and highly presentable when yours is a wreck." Ledger then pleads with his friend not to tell anybody that "I had my clothes made in a dry goods store." Daybrook replies: "Oh *I* won't tell anybody, of course, but I am afraid that the suit itself won't keep the secret so well."[3]

This story is a transparent sales pitch for Browning, King & Company, but it also taps into a broader discourse of clothing. Ledger and Daybrook live in a ready-made world, nominally governed by expertise but still oper-ating on principles of body politics and self-presentation (represented in the crucial desire that the coat remain "shapely and highly presentable"). Clothing was an important social marker for men as well as women. In fact, Ledger's suit cannot "keep a secret." Ledger and Daybrook also live in a sharply gendered world: Ledger's suspect garment is first identified as coming from a department store, which was considered a feminine space. Contemporary accounts described department stores as being populated by "a throng of well-dressed women, who, with preoccupied air, tread the spacious aisles," and historians have designated them simply as "female territory" because 90 percent of the customers and virtually all the sales clerks were women.[4] Later the story describes the offending suit as having been "made in a dry goods store," which, being principally a source of sewing supplies, was an even more unmistakably feminized designation. Ledger explains in an effort to fend off his friend's criticism, "Well, it was the wife persuaded me to get it."[5] The moral of the story is that any man worthy of the name wears a ready-made suit from a clothier.

Not all of clothing's cultural fables were consciously fictionalized. Think, for example, of William Browning's proud boast about the development and high standards of the men's clothing industry, Charlotte Perkins Gilman's incisive commentary into the symbolic economy of dress, Edward Bok's insistence on clothing as a true index of character, or Mary Antin's remembrance of her "real American machine-made garments." The meaning of clothes was widely understood and deployed at the end of the nineteenth century, even by those far removed from the affairs of New York's Four Hundred. Diaries, letters, and memoirs show that a farm girl in southwestern Iowa could enthusiastically describe her new dress with language that could have come straight from the *Ladies' Home Journal*: "It is made with a princess skirt, gathered waist, full sleeves, and a little short jacket without sleeves." A middle-class homemaker in Kansas thought it natural to write to her mother describing how carefully she matched her social engagements and her attire: "[The event] was gotten up on the spur of the moment so I did not dress up." A high school student in Cairo, Illinois, could confidently assess the fashion sense of the class ahead of her: "half the ninnies are getting white satins—think how inappropriate—graduates in satins!" And an immigrant girl in New York could vividly cast her ideals of class consciousness and domestic happiness in terms of clothing: "We shall be married, and I shall not be compelled to wear a gold watch and chain, a pearl necklace and silk dresses! We shall be married and together work for the people."[6]

Ultimately, the stories about clothing did not require words at all. The public accessibility and cultural importance of dress was expressed in the garments themselves, in the bulked-up chests of men's ready-made suits and the custom-made "frills and furbelows" of women's visiting gowns. These garments, like Ledger's suit, could not keep a secret when it came to gender roles, class relations, citizenship, or the many other cultural categories that were in transition at the end of the nineteenth century. The complex and shifting syntax of the dress code meant complicated issues and difficult cultural tensions could be confronted indirectly and resolved symbolically.

Crucial to fashion's accessibility was its dissemination via mass-market advertising, a cultural form just beginning in the 1890s to employ large-circulation periodicals and new technologies for illustration in a recognizably modern format. Clothing and advertising both thrived as cultural forms because they were accessible enough to provide the basis of shared understanding, ambiguous enough to offer multiple meanings or provide indirect communications on volatile subjects, and flexible enough to address the broad range of cultural categories that were shifting as the scope of daily life expanded under the influence of mass production and mass communications. Both helped create a fascination and accommodation to change, body politics, and self-presentation that have continued to define much of American popular culture and social interaction ever since.

A dynamism—the sense of trial and error, of cultural values under construction—is among the most salient characteristics of those cultural processes. The ever-changing appearances of fashion and advertising underwrote a "view of cultural situations as *always* in flux, in a perpetual historically sensitive state of resistance and accommodation."[7] Mass-produced goods and mass-media advertising not only reinforced this cultural view, to a degree they also constituted it. However, they also offered the tools by which the change could be understood, accommodated, and adjusted. The impact of social and economic change shook a host of cultural values out of alignment at the end of the nineteenth century. By looking at clothing habits and the ways they were advertised, one can see how people began to piece these values back together in new and sometimes tentative ways. Clothing styles, to be accepted, have somehow to fit prevailing attitudes about the nature of men and women, about citizenship, and about society as a whole.[8] Understanding this, one sees the true significance in the words written by a *Ladies' Home Journal* columnist in 1893. "Dress," she said, "has its influence over everybody."[9]

Notes

The following abbreviations appear in the notes.

CC   *Custom Cutter*
CDGR   *Chicago Dry Goods Reporter*
CG   *Clothing Gazette* (name changed to *Gibson's Clothing Gazette* in December 1894)
Designer *Designer* (name changed to *Standard Designer* in August 1898)
DGE   *Dry Goods Economist*
GH   *Good Housekeeping*
Godey's *Godey's Magazine* (known as *Godey's Lady's Book* until October 1892)
LHJ   *Ladies' Home Journal*
PCT   *Practical Cutter and Tailor*
PI   *Printers' Ink*
SAJ   *Sartorial Art Journal*
WHC   *Woman's Home Companion* (known as *Ladies' Home Companion* until January 1897)

Introduction

1. "Godey's Fashions," *Godey's Magazine* (June 1893): 785. This article ran with the subheading, "The Individual Significance of Clothes."

2. Elizabeth Robbins, "The Right Man," *WHC* (June 1898): 8–9.

3. Isabel Mallon, "Some Dresses for the House," *LHJ* (November 1892): 27.

4. Elizabeth Robbins, "The Right Man," 8.

5. Ruth Ashmore, "The Restlessness of the Age," *LHJ* (January 1895): 16; Edward Bok, "The Rush of American Women," *LHJ* (January 1899): 14.

6. T. J. Jackson Lears, *No Place of Grace: Antimodernism and the Transformation of American Culture, 1880–1920* (New York: Pantheon, 1981), 32; Robert Wiebe, *The Search for Order, 1877–1920* (New York: Hill and Wang, 1967), 12. For a summary of the sense of transition that characterized this decade, see John Higham, "The Reorientation of American Culture in the 1890s," in *The Origins of Modern Consciousness,* ed. John Weiss (Detroit: Wayne State University Press, 1965), 25–48.

7. John Whiteclay Chambers II, *The Tyranny of Change: America in the Progressive Era, 1890–1920,* 2nd ed. (New Brunswick, N.J.: Rutgers University Press, 2000), 19, 2. Good overviews of this period can be found in this book, as well as in Steven Diner, *A Very Different Age: America in the Progressive Era* (New York: Hill

and Wang, 1998); Mark Summers, *The Gilded Age, Or, A Hazard of New Functions* (Upper Saddle River, N.J.: Prentice-Hall, 1997); and Alan Trachtenberg, *The Incorporation of America: Culture and Society in the Gilded Age* (New York: Hill and Wang, 1982).

8. Brooks Adams, *America's Economic Supremacy* (New York: Macmillan, 1900), v–vi; Trachtenberg, *Incorporation of America*, 208. Turner's paper, "The Significance of the Frontier in American History," was first presented in 1893 and was published the following year by both the State Historical Society of Wisconsin and the American Historical Association. It has been reprinted many times since in various collections, including Turner's own *The Frontier in American History* (New York: Henry Holt, 1920), 1–38.

9. For comments on the general change in visual media during this period, see Raymond Williams, "When Was Modernism?" in *The Politics of Modernism: Against the New Conformists* (London: Verso Press, 1989), 33; and Neil Harris, "Iconography and Intellectual History: The Halftone Effect," in *Cultural Excursions: Marketing Appetites and Cultural Tastes in Modern America* (Chicago: University of Chicago Press, 1990), 307. Harris's essay also discusses the significance of the halftone process. For brief descriptions of other developments see the following: on comic strips (1897), Frank Luther Mott, *American Journalism: A History: 1690–1960*, 3rd ed. (New York: Macmillan, 1962), 585–587; on the first Kodak (1888) and Kinetoscope galleries (1894), Reese Jenkins, *Technology and the American Photographic Industry 1839 to 1925* (Baltimore: Johns Hopkins University Press, 1975), 113–116, 268–275; on the poster craze (mid-1890s), Patricia Hills, *Turn-of-the-Century America* (New York: Whitney Museum of American Art, 1975), 58–60; on picture postcards (1893), Donald Miller and Dorothy Miller, *Picture Postcards in the United States* (New York: Clarkson Potter, 1976), 1–14; on light and color, William Leach, "Strategists of Display and the Production of Desire," in *Consuming Visions: Accumulation and Display of Goods in America, 1880–1920*, ed. Simon Bronner (New York: W. W. Norton, 1989), 99–132, and Carolyn Marvin, *When Old Technologies Were New: Thinking About Electric Communication in the Late Nineteenth Century* (New York: Oxford University Press, 1988), 158–190; on new words, Thomas Richards, *The Commodity Culture of Victorian England: Advertising and Spectacle, 1851–1914* (Stanford, Calif.: Stanford University Press, 1990), 268.

10. Lela Barnes, ed., "North Central Kansas in 1887–1889: From the Letters of Leslie and Susan Snow of Junction City—Concluded," *Kansas Historical Quarterly* 29, no. 4 (Winter 1993): 404, 408, 414, 417, 422.

11. For an 1890s estimate of the spread of men's ready-made clothing, see William Browning, "The Clothing and Furnishing Trade," in *One Hundred Years of American Commerce*, vol. 2, ed. Chauncey M. Depew (New York: D. O. Haynes, 1895), 563–564. For recent estimates of a similar spread in the women's trade, see Joan Severa, *Dressed for the Photographer: Ordinary Americans and Fashion* (Kent, Ohio: Kent State University Press, 1995), 372–373, and Nan Enstad, *Ladies of Work, Girls of Adventure: Working Women, Popular Culture, and Labor Politics at the Turn of the Century* (New York: Columbia University Press, 1999), 17, 21. Many of Severa's statements on ready-made clothing are qualified by parallel assertions about the continuing importance of home sewing (297, 380, 455). Enstad associates ready-made women's fashion with working-class consumers and does not directly contradict my own description of mostly middle-class consumption.

12. Edward Bok, "Personal from the Editor," *LHJ* (November 1899): 16. Bok boasted in his autobiography that through his efforts the number of letters received from readers climbed to nearly 1 million a year by the late 1910s. Bok

required staff members to answer all letters promptly, regularly sending fake queries under an assumed name to check their efficiency. Given the magazine's preeminent skill at building both advertising and circulation, there is every reason to think that if Bok had believed he could encourage business or readership by promoting ready-to-wear clothing, he would have done so. See Edward Bok, *The Americanization of Edward Bok: The Autobiography of a Dutch Boy Fifty Years Later* (New York: Charles Scribner's Sons, 1922), 173–174; and Salme Steinberg, *Reformer in the Marketplace: Edward W. Bok and the Ladies' Home Journal* (Baton Rouge: Louisiana State University Press, 1979), 56.

13. Certainly some ready-made garments for women (cloaks in the 1870s, tailored suits in the 1880s, shirtwaists in the 1890s) made in-roads in the marketplace before the end of the century. Thus, it is not inaccurate to say, as Jean Funderburk does, that "a variety of women's ready-made garments were available in the 1870s." See Jean Arta Uhrig Funderburk, "The Development of Women's Ready-To-Wear, 1865 to 1914: Based on *New York Times* Advertisements" (Ph.D. diss., University of Maryland, 1994), 39. Similar comments can be made about the 1880s and 1890s as well. It is also credible, however, to conclude, as Nancy Green does, that such trends were not clearly established until almost 1920. She makes the still heavily qualified estimation that "by the First World War, almost all Americans were wearing *some garments* that had been made up without multiple fittings" (emphasis added). See Nancy Green, *Ready-To-Wear and Ready-To-Work: A Century of Industry and Immigrants in Paris and New York* (Durham, N.C.: Duke University Press, 1997), 46. Green's book offers the most recent and most thorough examination of the development of the women's clothing industry. I am not attempting to deny the erratic progress of women's ready-made clothing during the late 1800s, and indeed I discuss it in Chapter 2. The piecemeal introduction of ready-made clothing for women in fact fits my overall thesis. The evidence suggests, however, that the benchmark for when consumption and acceptance of such garments became the cultural norm should be properly placed after, perhaps well after, the turn of the century. Jenna Weissman Joselit has documented continuing resistance and controversy over the acceptability of ready-made clothing well into the 1920s. See Jenna Weissman Joselit, *The Perfect Fit: Clothes, Character, and the Promise of America* (New York: Henry Holt, 2001), 7–41.

14. The association of femininity and consumption pre-dates this era. In the 1890s, however, we see the new, self-styled advertising experts self-consciously promoting this equation. See, for example, Joel Benton, "The Woman Buyer," *Fame* (October 1898): 403; and Oscar Herzberg, "Women and Advertising," *Printers' Ink* (October 30, 1895): 20. For overviews of consumption, gender, and history, see Mary Louise Roberts, "Gender, Consumption, and Commodity Culture," *American Historical Review* 103, no. 3 (June 1998): 817–844; Victoria de Grazia, "Introduction," in *The Sex of Things: Gender and Consumption in Historical Practice*, ed. Victoria de Grazia with Ellen Furlough (Berkeley: University of California Press, 1996), 1–10; and Steven Lubar, "Men/Women/Production/Consumption" in *His and Hers: Gender, Consumption, and Technology*, ed. Roger Horowitz and Arwen Mohun (Charlottesville: University Press of Virginia, 1998), 7–37.

15. On magazines, see Richard Ohmann, "Where Did Mass Culture Come From? The Case of Magazines," *Berkshire Review* 16 (1981): 85–101. On the first daily newspaper to sell a million copies a day (the *New York World* in 1897), see Frank Luther Mott, *American Journalism*, 546–548.

16. William Dean Howells, "Bates and His Book," *Printers' Ink* (May 20, 1896):

18–20. This was a reprint of an article that appeared May 9, 1896, in *Harper's Weekly*.

17. Ellen Gruber Garvey, *The Adman in the Parlor: Magazines and the Gendering of Consumer Culture, 1880s to 1910s* (New York: Oxford University Press, 1996), 15. Many works on advertising history suggest that advertisements were mostly utilitarian, informative notices until the development of symbolic, psychological appeals in the 1920s.

18. The *Oxford English Dictionary* lists the first usage of the term "ready-to-wear" in 1895, citing the Montgomery Ward catalog, but the phrase was popping up regularly in newspaper ads by this time as well. The previous year, for example, a Chicago clothing store had advertised "the finest and most luxurious ready-to-wear suits and overcoats possible to make." See *Oxford English Dictionary*, 2nd ed., s.v. "ready-to-wear"; The Hub advertisement, *Chicago Tribune* (November 11, 1894): 30.

19. Daniel Boorstin offered an early and influential description of this era as marking the move from producer to consumer in *The Americans: The Democratic Experience* (New York: Random House, 1973), 99. This periodization has found favor with many other historians in the ensuing years. See, for example, Richard Wightman Fox and T. J. Jackson Lears, introduction, in *The Culture of Consumption: Critical Essays in American History, 1880–1980,* ed. Richard Wightman Fox and T. J. Jackson Lears (New York: Pantheon, 1983), xi; Susan Porter Benson, *Counter Cultures: Saleswomen, Managers and Customers in American Department Stores, 1890–1940* (Urbana: University of Illinois Press, 1986), 75; William Leach, *Land of Desire: Merchants, Power, and the Rise of a New American Culture* (New York: Pantheon, 1993), 8. In contrast, Cary Carson argues that the "consumer revolution" had already occurred by 1750, when "people up and down the social order had discovered and were indulging the most extraordinary passion for consumer goods in quantities and varieties that were unknown, even unimaginable, to their fathers and grandfathers." Alternatively, Lizabeth Cohen has demonstrated that as late as the 1920s working-class people were resisting and reformulating the "culture of consumption" in various crucial ways. And W. T. Lhamon, Jr., stated that "the middle of the fifties was when it became clear that the problem of production, at least in the United States, was yielding to the problem of consumption." On earlier consumer culture, see Cary Carson, "The Consumer Revolution in Colonial America: Why Demand?" in *Of Consuming Interests: The Style of Life in the Eighteenth Century,* ed. Cary Carson, Ronald Hoffman, and Peter J. Albert (Charlottesville: University Press of Virginia, 1994), 483–697; and John Brewer and Roy Porter, eds., *Consumption and the World of Goods* (London: Routledge, 1993). The quotation from Cary Carson appears on page 486. On later consumption, see Lizabeth Cohen, *Making a New Deal: Industrial Workers in Chicago, 1919–1939* (Cambridge: Cambridge University Press, 1990), 99–158; and W. T. Lhamon, Jr., *Deliberate Speed: The Origins of a Cultural Style in the American 1950s* (Washington, D.C.: Smithsonian Institution Press, 1990), 16. For review of the historical literature on consumer culture see Jean-Christophe Agnew, "Coming Up for Air: Consumer Culture in Historical Perspective," *Intellectual History Newsletter* 12 (1990): 3–21 (also in Brewer and Porter, *Consumption and the World of Goods,* 19–39).

20. Marshall Sahlins, *Culture and Practical Reason* (Chicago: University of Chicago Press, 1976), 168–169; Arjun Appadurai, "Introduction: Commodities and the Politics of Value," in *The Social Life of Things: Commodities in Cultural Perspective,* ed. Arjun Appadurai (Cambridge: Cambridge University Press, 1986), 6,

12–13; Mary Douglas and Baron Isherwood, *The World of Goods: Towards an Anthropology of Consumption* (London: Routledge, 1996), 36–40; Don Slater, *Consumer Culture and Modernity* (Cambridge: Polity Press, 1997), 132.

21. William Leiss distinguishes modern consumer culture as a "high intensity market setting" in *The Limits to Satisfaction: An Essay on the Problem of Needs and Commodities* (Toronto: University of Toronto Press, 1975), x.

22. For general observations on the qualities that make a commodity particularly expressive, see Appadurai, "Introduction: Commodities and the Politics of Value," 38, and Ann Smart Martin, "Makers, Buyers, and Users: Consumerism as a Material Cultural Framework," *Winterthur Portfolio* 28, nos. 2–3 (Summer-Autumn 1993): 156. Based on their analyses, one would expect a highly expressive commodity to exist in tight linkage with body, person, and personality, be capable of considerable semiotic virtuosity, and require specialized and culturally specific knowledge for appropriate use. Fashion fits these criteria exceptionally well.

23. De Grazia, "Introduction," 4.

24. Malcolm Barnard argues along these lines in *Fashion as Communication* (London: Routledge, 1996), 8–10.

25. Florence Howe Hall, *Social Customs* (Boston: Estes and Lauriat, 1887), 247.

26. Christopher Breward offers a rare exception to the equation of fashion and female in "Renouncing Luxury: Men, Fashion and Luxury, 1870–1914," in *Defining Dress: Dress as Object, Meaning and Identity*, ed. Amy de la Haye and Elizabeth Wilson (Manchester: Manchester University Press, 1999), 48–62.

27. On autonomous fashion cycles, see Agnes Young, *Recurring Cycles of Fashion, 1760–1937* (New York: Harper & Brothers, 1937), and Jane Richardson and A. L. Kroeber, "Three Centuries of Women's Dress Fashions: A Quantitative Analysis," *Anthropological Records* 5, no. 2 (October 1940): 111–153. The best business studies of fashion are Ben Fine and Ellen Leopold, *World of Consumption* (London: Routledge, 1993), 93–114; and Nancy Green, *Ready-to-Wear and Ready-to-Work*. The purest and most insightful scholarly example of an art-historical approach to fashion is Anne Hollander, *Seeing Through Clothes* (Berkeley: University of California Press, 1993). For class emulation, both Thorstein Veblen, "The Economic Theory of Woman's Dress," *Popular Science Monthly* (November 1894): 198–205, and Georg Simmel, "Fashion," *International Quarterly* 10 (October 1904): 130–151, continue to attract followers. On dress and eroticism, the classic statement is J. C. Flugel, *The Psychology of Clothes* (London: Hogarth Press, 1930); Valerie Steele offers a more complex and persuasive psychoanalytic interpretation in *Fashion and Eroticism: Ideals of Feminine Beauty from the Victorian Era to the Jazz Age* (New York: Oxford University Press, 1985). The influence of marketing and advertising is stressed in Stuart Ewen, *All Consuming Images: The Politics of Style in Contemporary Culture* (New York: Basic Books, 1984).

28. Here I adopt a semantic distinction made by Fred Davis, who notes that the principal definition of ambivalence involves contradictory and oscillating attitudes, while ambiguity is first of all concerned with having two or more meanings. See Fred Davis, *Fashion, Culture, and Identity* (Chicago: University of Chicago Press, 1992), 21n. Among the other relatively rare works to embrace ambiguity and multiple meanings as the essence of fashion are Elizabeth Wilson, *Adorned in Dreams* (Berkeley: University of California Press, 1987); and Christopher Breward, *The Culture of Fashion* (Manchester: Manchester University Press, 1994), 4, 147, 170–176.

29. Charles Beezley, *Our Manners and Social Customs* (Chicago: Elliott and Beezley, 1891), 312; John H. Young, *Our Deportment* (Detroit: F. B. Dickinson,

1881), 314; Florence Howe Hall, *The Correct Thing in Good Society* (Boston: Estes and Lauriat, 1888), 160.

30. John H. Young, *Our Deportment*, 315; Clara Moore [Mrs. H. O. Ward, pseud.], *Sensible Etiquette of the Best Society* (Philadelphia: Porter and Coates, 1878), 250.

31. Lela Barnes, "North Central Kansas," 422.

32. "Editorial," *CDGR* (May 13, 1899): 12. For similar comment on the crinoline, see "Godey's Fashions," *Godey's* (April 1893): 514.

33. For example, see Mrs. Burton Harrison, *The Well-Bred Girl in Society* (Philadelphia: Curtis Publishing, 1898), 20.

34. Herbert Blumer defines this process as "collective selection." He describes it as an "unwitting groping for suitable forms of expression . . . an effort to move in a direction which is consonant with the movement of modern life in general. Evidence indicates that the increasing sophistication and pervasiveness of the marketing system in the twentieth century did not diminish this uncertainty as to fashion's progress. Blumer pointed out that designers often offer thirty designs in a season with no idea which half-dozen the buyers will choose to take to the marketplace. Herbert Blumer, "Fashion: From Class Differentiation to Collective Selection," *Sociological Quarterly* 10, no. 3 (Summer 1969): 275–291. See also Jeanette Lauer and Robert Lauer, *Fashion Power: The Meaning of Fashion in American Society* (Englewood Cliffs, N.J.: Prentice-Hall, 1981), 263; and Davis, *Fashion, Culture, and Identity*, 115–116.

35. I draw here on both the cultural studies theorizing of scholars such as Abigail Solomon-Godeau, who contends that "capitalism is as much a semiotic system as an economic system," and business history research such as that of Nancy Green, who argues that "regardless of who dictates fashion, fashion dictates production insofar as it incarnates demand." See Abigail Solomon-Godeau, "The Other Side of Venus: The Visual Economy of Feminine Display," in *The Sex of Things: Gender and Consumption in Historical Perspective*, ed. Victoria de Grazia with Ellen Furlough (Berkeley: University of California Press, 1996), 114; and Green, *Ready-to-Wear and Ready-to-Work*, 19.

36. For assertions that fashion style has fixed social meanings, see Lois Banner, *American Beauty* (Chicago: University of Chicago Press, 1983), 203; and Helene Roberts, "The Exquisite Slave: The Role of Clothes in the Making of the Victorian Woman," *Signs* 2, no. 3 (Spring 1977): 567. For a description of fashion meaning as completely arbitrary, see Jean Baudrillard, *Symbolic Exchange and Death*, trans. Iain Hamilton Grant (London: Sage Publications, 1993), 87.

37. Isabel Mallon, "The Newest Spring Gowns," *LHJ* (March 1898): 3; Mary Katharine Howard, "The Newest Designs in Bodices," *WHC* (November 1899): 27.

38. See Stuart and Elizabeth Ewen, *Channels of Desire: Mass Images and the Shaping of American Consciousness*, 2nd ed. (Minneapolis: University of Minnesota Press, 1992), 169–172; and Julia Emberley, "The Fashion Apparatus and the Deconstruction of Postmodern Subjectivity," in *Body Invaders: Panic Sex in America*, ed. Arthur Kroker and Marilouise Kroker (Montreal: New World Perspectives, 1989), 47–60.

39. Elizabeth Wilson, *Adorned in Dreams*, 258; Gilles Lipovetsky is perhaps the most exuberant celebrant of fashion's liberating potential, arguing that it is "a way out of the world of tradition" and operates as a "globally positive power, with respect both to democratic institutions and the autonomy of consciousness." See Gilles Lipovetsky, *The Empire of Fashion: Dressing Modern Democracy*, trans. Catherine Porter (Princeton, N.J.: Princeton University Press, 1994), 4, 6.

40. Michel Foucault, *Discipline and Punish,* trans. Alan Sheridan (New York: Vintage Books, 1979), 136–139, 167–168.

41. Erving Goffman writes that to manage social interaction an individual "needs cosmetic and clothing supplies, tools for applying, arranging, and repairing them, and an accessible, secure place to store these supplies and tools—in short, the individual will need an 'identity kit' for the management of his personal front." Goffman argues that one suffers "personal defacement" if one loses control over one's identity kit. See *Asylums: Essays on the Social Situation of Mental Patients and Other Inmates* (Boston: Doubleday, 1961), 20–21.

42. Leslie Rabine has characterized fashion as creating simultaneously "two bodies" for its wearers, one promoting the values of dominant culture and one offering freedom from that dominance. She believes this reflects both an inherent duality of the fashion code and an endemic ambivalence in modern capitalism. See "A Woman's Two Bodies: Fashion, Magazines, Consumerism and Feminism" in *On Fashion,* ed. Shari Benstock and Suzanne Ferriss (New Brunswick, N.J.: Rutgers University Press, 1994), 59–75. Kim Sawchuk argues that "the body, lying in both the realm of the public and private, is a metaphor for the essential instability of objects in their relationship to each other." For that reason, she argues, the flow of fashion cannot be reduced to one or two variables, such as sex and class. See "A Tale of Inscription/Fashion Statements," in *Body Invaders: Panic Sex in America,* ed. Arthur Kroker and Marilouise Kroker (Montreal: New World Perspectives, 1987), 61–77. See also Anne Hollander's argument that "fashion in dress is committed to risk, subversion and irregular forward movement" in *Sex and Suits,* 14.

43. The theoretical dimensions of "impression management" have been elaborated by Erving Goffman, who also uses such evocative terms as "personal front," "body idiom," "embodied information," and "identity kit" (see note 41) to describe how appearances function in social interaction. See Erving Goffman, *The Presentation of Self in Everyday Life* (New York: Anchor, 1959) and *Behavior in Public Places: Notes on the Social Organization of Gatherings* (New York: Free Press, 1963). The historical dimensions of this concept are central to the work of Karen Halttunen, *Confidence Men and Painted Women: A Study of Middle-Class Culture in America, 1830–1870* (New Haven: Yale University Press, 1982), and John Kasson, *Rudeness and Civility: Manners in Nineteenth-Century Urban America* (New York: Hill and Wang, 1990).

44. Lela Barnes, "North Central Kansas," 406.

45. For comments on the "crisis of self-representation" in the late 1800s, see Kasson, *Rudeness and Civility,* 93–94; Carlo Ginzburg, "Clues: Morelli, Freud, and Sherlock Holmes," in *The Sign of Three,* ed. Thomas Sebeok and Umberto Eco (Bloomington: Indiana University Press, 1983), 81–118. For an argument that traces the effort to relate physical appearance and individual character back to ancient Greece, see Joanne Finkelstein, *The Fashioned Self* (Philadelphia: Temple University Press, 1991), 17–48. Erving Goffman argues that it is virtually inevitable that in social interactions one will attempt to ascertain essential attributes by examining surface appearance in *The Presentation of the Self in Everyday Life,* 249; *Behavior in Public Places,* 34–35; and *Gender Advertisements* (New York: Harper, 1979), 6–7.

46. Beezley, *Our Manners and Social Customs,* 307.

47. Edward Bok, "What Makes a Gentleman," *LHJ* (July 1898): 14.

48. By 1910, immigrants and their children accounted for more than 70 percent of the population in New York, Chicago, Boston, Cleveland, Detroit, Buffalo,

and Milwaukee and more than 50 percent of the population in San Francisco, Newark, Pittsburgh, St. Louis, Philadelphia, and Cincinnati. See Raymond A. Mohl, *The New City: Urban America in the Industrial Age, 1860–1920* (Arlington Heights, Ill.: Harlan Davidson, 1985), 25. Among many works on American imperialism, a valuable overview remains Walter LaFeber, *The New Empire: An Interpretation of American Expansionism* (Ithaca, N.Y.: Cornell University Press, 1963). For a recent study that examines both foreign policy and immigration, see Matthew Frye Jacobson, *Barbarian Virtues: The United States Encounters Foreign Peoples at Home and Abroad, 1876–1917* (New York: Hill and Wang, 2000).

49. "Editorial," *CDGR* (September 3, 1898): 12; Margaret F. Byington, *Homestead: The Households of a Mill Town* (1910; reprint, Pittsburgh: University Center for International Studies, 1974), 150.

50. Nan Enstad has shown how in precisely this manner working-class women wrested a political identity from the new symbolic systems, including fashion, that became available to them around the turn of the century. See *Ladies of Labor, Girls of Adventure,* 5–6.

51. Edward Bok, "At Home with the Editor," *LHJ* (August 1892): 12; John Ruth, *Decorum: A Practical Treatise on Etiquette and Dress of the Best American Society* (New York: Union Publishing, 1882), 263; Walter R. Houghton et al., *American Etiquette and Rules of Politeness* (Indianapolis: A. E. Davis, 1882), 266.

52. On the manner in which reality is "produced, maintained, repaired, and transformed" by symbols that impose social distinction and cultural categories on an essentially continuous natural world, see James Carey, *Communication as Culture: Essays on Media and Society* (New York: Routledge, 1989); Grant McCracken, *Culture and Consumption* (Bloomington: Indiana University Press, 1988); Clifford Geertz, *The Interpretation of Cultures* (New York: Basic Books, 1973); Marshall Sahlins, *Culture and Practical Reason;* idem, *Islands in History* (Chicago: University of Chicago Press, 1985); and Michael Walzer, "On the Role of Symbolism in Political Thought," *Political Science Quarterly* 82, no. 2 (June 1967): 191–204. See also Joan Scott's ideas of examining ideology through its "categories of representation" in "The Evidence of Experience," *Critical Inquiry* 7, no. 4 (Summer 1991): 777–778.

53. Two excellent brief introductions to the development of mass magazines are Mary Ellen Waller-Zuckerman, "'Old Homes, in a City of Perpetual Change': Women's Magazines, 1890–1916," *Business History Review* 63, no. 4 (Winter 1989): 715–756; and Richard Ohmann, "Where Did Mass Culture Come From?"

54. Quoted in Frank Luther Mott, *A History of American Magazines,* vol. 3 (Cambridge, Mass.: Harvard University Press, 1938), 183. The statement comes from the *Journalist,* itself a trade publication only six years old, on September 13, 1890.

55. Correspondence published in *Printers' Ink* during the 1890s indicated the magazine had regular readers in places such as Janesville, Wisconsin, Caney, Kansas, and Marysville, Ohio, as well as in larger manufacturing and retailing centers. During the same period, the *Clothing Gazette* frequently printed "retail ramblings" from locations including Caribou, Maine, Sioux City, Iowa, and Missoula, Montana.

56. Kenneth Ames, "Trade Catalogues and the Study of History," in *Accumulation and Display: Mass Marketing Household Goods in America, 1880–1920,* by Deborah Anne Federhen et al. (Winterthur, Del.: Henry Francis du Pont Winterthur Museum, 1986), 8, 10; Rae Elizabeth Rips, "An Introductory Study of the Role of the Mail Order Business in American History" (M.A. thesis, University of

Chicago, 1938), 18–19, 27, 30; Thomas Schlereth, "Country Stores, County Fairs and Mail-Order Catalogues: Consumption in Rural America," in *Consuming Visions: Accumulation and Display of Goods in America, 1880–1920,* ed. Simon Bronner (New York: W. W. Norton, 1989), 343–346; Susan Strasser, *Satisfaction Guaranteed: The Making of the American Mass Market* (New York: Pantheon Books, 1989), 58–88. Properly speaking, a "trade catalog" is one intended for the trade, that is, a catalog sent by the wholesaler to the retailer, while a "mail-order catalog" is sent from the manufacturer directly to the consumer. In common practice, however, both types of catalogs are lumped under the term "trade catalog," and even curators and archivists often treat them as a single genre. See E. Richard McKinstry, "The Trade Catalog Collection in the Winterthur Museum Library," in *Accumulation and Display: Mass Marketing Household Goods in America 1880–1920,* by Deborah Anne Federhen et al. (Winterthur, Del.: Henry Francis du Pont Winterthur Museum, 1986), 3. In examining both types, one might notice some variations in the introductory material and sales pitches. Except for those catalogs that were nothing but price lists, however, the display and description of the goods themselves are virtually indistinguishable between the two types. Where I have used the two terms interchangeably, it is because no difference between them was evident in the context under discussion.

57. Mary Ellen Bobbitt, *A Bibliography of Etiquette Books Published in America Before 1900* (New York: New York Public Library, 1947). See also Kasson, *Rudeness and Civility,* 5; and Arthur M. Schlesinger, *Learning How to Behave: A Historical Study of American Etiquette Books* (New York: Macmillan, 1946), 32.

58. Rose Pastor Stokes, *"I Belong to the Working Class": The Unfinished Autobiography of Rose Pastor Stokes,* ed. Herbert Shapiro and David L. Sterling (Athens: University of Georgia Press, 1992), 56; F. M. Atwood advertisement, *Chicago Tribune* (April 20, 1895): 4; Ruth, *Decorum,* 266.

59. Theodore Dreiser, *Sister Carrie* (New York: W. W. Norton, 1991), 3, 5, 13, 25, 31, 51, 75, 231.

60. Mary Katharine Howard, "Some Charming House Gowns," *WHC* (June 1897): 14.

61. In this section, I have paraphrased Douglas and Isherwood, who assert: "The essential function of consumption is its capacity to make sense." See *World of Goods,* 40.

Chapter 1. Men's Clothing

1. William C. Browning, "The Clothing and Furnishing Trade," in *One Hundred Years of American Commerce,* vol. 2, ed. Chauncey M. Depew (New York: D. O. Haynes, 1895), 561–565. The "Publishers' Introduction" to the two-volume set mentioned the editorial committee as being responsible for selecting contributors who were "fitted by ability and experience to represent the industry with which he was identified" (vol. 1, p. viii), but it does not name the committee members. The claim of "largest manufacturer and retailer" was quoted from a company catalog, *Correct Styles in Apparel for the Spring and Summer of 1897* (New York, 1897): front cover. Locations of 1895 stores are listed in "Premier Clothiers of America," *CG* (February 1895): 11. Browning, King continued to flourish in the twentieth century under William C. Browning's son. In the late 1920s, Paul Nystrom described it as "one of the largest chain store organizations in the men's clothing field." See Paul Nystrom, *The Economics of Fashion* (New York:

Ronald Press, 1928), 409. The Depression forced the breakup of the chain, whose stores were sold off individually in 1933 and 1934.

2. "The Story of a Great House," *CG* (May 1893): 52; Browning, King advertisement in "Modern Clothing Advertising," *CG* (June 1895): 62; "Ready-Made Versus Custom-Made," *Browning, King & Co.'s Illustrated Monthly* (January 1898): 4; "The Style's the Thing," *Browning, King & Co.'s Illustrated Monthly* (August 1895): 14.

3. Anne Hollander states that men's ready-made suits "were already on their way to phenomenal success in the 1820s"; Claudia B. Kidwell and Margaret C. Christman describe the "easy acceptance" of the ready-made product in the 1830s; Sean Wilentz asserts that there "was some initial resistance to this noncustom work among the most cosmopolitan customers—but by the late 1840s clothiers had changed people's minds"; Egal Feldman argues for the "universal acceptance" of ready-mades before the Civil War. See Anne Hollander, *Sex and Suits: The Evolution of Modern Dress* (New York: Kodansha International, 1994), 106; Claudia B. Kidwell and Margaret C. Christman, *Suiting Everyone: The Democratization of Clothing in America* (Washington, D.C.: Smithsonian Institution Press, 1974), 55; Sean Wilentz, *Chants Democratic: New York City and the Rise of the American Working Class, 1788–1850* (New York: Oxford University Press, 1984), 120; Egal Feldman, *Fit for Men: A Study of New York's Clothing Trade* (Washington, D.C.: Public Affairs Press, 1960), 74.

4. "The Clothing Trade," *CG* (January 1893): 62; Kirschbaum advertisement, *CG* (January 1895): 18.

5. Kidwell and Christman, *Suiting Everyone,* mention Jacksonian democracy and the rising middle class (pp. 37–39) along with other factors, including the development of a native American wool industry (pp. 63–69); Harry Cobrin, *The Men's Clothing Industry: Colonial Through Modern Times* (New York: Fairchild, 1970), leans heavily toward urban development and the growing number of white-collar workers (p. 18), as does Jesse Pope, *The Clothing Industry in New York* (Columbia: University of Missouri Press, 1905), 3; Feldman, *Fit for Men,* mentions "America's democratic system" as a contributing factor (p. 75) but by implication places more stress on the expansion of markets south and westward (pp. 35–58); the emergence of a female labor supply (often with needle skills) is stressed in Ava Baron and Susan E. Klepp, "'If I Didn't Have My Sewing Machine . . .': Women and Sewing Machine Technology," in *A Needle, a Bobbin, a Strike: Women Needleworkers in America,* ed. John Jensen and Sue Davidson (Philadelphia: Temple University Press, 1984), 23. Christine Stansell makes the same point in "The Origins of the Sweatshop: Women and Early Industrialization in New York City," in *Working-Class America: Essays on Labor, Community and American Society,* ed. Michael H. Frisch and Daniel Walkowitz (Urbana: University of Illinois Press, 1983), 82–83; Ben Fine and Ellen Leopold, *World of Consumption* (London: Routledge, 1993), stress the importance of expansion south and west (pp. 98–100). Michael Zakim, "A Ready-Made Business: The Birth of the Clothing Industry in America," *Business History Review* 73, no. 1 (Spring 1999), likewise focuses on emerging markets in the interior of the United States but also stresses the concurrent development of an "entrepreneurial logic" in American commerce (p. 67) and ties the clothiers' success to their ability to link these new markets to expanding urban labor pools and the trans-Atlantic cloth trade (p. 62). Wilentz, *Chants Democratic,* gives high priority to the "aggressive merchandising methods" and liberal credit policies of New York merchants (p. 120), a factor also mentioned by Feldman (*Fit for Men,* 124).

6. Browning, "The Clothing and Furnishing Trade," 561–562; Henry Hall, ed., *America's Successful Men of Affairs*, vol. 1 (New York: New York Tribune, 1895), 117–118.

7. On the derivation of the term "sloppy," see *Oxford English Dictionary*, 2nd ed. s.v. "slop," "sloppy." Feldman quotation on slop shops is in *Fit for Men*, 74. On slop shops in general, see also Cobrin, *Men's Clothing Industry*, 19; "History of the Men's Wear Industry," *Men's Wear* (February 10, 1950): 195; Browning, "Clothing and Furnishing Trade," 561.

8. Feldman, *Fit for Men*, 102–103; U.S. Department of Commerce, Bureau of Foreign and Domestic Commerce, *The Men's Factory-Made Clothing Industry* (Washington, D.C.: Government Printing Office, 1916), 10; Fine and Leopold, *World of Consumption*, 96–100; Cobrin, *Men's Clothing Industry*, 32–47. The Southern trade also involved a limited amount of ready-made and made-to-measure garments for city dwellers and rural gentry.

9. "History of the Men's Wear Industry," 195. In the 1850s, Cincinnati and St. Louis became substantial clothing centers as well, and after the Civil War, Chicago and Rochester grew in importance. See Feldman, *Fit for Men*, 57–58, "History of the Men's Wear Industry," 201. In 1899 these eight cities remained the only ones in the country producing more than $10 million of manufactured men's clothing annually. See United States Census Office, *Twelfth Census of the United States*, vol. 9, *Manufactures*, part 3: *Special Reports on Selected Industries* (Washington, D.C.: United States Census Office, 1902), 282.

10. Some writers accord the Civil War a decisive role in the history of men's clothing because the demand for uniforms provided an impetus to standardize sizes and create manufacturing infrastructure. See Daniel J. Boorstin, *The Americans: The Democratic Experience* (New York: Random House, 1973), 98–99; U.S. Department of Commerce, *The Men's Factory-Made Clothing Industry*, 10–11; Cobrin, *Men's Clothing Industry*, 46. However, the war had many negative consequences for the industry as well. Some firms that relied on the trade with the South were ruined; the uniforms produced were often of such poor quality that the industry's overall reputation suffered; the extent to which sizing was standardized is often overestimated, and the extent to which hand-made uniforms were used is often underestimated. See Kidwell and Christman, *Suiting Everyone*, 105; "History of the Men's Wear Industry," 198–199, 204; "Mr. William H. Whitford's Recollections," *CG* (April 1893): 52. Wartime needs undoubtedly improved the manufacturing techniques and capacity of the clothing producers, but they did not provide the decisive turning point for the industry.

11. Boorstin, *The Americans: The Democratic Experience*, 99 (Boorstin gives no source for his statistics); U.S. Census Office, *Twelfth Census*, vol. 9, 261, 301. These statistics refer mainly to suits—coats, vests, and pants—and overcoats. This is what both census enumerators and industry trade publications generally meant when they referred to the "men's clothing industry." Furnishings (shirts, ties, underwear, socks), work clothes, and sports clothes were almost always treated separately. See Cobrin, *Men's Clothing Industry*, 5. Including these other product lines would complicate the story I am telling but not change its overall outline. This is especially true because of the nearly widespread acceptance of the suit as a basic clothing standard at the end of the century.

12. Up until 1890 no distinction in census statistics was made between custom-made and ready-made clothing, so calculation of the differential between them is impossible. Further, home production and secondhand clothing, both sizable contributors to early clothing use, were not taken into account at all. At various

times throughout the latter nineteenth century, the census reports themselves suggested the returns had been distorted by incomplete counts, poorly trained enumerators, changing instructions, and the difficulty of collecting information on an industry that relied on outworkers scattered in tenements throughout metropolitan areas. Egal Feldman found he could not reconcile census figures for New York with data he obtained independently from local records. Looking at figures from the late nineteenth and early twentieth centuries, Kenneth Dameron, who wrote a clothing history in the 1920s, complained that "every valet, presser, and local cleaner calls himself a tailor, and the census can not accurately distinguish between them." Also, inflation during and immediately after the Civil War followed by a long, slow decline in prices from the 1870s through the 1890s can make comparisons between decades misleading. See U.S. Department of Commerce, *Biennial Census of Manufactures 1921* (Washington, D.C.: Government Printing Office, 1924), 252; U.S. Census Office, *Ninth Census, 1870,* vol. 3, *The Statistics of Wealth and Industry of the United States* (Washington, D.C.: Government Printing Office, 1872), 380; U.S. Census Office, *10th Census,* vol. 2, *Report on the Manufactures of the United States* (Washington, D.C.: Government Printing Office, 1883), ix; U.S. Census Bureau, *Eleventh Census,* vol. 6, *Report on Manufacturing Industries in the United States* (Washington, D.C.: Government Printing Office, 1895), clvi; Feldman, *Fit for Men,* 127n; Kenneth Dameron, *Men's Wear Merchandising* (New York: Ronald Press, 1930), 121; U.S. Department of Commerce and Labor, *Statistical Abstract of the United States 1908,* (Washington, D.C.: Government Printing Office, 1909), 569.

13. William C. Browning, "The Clothing and Furnishing Trade," 563.

14. Baron and Klepp, "'If I Didn't Have My Sewing Machine,'" 31–32, 37.

15. Pope, *Clothing Industry in New York,* 1; Philip Kahn Jr., *A Stitch in Time: The Four Seasons of Baltimore's Needle Trades* (Baltimore: Maryland Historical Society, 1989), 23n; Browning, "The Clothing and Furnishing Trade," 563. Among historians who have attributed much greater significance to textile industrialization, see Kidwell and Christman, *Suiting Everyone,* 65–69; Fine and Leopold, *World of Consumption,* 91–92.

16. Edwin T. Freedley, *Leading Pursuits and Leading Men* (1856; reprint, New York: Garland, 1974), 129; Charles Cist, *Sketches and Statistics of Cincinnati in 1859* (n.p., 1859), 364; Pope, *Clothing Industry in New York,* 70.

17. Daniel Rodgers, *The Work Ethic in Industrial America, 1850–1920* (Chicago: University of Chicago Press, 1978), 27. Rodgers notes that between 1860 and 1920 the population of the United States increased a little more than threefold, while the volume of manufactured goods increased by a factor of twelve to fourteen.

18. "Effective Advertising," *CG* (October 1895): 1 (part of an eight-page section paginated separately from rest of issue); Arthur B. Chivers, "Illustrating Retail Advertising," *Advertising Experience* (December 1896): 8–10.

19. In the old system, as Richard Sennett describes it, the bargaining process was interactive and participatory: "The stylized interplay weaves the buyer and seller together socially." In the less nostalgic terms of one of John Wanamaker's biographers, the system simply meant that "every sale was an argument." In any case, as Susan Strasser points out, the new method of buying and selling was no longer "embedded in human relationships" in quite the same way. Instead, people became "participants in a national market composed of masses of people associated with big, centrally organized, national-level companies." Richard Sennett, *The Fall of Public Man* (New York: Knopf, 1977), 142; Herbert Gibbons, *John Wanamaker,* vol. 1 (New York: Harper and Row, 1926), 87; Susan Strasser,

Satisfaction Guaranteed: The Making of the American Mass Market (New York: Pantheon, 1989), 26, 15.

20. Arjun Appadurai, "Introduction: Commodities and the Politics of Value," in *The Social Life of Things: Commodities in Cultural Perspective*, ed. Arjun Appadurai (Cambridge: Cambridge University Press, 1986), 48–54; William Leiss, *The Limits to Satisfaction: An Essay on the Problem of Needs and Commodities* (Toronto: University of Toronto Press, 1976), 15–16.

21. Nathan Rosenberg asserted that the adoption of factory-made suits hinged on a peculiar American temperament that "readily accepted a high degree of standardization"; *Technology and American Economic Growth* (New York: Harper and Row, 1972), 44–45.

22. "Extensive Clothing Establishments," *Merchants' Magazine and Commercial Review* (March 1849): 348; Freedley, *Leading Pursuits*, 125.

23. Freeman Hunt, "The Editor to His Friends and Patrons," *Merchants' Magazine and Commercial Review* (July 1849): 144.

24. George Foster, *New York in Slices* (New York: W. D. Burgess, 1848), 14. Foster's book was based on sketches he had published in the *New York Tribune*. Chatham Street was famous as a center of secondhand clothing, although the merchants there sold new ready-made garments as well. In fact, scholars such as Jesse Pope believe the ready-made trade as a whole did not exceed the secondhand trade until after the Civil War; *Clothing Industry in New York*, 6–7.

25. Harvey Morris, *The Story of Men's Clothes* (Rochester: Hickey-Freeman, 1926), 31–32.

26. Charles Cist, *Sketches and Statistics of Cincinnati*, 271; information on clothing establishments of various kinds comes from editions of *Williams' Cincinnati Directory* (Cincinnati: C. S. Williams, 1850–1859); *Fortieth Annual Report of the Cincinnati Chamber of Commerce and Merchants' Exchange for the Commercial Year Ending August 21, 1889* (Cincinnati: Ohio Valley Company, 1889), 151. By the 1890s there was considerable variation and overlap in the prices of ready-made and custom-made suits. Browning, King's ready-made suits ranged from $15 to $30, although others sold them for $10 or less. Made-to-measure suits were advertised for as little as $15, but at more exclusive tailors prices started at $30.

27. "Premier Clothiers of America," 11.

28. U.S. Department of Commerce, *Men's Factory-Made Clothing Industry*, 9, 12; Morris, *The Story of Men's Clothes*, 15; "History of the Men's Wear Industry," 209. In addition, Paul Nystrom argues that men's ready-made clothing production did not "forge ahead" of custom production until after 1893, and Jesse Pope still felt compelled in 1905 to make the case that "the high degree of perfection to which ready-made clothing has attained has brought it into direct competition with the custom trade." See Nystrom, *The Economics of Fashion*, 415, and Pope, *The Clothing Industry in New York*, 292.

29. Booth Tarkington described 1880s fashion in a novel he wrote in the 1910s: "Trousers with a crease were considered plebeian; the crease proved that the garment had lain upon a shelf, and hence was "ready-made"; these betraying trousers were called 'hand-me-downs,' in allusion to the shelf." See *The Magnificent Ambersons* (1918; reprint, Bloomington: Indiana University Press, 1989), 5.

30. Isaac Walker, *Dress: As It Has Been, Is, and Will Be* (New York: Isaac Walker, 1885), vii, 15–16.

31. Priscilla Dalrymple, *American Victorian Costume in Early Photographs* (New York: Dover, 1991); Jo Barraclough Paoletti, "Changes in the Masculine Image

in the United States, 1880–1910: A Content Analysis of Popular Humor About Dress" (Ph.D. diss., University of Maryland, 1980); idem, "Ridicule and Role Models as Factors in American Men's Fashion Change, 1880–1910," *Costume* 19 (1985): 121.

32. Kahn, *A Stitch in Time*, 48; Kidwell and Christman, *Suiting Everyone*, 115.

33. The stylistic development of the three-piece suit can be traced back to the late seventeenth century, when coat, vest, and knee-breeches became the costume of choice for fashionable men. By the 1820s, pants had for the most part replaced knee-breeches and the whole outfit was worn over a white shirt. At mid-century the turned-down collar became a fashionable substitute for the "standing" collar, and the flowing cravat that had typified men's neckwear was squeezed into the thinner necktie in order to fit beneath the new collar style. Thus the suit assumed its "modern" form, although for some time it would commonly utilize wildly contrasting fabric patterns for each of the three pieces. The sack suit emerged in the 1850s as a garment appropriate for only the most informal circumstances, but it gradually became fashionable for more and more occasions. After the introduction of the tuxedo, a variation of the sack suit first worn in 1886, this style even began to be accepted as an alternative to the tailcoat at formal occasions.

34. "Fashions, Fads and Follies," *CG* (September 1894): 51.

35. The term "crisis" has been applied to male gender roles during this period since the publication of Joe Dubbert, "Progressivism and the Masculinity Crisis," in *The American Man*, ed. Elizabeth Pleck and Joseph Pleck (Englewood Cliffs, N.J.: Prentice-Hall, 1980), 303–320. Clyde Griffen expresses reservations somewhat similar to my own about the "crisis" designation in "Reconstructing Masculinity from the Evangelical Revival to the Waning of Progressivism: A Speculative Synthesis," in *Meanings for Manhood: Constructing Masculinity in Victorian America*, ed. Mark C. Carnes and Clyde Griffen (Chicago: University of Chicago Press, 1990), 184.

36. Gail Bederman, *Manliness and Civilization* (Chicago: University of Chicago Press, 1995); Joe L. Dubbert, *A Man's Place: Masculinity in Transition* (Englewood Cliffs, N.J.: Prentice-Hall, 1979); Peter Filene, *Him/Her/Self: Sex Roles in Modern America*, 2nd ed. (Baltimore: Johns Hopkins University Press, 1986); Griffen, "Reconstructing Masculinity," 183–205; Michael Kimmel, *Manhood in America: A Cultural History* (New York: Free Press, 1996); Charles Rosenberg, "Sexuality, Class and Role in Nineteenth-Century America," in *The American Man*, ed. Elizabeth and Joseph Pleck (Englewood Cliffs, N.J.: Prentice-Hall, 1980), 219–254; Anthony Rotundo, *American Manhood: Transformations in Masculinity from the Revolution to the Modern Era* (New York: Basic Books, 1993).

37. Bederman, *Manliness and Civilization*, 12; and Michael Kimmel, "Consuming Manhood: The Feminization of American Culture and the Recreation of the Male Body, 1832–1920," *Michigan Quarterly Review* 33, no. 1 (Winter 1994): 13.

38. Stanley Jones, *The Presidential Election of 1896* (Madison: University of Wisconsin Press, 1964), 276–350.

39. Bederman, *Manliness and Civilization*, 12–19; Kimmel, *Manhood in America*, 81–100, 135–141; Rotundo, *American Manhood*, 279–283; Amy Kaplan, "Romancing the Empire: The Embodiment of American Masculinity in the Popular Historical Novel of the 1890s," *American Literary History* 2, no. 4 (Winter 1990): 659–690; John Higham, "The Reorientation of American Culture in the 1890s," in *The Origins of Modern Consciousness*, ed. John Weiss (Detroit: Wayne State University Press, 1965), 27–33. "Empire figures" quotation from Kaplan, 664. On the

"cult of muscularity" and athletics in the late nineteenth century, see also Eliott J. Gorn, *The Manly Art: Bare-Knuckle Prize Fighting in America* (Ithaca: Cornell University Press, 1986) 185–194; and Elliot Gorn and Warren Goldstein, *A Brief History of American Sports* (New York: Hill and Wang, 1993), 138–149.

40. Roosevelt coined the term "The Strenuous Life" to summarize his philosophy of manliness in a speech he delivered in 1899 to a Chicago men's club. For discussions of Roosevelt, the strenuous life, and gender, see Kimmel, *Manhood in America*, 181–187; Bederman, *Manliness and Civilization*, 170–215; and Arnaldo Testi, "The Gender of Reform Politics: Theodore Roosevelt and the Culture of Masculinity," *Journal of American History* 84, no. 1 (March 1995): 1509–1533.

41. On the increasing emphasis on rigid distinctions between men and women, see Filene, *Him/Her/Self*, 92–93; for a description of a similar process with regard to homosexuals, see George Chauncey, *Gay New York: Gender, Urban Culture and the Making of the Gay Male World, 1890–1940* (New York: Basic Books, 1994), 111–127.

42. Kimmel, "Consuming Manhood," 14. Roosevelt's father is quoted in Peter Filene, "Between a Rock and a Hard Place: A Century of American Manhood," *South Atlantic Quarterly* 84, no. 4 (Autumn 1985): 342; Rotundo, *American Manhood*, 254.

43. "Fashions, Fads and Follies," 51; Rafford Pyke, "What Men Like in Men," *Cosmopolitan* (August 1902): 405–406; Theodore Roosevelt, *Theodore Roosevelt: An Autobiography* (New York: Macmillan, 1913), 49. Roosevelt apparently was recycling a "champagne bottle" simile from a magazine article he wrote in 1897. See Mark Carnes, "Scottish Rite and the Visual Semiotics of Gender," in *Theatre of the Fraternity: Staging the Ritual Space of the Scottish Rite of Freemasonry, 1896–1929*, compiled by C. Lance Brockman (Jackson: University Press of Mississippi, 1996), 78, 91n.

44. Indeed, even when its gender status is clear a garment could have many meanings depending on context. For example, a suit means one thing when worn to work and quite another when worn to a funeral. See Jib Fowles, "Why We Wear Clothes," *ETC.: A Review of General Semantics* 31, no. 4 (December 1974): 348–349.

45. Kimmel, "Consuming Manhood," 8; Censor [Oliver Bunce], *Don't: A Manual of Mistakes and Improprieties More or Less Prevalent in Conduct and Speech* (New York: D. Appleton, 1884), 27; "Proof that Tailoring Is Artistic," *SAJ* (April 1896): 197; Paoletti, "Ridicule and Role Models," 129–131; Depew's speech is quoted in L. White Busbey et al., *The Battle of 1900* (Chicago: Wabash Publishing House, 1900), 257. Kristin Hoganson describes an interesting effort to rehabilitate the image of the dude after the Spanish-American War as a means of legitimating political power for the elite classes. See Kristin L. Hoganson, *Fighting for American Manhood: How Gender Politics Provoked the Spanish-American and Philippine-American Wars* (New Haven: Yale University Press, 1998), 118–124. She also alludes to the Depew speech about Roosevelt on p. 113.

46. The history of the separate spheres concept is detailed in Linda Kerber, "Separate Spheres, Female Worlds, Woman's Place: The Rhetoric of Women's History," *Journal of American History* 75, no. 1 (June 1988): 9–39. Kerber gives much credence to separate spheres as constituting physical as well as ideological space, but I am using the term more in line with her comment that "the phrase 'separate spheres' is a metaphor for complex power relations in social and economic context" (p. 28). See also Nancy Cott's statement: "The language of men's and women's 'spheres' had as much to do with the ruling fiction of differentiation

between the sexes as it did with physical sites" in "On Men's History and Women's History," in *Meanings for Manhood: Constructions of Masculinity in Victorian America*, ed. Mark C. Carnes and Clyde Griffen (Chicago: University of Chicago Press, 1990), 207.

47. Browning, King advertisement in "Modern Clothing Advertising," *CG* (June 1895): 62; Hackett, Carhart advertisement in "How the New Yorker Advertises," *CG* (February 1893): 53; "Men's Gauds," *CG* (February 1895): 28—this article is listed as a reprint from the *Outfitters' Chronicle*; "Friendly Chats with Clerks," *CG* (February 1895): 31.

48. B. Schleestein advertisement, *CG* (January 1895): 71. For a biography of Eugen Sandow, see David L. Chapman, *Sandow the Magnificent: Eugen Sandow and the Beginnings of Bodybuilding* (Urbana: University of Illinois Press, 1994); for a discussion of Sandow and masculinity in the 1890s, see John F. Kasson, *Houdini, Tarzan, and the Perfect Man: The White Male Body and the Challenge of Modernity in America* (New York: Hill and Wang, 2001), 21–76.

49. Kimmel, "Consuming Manhood," 17.

50. N. Snellenburg advertisement in "Examples of Advertising," *CG* (October 1895): 5; McFarlins' advertisement in "Examples of Advertising," *CG* (October 1895): 6; Hackett, Carhart advertisement in "Some Advertising Phrases," *CG* (December 1895): 86; F. M. Atwood advertisement, *Chicago Tribune* (June 22, 1898): 3; Rogers, Peet advertisement in "Examples of Advertising," *CG* (November 1895): 10.

51. Montgomery Ward, *Catalogue and Buyers' Guide, Spring and Summer 1895* (1895; reprint, New York: Dover, 1969), 267–268; Rogers, Peet advertisement, *New York Tribune* (May 4, 1898): 14; "History of the Men's Wear Industry," 222; Fine and Leopold, *World of Consumption*, 113. See also a more general discussion of turn-of-the-century product differentiation in Adrian Forty, *Objects of Desire: Design and Society Since 1750* (New York: Thames and Hudson, 1992), 62–66.

52. Edward Bok, "What Makes a Gentleman," *LHJ* (July 1898): 14; advertisement for Straus Brothers reproduced in Morris, *The Story of Men's Clothes*, 14. For a similar argument, see Christopher Breward, "Renouncing Luxury: Men, Fashion and Luxury, 1870–1914" in *Defining Dress: Dress as Object, Meaning and Identity*, ed. Amy de la Haye and Elizabeth Wilson (Manchester: Manchester University Press, 1999), 48–62.

53. Union Clothing advertisement in "Examples of Advertising," *CG* (December 1895): 21; Harvey Morris, *Story of Men's Clothes*, 23; Hackett, Carhart advertisement in "Examples of Advertising," *CG* (December 1895): 24 (emphasis added); H. B. Rosenthal. advertisement, *CG* (July 1895): 20; Browning, King advertisement in "Some Advertising Phrases," *CG* (December 1895): 85; A. C. Yates advertisement, *CG* (December 1893): 70; Rogers, Peet advertisement in "Some Advertising Phrases," *CG* (December 1895): 84; Putnam advertisement, *CG* (July 1895): 14.

54. David Marks & Sons advertisement, *CG* (July 1894): 3.

55. "Salutation," *CC* (June 1890): 1; "The Merchant Tailor and Ready-Made Clothing," *CC* (June 1890): 2.

56. "Uncertain Points in Cutting," *CC* (March 1895): 72; "The Season Now Open," *CC* (October 1895): 225; "Past, Present and Future," *CC* (December 1895): 270; "Cutting as Profession," *CC* (March 1895): 56; "Tailors and the Tariff," *CC* (June 1890) 7; "Why Not a National Association?" *CC* (June 1890): 3; "Death of Worth," *CC* (April 1895): 88; "Mind and Hand Unite," *CC* (April 1895): 80; "Our Mission," *CC* (September 1890): 1. Michael Zakim offers an interpretation of the

adaptation of the custom trade to the "economic facts of industrial life" in "Customizing the Industrial Revolution: The Reinvention of Tailoring in the Nineteenth Century," *Winterthur Portfolio* 33, no. 1 (Spring 1998): 41–58.

57. "Hints to Cutters," *PCT* (September 1897): 177; "How to Treat 'Some Cranks,'" *PCT* (July 1895): 172.

58. "Why Some Reputations Wobble," *SAJ* (December 1895): 101; "Where Will It All End?" *PCT* (June 1895): 157.

59. "What They Say," *CC* (February 1895): 23; *PCT* (June 1897): 142; "Learning Ladies' Tailoring," *CC* (August 1895): 178–179; "Women's Tailor-Made Garments," *SAJ* (April 1895): 245; *PCT* (November 1896): 31; "Royalty and the Tailors," *PCT* (October 1896): 3.

60. Charles Austin Bates, *The Tailoring Book* (New York: Charles Austin Bates Syndicate, 1899), 3; John S. Grey, "Compulsory Advertising," *Fame* (April 1909): 94; Clifton S. Wady, "Problem of the Merchant Tailor and the Answer to It," *Fame* (June 1909): 139.

61. Cobrin, *Men's Clothing Industry,* 152–157.

62. Letter dated December 16, 1903, addressed by the International Tailoring Company to Geo. W. Smith of Mattawamkeag, Maine; *The Label Mystery: Being a Short Story* (New York: International Tailoring, n.d.). Evidence in the story dates this publication from 1904. Both items are in the Warshaw Collection at the Smithsonian Institution's National Museum of American History.

63. "Selling Arguments." The unpaginated production of the Spencer-Tracy Company is copyrighted 1907. It is in the Warshaw Collection at the National Museum of American History. Emphasis in the original.

64. "Necrology," *PCT* (December 1895): 261; "History of Men's Wear," 228–229. According to the firm's advertising, Nicoll the Tailor shops in twenty cities did a combined business of $1 million a year by 1894. See advertisement in the *Chicago Tribune* (April 4, 1894): 7.

65. Quotation is from "The Future of Tailoring," *PCT* (January 1897): 50, emphasis added. The series "Eminent Men and Their Dress" ran throughout the mid-1890s in the *Custom Cutter*.

66. "Essays on Advertising," *CG* (June 1890): 43.

67. See, for example, Stuart and Elizabeth Ewen's assertion that modern consumer society was "soaked in the blood of decimated traditional cultures" in *Channels of Desire: Mass Images and the Shaping of American Consciousness,* 2nd ed. (Minneapolis: University of Minnesota Press, 1992), 32. William Leach argues that "American capitalism began to produce a distinct culture, *unconnected* to traditional family or community values, to religion in any conventional sense, or to political democracy" (emphasis added) in *Land of Desire: Merchants, Power, and the Rise of a New American Culture* (New York: Pantheon, 1993), 3. Jackson Lears states that "under capitalism, visual and verbal signs become detached from all traditional associations" in "From Salvation to Self-Realization: Advertising and the Therapeutic Roots of the Consumer Culture, 1880–1930" in *The Culture of Consumption: Critical Essays in American History 1880–1980,* ed. Richard Wightman Fox and T. J. Jackson Lears (New York: Pantheon, 1983), 21.

Chapter 2. Women's Clothing

1. Edward Bok, "The Rush of American Women," *LHJ* (January 1899): 14. See also Edward Bok, "At Home with the Editor," *LHJ* (May 1894): 12; idem, "At

Home with the Editor," *LHJ* (April 1893): 18; idem, "At Home with the Editor," *LHJ* (April 1894): 14. For background on women's expanded activities in these areas, see Peter Filene, *Him/Her/Self: Sex Roles in Modern America,* 2nd ed. (Baltimore: Johns Hopkins University Press, 1986), 16–28; Sara Evans, *Born for Liberty* (New York: Free Press, 1989), 147–164.

2. Edward Bok, "Back to First Principles," *LHJ* (November 1897): 14.

3. Edward Bok, "At Home with the Editor," *LHJ* (December 1989): 16; idem, "On Being Old Fashioned," *LHJ* (September 1897): 14; idem, "The Side Next to the Sun," *LHJ* (May 1898): 14.

4. Carroll Smith-Rosenberg has discussed how attitudes and symbolism involving the human body can reflect a sublimated discussion of controversial social issues. In effect, I am extending her argument to include the symbolism of clothing, which, in Kaja Silverman's words, is what "makes the human body culturally visible." Carroll Smith-Rosenberg, "The New Woman as Androgyne: Social Disorder and the Gender Crisis, 1870–1936," in *Disorderly Conduct: Visions of Gender in Victorian America* (New York: Oxford University Press, 1985), 268; Kaja Silverman, "Fragments of a Fashionable Discourse," in *Studies in Entertainment: Critical Approaches to Mass Culture,* ed. Tania Modleski (Bloomington: Indiana University Press, 1986), 145. The Silverman essay also appeared in *On Fashion,* ed. Shari Benstock and Suzanne Ferriss (New Brunswick, N.J.: Rutgers University Press, 1994), with quoted material on p. 189.

5. "Dainty Stitchery for Artistic Fingers," *Godey's* (January 1894):124; Emma Hooper, "The Baby's Dainty Layette," *LHJ* (January 1897): 20.

6. Emily French, *Emily: The Dairy of a Hard-Worked Woman,* ed. Janette LeCompte (Lincoln: University of Nebraska Press, 1987), 61, 67, 71.

7. Louis Levine [Lewis Lorwin], *The Women's Garment Workers* (1924; reprint, New York: Arno Press, 1969), 6, 410. Levine believed the main customers for these garments were rural and working-class women.

8. On capes as "pneumonia wraps," see Mary Katharine Howard, "What Women are Wearing," *WHC* (July 1892): 14. On remaining inconspicuous in the street, see Helena Rowe, "Family Fashions and Fancies," *GH* (May 1891): 244; and John H. Young, *Our Deportment* (Detroit: F. B. Dickerson, 1881) 143. Many etiquette books contained similar advice.

9. For example, the *Ladies' Home Journal* offered to sell readers sewing patterns for the coats and wraps discussed in its fashion columns. See Isabel Mallon, "Coats and Wraps for the Winter," *LHJ* (September 1897): 33.

10. National Cloak advertisement, *LHJ* (September 1895): 29. The company's 1908 catalog claimed the company had begun nineteen years earlier and now had 500,000 customers. See *New York Fashions, 1908* (New York, 1908), 5. The company began to add a few ready-made items in the 1900s and continued to thrive. By the time it merged with Bellas, Hess and Co. in 1927, National Cloak's assets were listed at more than $25 million. The new company, National Bellas Hess Co. was in the 1960s one of the five largest mail-order firms in the country. An ill-advised shift in business strategy from mail-order to discount store in the 1970s led to the firm's bankruptcy in 1976. See "Cloak Concerns Merge," *New York Times* (February 20, 1927): sect. 2, p. 14; Rocco Famighetti, "What Was National Bellas Hess?" *DM News* (June 8, 1992): 3.

11. Hester M. Poole, "Notions and Novelties," *GH* (December 1898): 208.

12. The *Ladies' Home Journal* advised in 1899 that tailored suits were "not successfully handled by dressmakers unless they have a tailoring department, for a man must do the pressing and finishing." See Emma Hooper, "The Home

Dressmaker," *LHJ* (March 1899): 42. For background on the tailored-suit trade, see Claudia B. Kidwell and Margaret C. Christman, *Suiting Everyone* (Washington, D.C.: Smithsonian Institution Press, 1974), 139, 143.

13. "Up-to-Date Advertising," *CDGR* (May 9, 1896): 35 (emphasis added).

14. H. C. F. Koch and Co. advertisement, *WHC* (April 1898): 23; H. O'Neill and Co., *Fall and Winter Fashion Catalogue, 1898–99* (New York, 1898), 128; Isabel Mallon, "Costumes of Early Autumn," *LHJ* (October 1892): 12; editorial, *CDGR* (October 1, 1898): 12. Mallon's article in the *Ladies' Home Journal* enumerated the number of fittings a tailored suit required: "The first fitting is an ordinary cotton lining; the second one a silk lining, the third one the silk and the material, the fourth one the almost finished bodice."

15. "Editorial," *CDGR* (January 25, 1896): 10; Jessica Daves, *Ready-Made Miracle: The American Story of Fashion for the Millions* (New York: G. P. Putnam, 1967), 29–31; Kidwell and Christman, *Suiting Everyone*, 145; Levine, *Women's Garment Workers*, 144–145.

16. Levine, *Women's Garment Workers*, 145, 391.

17. Kidwell and Christman, *Suiting Everyone*, 145.

18. "Cloaks, Suits and Waists," *CDGR* (June 13, 1896): 29; Carson Pirie Scott advertisement, *LHJ* (March 1895): 16; Carson Pirie Scott advertisement, *LHJ* (September 1895): 28; "Shirt-Waists Which Are Not in the Shops," *LHJ* (May 1899): 17; *McCall's* advertisement, *LHJ* (April 1899): 45.

19. Kidwell and Christman, *Suiting Everyone*, 139, 145, 147.

20. Emma Hooper, "The Practical Side of Shopping," *LHJ* (January 1899): 24. Hooper's byline had begun to appear in the *Ladies' Home Journal* by early 1888 when the magazine was barely four years old. She was listed on the magazine's masthead by 1890 and was still contributing regularly in 1900.

21. "New Year Greeting," *WHC* (January 1897): n.p.; Mary Katharine Howard, "The New Summer Frocks," *WHC* (June 1899): 27. Mary Katharine Howard's contributions to the magazine began in late 1895 and continued in virtually every issue for the rest of the decade.

22. "Spring Dress Materials," *Delineator* (April 1890): 311; The series "Fashions and Fabrics" by Margaret Bisland ran in *Good Housekeeping* from June 1899 to November 1899 with the subtitle "Suggestions for Home Dressmaking."

23. See, for example, George Lawrence, "Godey's Fashions," *Godey's* (January 1893): 137–138 (subtitled "Hints on Home Dressmaking"); idem, "Godey's Fashions," *Godey's* (March 1893): 387 (subtitled "Useful Hints for Home Dressmakers"); Ada Simpson Sherwood, "Plain Sewing and Dressmaking," *GH* (April 1893): 157–158; Emma Hooper, "Hints on Home Dressmaking," *LHJ* (April 1894): 39; Sybil Lanigan, "Old-Fashioned Plain Sewing," *LHJ* (June 1894): 12; "Dressmaking at Home," *Delineator* (July 1895): 62–67; Emma Hooper, "Easy Lessons in Dressmaking," *LHJ* (October 1895): 20; Mary Katharine Howard, "Practical Lessons in Dressmaking," *WHC* (February 1897): 11; idem., "Practical Lessons in Sewing," *WHC* (April 1897): 14; Emma Hooper, "The Home Dressmaker," *LHJ* (April 1898): 45; Mary Katharine Howard, "Problems in Dressmaking," *WHC* (November 1898): 30; Margaret Bisland, "Fashions and Fabrics," *GH* (June 1899): 275 (subtitled "Suggestions for Home Dressmaking"); Mary Katharine Howard, "Dressmaking at Home," *WHC* (July 1899): 19. "What to Wear and How to Make It" appeared as a regular feature in *Woman's Home Companion* from August 15, 1893, through November 15, 1895; for most of that time, Dinah Sturgis was in charge of the department. The magazine's end-of-the decade promise to the home dressmaker can be found in "Notes by the Editors," *WHC* (March 1899): 35.

24. Margaret Bisland, "Fashions and Fabrics," *GH* (October 1899): 171. Instructions on garment construction can be found in any of the sewing columns mentioned in notes 22 and 23. For specific advice on organizing the work, see Ada Simpson Sherwood, "Plain Sewing and Dressmaking," 157; on organizing the workspace, see Emma M. Hooper, "Hints on Home Dressmaking," *LHJ* (January 1892): 20—section subtitled "What to Have in a Sewing Room"; Emma M. Hooper, "Making a Dress at Home," *LHJ* (December 1892): 26—section subtitled "The Room for Sewing"; and Ada Simpson Sherwood, "Plain Sewing and Dressmaking," 157. On homemade dress forms, see Marie Jonreau, "A Home-Made Bust Model," *WHC* (March 1, 1895): 11; and Clara B. Miller, "Economy in Dress," *GH* (January 1894): 31. On dealing with dressmakers, see Emma Hooper, "Making a Dress at Home," 26; and Helen Jay, "Getting Ready for the Dressmakers," *LHJ* (February 1891): 4.

25. Ethel Spencer, *The Spencers of Amberson Avenue: A Turn-of-the-Century Memoir* (Pittsburgh: University of Pittsburgh Press, 1983), 38, 40–41.

26. Sherman, "Plain Sewing and Dressmaking," 157; Isabella Maud Rittenhouse, *Maud*, ed. Richard Lee Strout (New York: Macmillan, 1939), 103, 106, 472. Diary entries quoted were dated June 8, 1882 (dress arrives), June 10, 1882 (dressmaker), and September 11, 1889 (mail-order); *Ladies' Home Companion* advertisement, *LHC* (March 1, 1894): 20.

27. George Lawrence, "Godey's Fashions," *Godey's* (March 1893): 387; Helena Rowe, "Family Fashions and Fancies," *GH* (June 1891): 315; Emma Hooper, "Cotton and Woolen Gowns," *LHJ* (October 1892): 12; Emma Hooper, "The Home Dressmaker," *LHJ* (February 1899): 30; Dinah Sturgis, "Does It Pay to Make Over?" *WHC* (September 15, 1893): 91; Isabel Mallon, "Costumes of Early Autumn," 21; Elsie Gray, "Home Tailoring," *GH* (October 1897): 155; "Publisher's Department," *Delineator* (April 1890): 329.

28. French, *Emily*, 44, 46. The diary entry mentioning the *Ladies' Home Journal* was dated March 30, 1890, and the entry on making over a dress for Olive was dated April 7, 1890.

29. Descriptions of the growth of the paper pattern industry from the 1860s to the 1890s can be found in Margaret Walsh, "The Democratization of Fashion: The Emergence of the Women's Dress Pattern Industry," *Journal of American History* 66, no. 2 (September 1979): 299–313; and Nancy Page Fernandez, "Pattern Diagrams and Fashion Periodicals, 1840 to 1900," *Dress* 13 (1987): 4–10.

30. *Godey's* jumped in and out of the pattern business several times during this decade. At one time each issue of the magazine included a coupon that entitled the subscriber to a free pattern based on that month's fashion plates; see "Prospectus for 1890," *Godey's* (January 1890): n.p. *Good Housekeeping* launched a pattern department in 1900 that promised "to furnish patterns of garments for all members of the family" but offered none for men's clothing. The styles for women included jackets, shirtwaists, and skirts, even though these were among the garments that had become increasingly available in ready-made form by this time; see "Stylish Dress Patterns," *GH* (October 1900): 208. The *Woman's Home Companion* offered patterns to accompany its fashion illustrations in 1897, but abandoned the idea a few months later, not because it was unpopular but because orders flooded in so fast the fashion editors could not attend to the business of getting the magazine published. The magazine regrouped and was offering patterns again two years later; see Mary Katharine Howard, "Spring and Summer Costumes," *WHC* (April 1897): 14; idem, "What Women Are Wearing," 14; *Woman's Home Companion* advertisement, *WHC* (May 1899): 37–38. The *Ladies'*

Home Journal experimented with patterns in the late 1890s, then temporarily dropped the idea. When the magazine got into business in earnest in 1905, its publishers set up an entire new company—the Home Pattern Company—to create and distribute the patterns. Their effort met with such success that by the third month the magazine reported that "thousands of orders had been received where hundreds were expected"; see Mallon, "Coats and Wraps for the Winter," 33; "Some Plans for a New Year," *LHJ* (January 1905):1; "The Journal's New Departure," *LHJ* (May 1905): 1. The *Delineator* was founded by the Butterick Pattern Co., whose promotional literature advanced Ebenezer Butterick's claim as the inventor of the paper dress pattern. The Butterick Co. asserted that since the *Delineator's* founding in 1872 and its subsequent "expansion and modernization," its readership had come to include "queens and princesses, farmers' wives and society people"; see Butterick promotional pamphlet, "A Century of Delineator Girls," 1904 (in the collection of the Hagley Museum and Library). *McCall's* owed its existence to the McCall Pattern Co. and in 1899 continued to offer a free pattern to each new subscriber; see *McCall's* advertisement, *LHJ* (April 1899): 45. The *Pictorial Review* was started in 1899 by pattern entrepreneur William Ahnelt.

31. "Hints to Retailers," *CDGR* (January 25, 1896): 35; Emma Hooper, "Dress Goods as Christmas Presents," *LHJ* (December 1899): 28.

32. Nancy Page Fernandez, "'If a Woman Had Taste . . .': Home Sewing and the Making of Fashion, 1850–1910" (Ph.D. diss., University of California at Irvine, 1987), 14, 26, 25.

33. This interpretation of the mail-order business contrasts somewhat with that of historians who have seen catalogs as "modernizing 'agencies of change'" that "unequivocally endorsed the new." See Thomas Schlereth, "Country Stores, County Fairs and Mail-Order Catalogues: Consumption in Rural America," in *Consuming Visions: Accumulation and Display of Goods in America, 1880–1920*, ed. Simon Bronner (New York: W. W. Norton, 1989), 340, 374; and Fred E. H. Schroeder, "The Wishbook as Popular Icon," in *Outlaw Aesthetics* (Bowling Green, Ohio: Bowling Green University Popular Press, 1977): 50–61. For a contrasting view closer to my own, see William Leiss, Stephen Klein, Sut Jhally, *Social Communication in Advertising: Persons, Products, and Images of Well-Being*, 2nd ed. (New York: Routledge, 1990), 71–79. Leiss et al., however, argue that this contradiction between the catalogs' backward-looking artisanal imagery and their implicit forward-looking promise of mass consumption was a problem for merchandisers. I argue rather that it represented a solution for consumers, an answer to the problem of how consumers were to find safe passage to a world organized by the symbolic system of mass-produced merchandise.

34. Viola Paradise, "By Mail," *Scribner's Magazine* (April 1921): 474, 477.

35. Jordan, Marsh, *1895–96, Fall and Winter* (Boston, 1895), 75; Boston Store, *Spring and Summer, 1898* (Worcester, Mass., 1898), 1; Boggs & Buhl, *Dry Goods Price Book and Hints on Fashion, 1899–1900* (Allegheny, Pa., 1899), 4, 52; H. O'Neill, *Fall and Winter Fashion Catalogue, 1899–1900* (New York, 1899), 50; for the Harvard study, see "Sewing at Home Decreases as 'Ready-Mades' Gain Favor," *New York Times* (December 18, 1927): sec. 10, p. 10. Note that the headline suggests ready-mades are still working for acceptance in the late 1920s.

36. Helena Rowe, "The Housekeeper's Shopping Bag," *GH* (September 1893): 117–118 (emphasis added).

37. Anne Helme, "How to Dress Well for Little Money," *Harper's Bazar* (February 23, 1895): 153.

38. Hester M. Poole, "Social Graces," *GH* (December 1897): 236; Sybil Lanigan,

"Old-Fashioned Plain Sewing," *LHJ* (June 1894): 12; Hester M. Poole, "Notions and Novelties," *GH* (January 1899): 15. For a description of the role of women reformers in promoting antisweatshop legislation, see Kathryn Kish Sklar, "Hull House in the 1890s: A Community of Women Reformers," *Signs* 10, no. 4 (Summer 1985): 657–677.

39. Advertisement quotation is from Ideal Button Hole Cutter Co. advertisement, *WHC* (June 1897): 16; Sybil Lanigan, "Old-Fashioned Plain Sewing," 12.

40. "The Poetry of Progress," *Godey's* (October 1895): 448–451. By 1895 the company that made Fibre Chamois had reportedly spent $250,000 advertising its profitable new product, which cost about 2 cents per pound to make and sold for the equivalent of $1 an ounce. See "Their Advertisements Decline," *PI* (October 16, 1895): 28, and *PI* (October 23, 1895): 35.

41. Nathaniel C. Fowler, Jr., included a twenty-five-page chapter called "Writing Puffs" in his book, *Building Business: An Illustrated Manual for Aggressive Business Men* (Boston: Trade Co., 1893).

42. "Interlinings," *Godey's* (January 1896): 112–113; Midge Preston, "Fibre Chamois," *Godey's* (March 1896): 338–339. At least occasionally in 1895, *Godey's* also ran a department of brief items called "Fashion Novelties in New York Shops" that appears to "puff" various stores by name (see editions of February 1895: 225 and May 1895: 560). Ellen Garvey mentions a similar column, "Current Notes," that appeared in *Lippincott's,* and she describes an example from the *Ladies' Home Journal* as well. She says the practice "met with disfavor" and died out in the early 1900s. See Ellen Garvey, *The Adman in the Parlor: Magazines and the Gendering of Consumer Culture, 1880s to 1910s* (New York: Oxford University Press, 1996), 94–97.

43. Fibre Chamois advertisement, *LHJ* (March 1895): 35; Fibre Chamois advertisement, *WHC* (May 1896): 16.

44. Brown, Durrell and Co., *The Trade Monthly* (Boston, April 1895): 41; Brown, Durrell and Co., *The Trade Monthly* (Boston, February 1895): 47.

45. "It is but slight exaggeration, if any, to say that modern advertising got its first real energy in 1891 from two slogans: 'You press the button; we do the rest' and 'See that hump?' The rapidity with which these phrases struck the popular fancy and became a part of everyday language brought out in a few years so many slogans that a collection for the first ten-year period alone would make a book." Frank Presbrey, *The History and Development of Advertising* (1929; reprint, New York: Greenwood Press, 1968), 365.

46. *Ladies' Home Journal* advertisement, *CDGR* (May 30, 1896): 41. The magazine's paid circulation was well below 3.5 million, but such an estimate is perhaps justified if one includes pass-along readers as well as purchasers.

47. Addison Archer, "Ladies Home Journalism," *PI* (May 22, 1895): 3–7; Oscar Herzberg, "About Women's Publications," *PI* (May 25, 1898): 28–29; "Improve the Appearance of Advertising Pages," *Profitable Advertising* (December 15, 1893): 198–199.

48. I have borrowed here from Benedict Anderson's concept that modern nations be considered "imagined communities" because "the members of even the smallest nation will never know most of their fellow-members, meet them, or even hear of them, yet in the minds of each lives the image of their communion." See Benedict Anderson, *Imagined Communities,* rev. ed. (London: Verso, 1991), 6.

49. National Cloak and Suit Co., *New York Fashions 1908,* 9 (emphasis in original). For other examples of this "do not cut or mutilate" advice, see Beifeld Brothers, *Illustrated Catalogue of Ladies' and Children's Cloaks, Etc.* (Chicago, 1881),

inside front cover; D. B. Loveman, *Catalogue No. 7* (Chattanooga, Tenn., 1887), 1; Bloomingdale Brothers, *Spring and Summer, 1886* (New York, 1886), inside front cover; John Daniell and Sons, *Spring and Summer, 1890* (New York, 1890), 2; and Boggs & Buhl, *Spring and Summer, 1893* (Allegheny, Pa., 1893), 2.

50. Jordan, Marsh, *The Latest Styles, Fall and Winter, 93–94* (Boston, 1893): inside back cover. This same claim, using very similar phrasing, can be found in Hilton, Hughes and Co., *Catalog No. 1, Fall and Winter, 1894 and 1895* (New York, 1894), inside front cover; Boston Store, *Spring and Summer, 1898*, inside front cover; and W. H. Frear and Co., *Spring and Summer Catalogue* (Troy, N.Y., 1903), inside front cover.

51. W. H. Frear and Co., *Spring and Summer Catalogue*, 5, 46, 72, 77, 78, 81.

52. Diamond Dyes advertisement, *LHJ* (March 1895): 35.

53. Coronet Corset Company advertisement, *LHJ* (September 1897): 29; Merritt's Princess Skirt advertisement, *Delineator* (April 1898): xxxi.

54. Mary Blanchard has argued that a certain fluidity with respect to gender boundaries can be documented by examining the aesthetic dress movement in the 1870s and 1880s, but that this fluidity ended abruptly in the militarized and remasculinized 1890s. See Mary W. Blanchard, "Boundaries and the Victorian Body: Aesthetic Fashion in Gilded Age America," *American Historical Review* 100, no. 1 (February 1995): 48–50.

55. Sarah T. Rorer, "Cooperation in Housekeeping," *LHJ* (January 1895): 14.

56. May Allinson, U.S. Department of Labor Bureau of Labor Statistics, *Dressmaking as a Trade for Women in Massachusetts* (Washington, D.C.: Government Printing Office, 1916), 18.

57. Isabel Mallon, "Coats to be Worn This Season," *LHJ* (November 1891): 25; Maud Cooke, *Our Social Manual for All Occasions* (Chicago: Monarch Books, 1896), 395.

58. Mary Katharine Howard, "Dressmaking at Home," *WHC* (May 1899): 25; Edward Bok, "At Home with the Editor," *LHJ* (December 1893): 16; Charlotte Perkins Gilman, "The Shape of Her Dress," *Woman's Journal* (July 16, 1904): 226—this article originally appeared in 1896 in the *Pacific Rural Press;* Maud Cooke, *Twentieth Century Hand-book of Etiquette* (Philadelphia: Co-Operative Publishing, 1899), 388, 389. This book appeared under the title *Social Etiquette* in editions by four publishers in 1896 and was published under the titles *Social Life* and *Our Social Manual* by two other publishers that same year. It then reemerged three years later under the titles *Twentieth Century Hand-book of Etiquette* and *Twentieth Century Culture and Deportment*. It appeared once again in 1902, this time known as *Our Deportment;* Emily Wight, "The Pretty and Simple Fall Coats," *LHJ* (October 1899): 31; Margaret Bisland, "Fashions and Fabrics," *GH* (July 1899): 17.

59. Mary Katharine Howard, "The Well-Dressed Woman," *WHC* (August 1898): 18.

60. Annie R. White, *Polite Society Here and Abroad* (Chicago: Monarch Books, 1891): 279; Richard Wells, *Manners of Culture and Dress in the Best American Society* (Springfield, Mass.: King Richardson, 1892): 328. The conservatism of this advice is indicated by the fact that this latter work substantially reprints an earlier volume that originally appeared almost a quarter of a century earlier as *Decorum: A Practical Treatise on Etiquette and Dress of the Best American Society* (Chicago: J. A. Ruth, 1878).

61. Filene, *Him/Her/Self,* 64; Smith-Rosenberg, "New Woman as Androgyne," 261–262.

62. Frances Steele, *Beauty of Form and Grace of Vesture* (New York: Dodd, Mead and Co., 1892), 14; Charles Beezley, *Our Manners and Social Customs* (Chicago: Elliot and Beezley, 1891), 307.

63. *American Dressmaker* (September 1902): 4.

64. Alice Ives et al., *Our Society* (Detroit: Darling Publishing, 1893), 275; Carrie Earle Garrett, "The Womanish Woman in Public," *WHC* (June 1896): 8; Edward Bok, "The Offense of the Colored Shirt," *LHJ* (June 1897): 14. Phrases such as the "eternal fitness of things" had been in the popular vocabulary for many years and entered the language to describe a worldview in which a natural, intuitive, a priori understanding of "right" and "wrong" was possible. The phrase was originally associated with the eighteenth-century ethical theories of Samuel Clark, who believed that humans could discern a "right" and "wrong" that was inherent in the nature of things. See *Oxford English Dictionary*, 2nd ed., s.v. "fitness."

65. Nancy Cott, *The Grounding of American Feminism* (New Haven: Yale University Press, 1987), 5–8.

66. Emma Hooper, "The Home Dressmaker," *LHJ* (February 1900): 44; Lanigan, "Old-Fashioned Plain Sewing," 12.

67. Susan Strasser, *Never Done: A History of American Housework* (New York: Pantheon Books, 1982), 133–134, 144. See also Marguerite Connolly, "The Transformation of Home Sewing and the Sewing Machine In America, 1858–1929" (Ph.D. diss., University of Delaware, 1994), 99–101.

68. Wendy Gamber, *The Female Economy: The Millinery and Dressmaking Trades, 1860–1930* (Urbana: University of Illinois Press, 1997), 2, 100–103, 106–107, 193–200. Gamber also points out some ways in which the production of women's custom clothing entailed close ties with the world of mass production and large-scale enterprise (99). For a firsthand account of the give-and-take between dressmakers and their clients, see Amelia Des Moulins, "The Dressmaker's Life Story," *Independent* (April 28, 1904): 944–946.

69. In 1910, according to the Census Bureau, 99.6 percent of people earning their living as dressmakers outside of factories were women. Of several hundred job categories, it was the one where female domination was most complete. Earlier statistical studies found dressmaking among the highest paid of women's employments, and census data from slightly later suggested it was one of the rare occupations that enabled a woman to sustain herself through her life. In 1920, 42 percent of dressmakers were over forty-five years old and 5.1 percent were over sixty-five. In comparison, among women workers in shirt, collar, and cuff factories, only 11 percent were older than forty-five. Even in a nonmanufacturing job such as sales clerking at a store, only 15.5 percent of the women workers were older than forty-five. See U.S. Bureau of the Census, *Women in Gainful Occupations, 1870 to 1920* (Washington, D.C.: Government Printing Office, 1929), 63–66, 166–169, 180–181; Carroll D. Wright, *The Working Girls of Boston* (1889; reprint, New York: Arno Press, 1969), 83, 92, 96.

70. "What to Say to Customers When They Ask," *American Dressmaker* (November 1901): 10; "Dressmaking on a Business Basis," *American Dressmaker* (November 1902): 28.

71. *American Dressmaker* (December 1901): 3.

72. *American Dressmaker* (July 1902): 3.

73. *American Dressmaker* (June 1902): 3; *American Dressmaker* (January 1902): 3; "Art the Key-Note," *SAJ* (August 1902): 69. The latter citation is from one of the increasing number of special issues the *Sartorial Art Journal* devoted to women's clothing just before and after the turn of the century. In 1903, the

company began issuing these reports as a separate publication, *American Ladies' Tailor.*

74. "The Tailor-Maid and Her New Attire," *SAJ* (August 1900): 96; "Be a Type Unto Yourself," *American Dressmaker* (August 1903): 4.

75. *American Dressmaker* (December 1902): 3.

76. Wendy Gamber, *Female Economy,* 202–203, 269 n.37.

77. B. O. Flower, "Fashion's Slaves," *Arena* 4 no. 22 (September 1891): 401–430; "Fashionable Dress Justified," *Woman's Journal* (January 1, 1887): 2; "The Tyranny of Fashion," *Godey's* (July 1893): 113–114; George H. Lawrence, "The Beneficent Influence of Dress," *Godey's* (February 1893): 243–244; Frances E. Russell, "Woman's Dress," *Arena* 3 no. 15 (February 1891): 353; "Godey's Fashions," *Godey's* (August 1893): 244. For the debate on dress reform in America, the secondary literature is extensive but rather fragmented. The most extensive work is Stella Mary Newton, *Health, Art and Reason: Dress Reformers of the Nineteenth Century* (London: John Murray, 1974). Informative shorter treatments include Robert Riegel, "Women's Clothes and Women's Rights," *American Quarterly* 15, no. 3 (Fall 1963): 390–401; William Leach, *True Love and Perfect Union: The Feminist Reform of Sex and Society* (New York: Basic Books, 1980), 245–260; Valerie Steele, *Fashion and Eroticism: Ideals of Feminine Beauty from the Victorian Era to the Jazz Age* (New York: Oxford University Press, 1985), 145–158.

78. Edward Bok, "At Home with the Editor," *LHJ* (January 1894): 12; Isabel Mallon, "For Woman's Wear," *LHJ* (February 1891): 20. In 1895 the magazine printed an article by prominent New York clergyman Charles Parkhurst that stated: "Any feminine attempt to mutiny against wifehood, motherhood and domestic 'limitations' is a hopeless and rather imbecile attempt to escape the inevitable." See Charles Parkhurst, "The True Mission of Woman," *LHJ* (April 1895): 15.

79. J. H. Kellogg, *Plain Facts for Old and Young* (1888; reprint, New York, Arno Press, 1974), 597, 49, 532–533. John Harvey Kellogg was a physician, a crusader on behalf of dietary regimens, a best-selling author, the inventor of corn flakes, and the operator of a well-known sanitarium. Self-control and self-denial were his constant themes, especially in the area of sexuality. He claimed a person who "resolutely determines to combat unchaste thoughts" ought to control even his or her dreams. According to Kellogg, "unchaste acts" were encouraged by dancing, novel-reading, smoking, coffee-drinking, overheated rooms, spicy food, "vile pictures"—and, of course, fashionable dress. See *Plain Facts for Young and Old,* 169–198, 227–245, 302–308, 367–374, 407–411.

80. "Fashionable Dress Justified," 2. This article appeared in response to a letter from Gilman (then Charlotte Perkins Stetson) that was published under the headline "Why Women Do Not Reform Their Dress," October 26, 1886, p. 338; "Dress Reform Notes," *Woman's Journal* (June 9, 1894): 177; "Fashion Notes," *Woman's Journal* (September 15, 1894): 292; "National Women's Council," *Woman's Journal* (March 9, 1895): 73. The text of the NWC's resolution in favor of dress reform is printed on p. 80 of the same issue; Georgina P. Curtis, "Dressmaking for Ladies at Home," *Woman's Journal* (September 28, 1985): 306; idem (October 5, 1895): 314; idem (October 12, 1895): 322; Springer Bros. advertisement, *Woman's Journal* (June 8, 1895): 183; idem, (November 2, 1895): 349. Although associated mainly with the suffrage movement, *Woman's Journal* sought to cover "the whole field of women's rights." See Alice Stone Blackwell, "The Why and Who of the Woman's Journal in 1870," *Woman's Journal* (December 1929): 9.

81. For example, see Simone de Beauvoir, *The Second Sex,* trans. H. M. Parshley (New York: Alfred A. Knopf, 1953), 529; and Susan Faludi, *Backlash: The Undeclared War Against American Women* (New York: Crown, 1991), 173.

82. Carol Ascher, "Narcissism and Women's Clothing," *Socialist Review* 11, no.3 (May-June 1981): 75–86; Jane Gaines, "Introduction: Fabricating the Female Body," in *Fabrications: Costume and the Female Body,* ed. Jane Gaines and Charlotte Herzog (New York: Routledge, 1990), 3–11; Elizabeth Wilson, "All the Rage," in *Fabrications: Costume and the Female Body,* ed. Jane Gaines and Charlotte Herzog (New York: Routledge, 1990), 28–38; Karen Hanson, "Dressing Down Dressing Up—The Philosophic Fear of Fashion," *Hypatia* 5, no. 2 (Summer 1990): 107–121; Iris Young, "Women Recovering Our Clothes," in *On Fashion,* ed. Shari Benstock and Suzanne Ferriss (New Brunswick, N.J.: Rutgers University Press, 1994), 197–210; Elizabeth Wilson, *Adorned in Dreams* (Berkeley: University of California Press, 1987), 13, 228–247; Anne Hollander, *Sex and Suits: The Evolution of Modern Dress* (New York: Kodansha International, 1994), 20; Pamela Church Gibson, "Redressing the Balance: Patriarchy, Postmodernism, and Feminism," in *Fashion Cultures: Theories, Explorations and Analysis,* ed. Stella Bruzzi and Pamela Church Gibson (London: Routledge, 2000), 349. Gibson believes an appropriate feminist response to fashion should "position itself somewhere between . . . celebration and repudiation—or in an oscillation between them" (362).

83. Gene Stratton-Porter, *Freckles* (New York: Grosset & Dunlap, 1904), 310.

Chapter 3. Dress, Darwinism, and Sex Differentiation

1. Charlotte Perkins Gilman, *The Living of Charlotte Perkins Gilman: An Autobiography* (New York: D. Appleton-Century, 1935), 240.

2. Delores Hayden, *The Grand Domestic Revolution: A History of Feminist Designs for American Homes, Cities, and Neighborhoods* (Cambridge, Mass.: MIT Press, 1980), 183–205.

3. Reviews of the events mentioned appeared in the *New York Evening Post* in 1898 on January 28 (p. 7), January 29 (p. 2), and January 31 (p. 7). The reviews were published without bylines, but supplemental biographical information on Finck makes it all but certain he was responsible for them.

4. Henry T. Finck, *Romantic Love and Personal Beauty: Their Development, Causal Relations, Historic and National Peculiarities* (London: Macmillan: 1887), 359–361, 375–377, 389–393, 427.

5. Charlotte Perkins Gilman, "The Dress of Women," *Forerunner* 6, no. 9 (September 1915): 246–247.

6. Hall is quoted in Anthony Rotundo, *American Manhood: Transformations of Masculinity from the Revolution to the Modern Era* (New York: Basic Books, 1993), 269. The quotation is from a 1908 article, although Hall had been expressing similar sentiments in similar words since the 1890s. See Michael Kimmel, *Manhood in America: A Cultural History* (New York: Free Press, 1996), 160–167. Hall's intellectual debt to Darwin and various strands of evolutionary theory is documented in Dorothy Ross, *G. Stanley Hall: The Psychologist as Prophet* (Chicago: University of Chicago Press, 1972).

7. Carrie B. Sanborn, "Renovating Men's Clothing," *GH* (November 1897): 211; "How to Fold a Man's Coat," *LHJ* (August 1891): 8.

8. Ethel Spencer, *The Spencers of Amberson Avenue: A Turn-of-the-Century Memoir* (Pittsburgh: University of Pittsburgh Press, 1983), 40.

9. See, for example, Nancy Green, *Ready-to-Wear and Ready-to-Work: A Century of Industry and Immigrants in Paris and New York* (Durham, N.C.: Duke University Press, 1997), 23; Margaret Brew, "American Clothing Consumption, 1879–1909" (Ph.D. diss., University of Chicago, 1945), 111; Jessica Daves, *Ready-Made Miracle: The American Story of Fashion for the Millions* (New York: G. P. Putnam, 1967), 31; Claudia R. Kidwell and Margaret C. Christman, *Suiting Everyone: The Democratization of Clothing in America* (Washington, D.C.: Smithsonian Institution Press, 1974), 135; Sandra Ley, *Fashions for Everyone: The Story of Ready-To-Wear, 1870s to 1970s* (New York: Charles Scribner's Sons, 1975), 44.

10. Bernard Smith, "A Study of Uneven Industrial Development: The American Clothing Industry of the Late Nineteenth and Early Twentieth Centuries" (Ph.D. diss., Yale University, 1989); Thomas Tuchscherer, "Fashion and the Development of the Dress Industry, 1890–1930" (Ph.D. diss., Northwestern University, 1973). Smith rebuts supply-side theories with a demand-driven argument, asserting that "the nature and evolution of product markets determine the technological and organizational structure and development of an industry" (p. 70). But he does not really explain why demand for machine-made garments was so uneven. Tuchscherer provides a rather straightforward economist's version of the "blame it on fashion" thesis, and his analysis of fashion change leans heavily toward a theory of autonomous cycles.

11. Marguerite Connolly, "The Transformation of Home Sewing and the Sewing Machine in America, 1858–1929" (Ph.D. diss., University of Delaware, 1994): 111–115; Ava Baron and Susan E. Klepp, "'If I Didn't Have My Sewing Machine . . .': Women and Sewing Machine Technology," in *A Needle, a Bobbin, a Strike: Women Needleworkers in America*, ed. John Jensen and Sue Davidson (Philadelphia: Temple University Press, 1984), 23; Emily Wight, "How a Frock May Be Transformed," *LHJ* (December 1899): 27.

12. Ben Fine and Ellen Leopold, *World of Consumption* (London: Routledge, 1993), 96–100.

13. Valerie Steele, *Fashion and Eroticism: Ideals of Feminine Beauty from the Victorian Era to the Jazz Age* (New York: Oxford University Press, 1985), 28; Claudia Brush Kidwell, "Gender Symbols or Fashionable Details?" in *Men and Women, Dressing the Part*, ed. Claudia Brush Kidwell and Valerie Steele (Washington, D.C.: Smithsonian Institution Press, 1987), 126–128.

14. J. C. Flugel, *The Psychology of Clothes* (London: Hogarth Press, 1930), 110–117; Valerie Steele, *Fashion and Eroticism*, 82. Other summaries of the "great masculine renunciation" in men's fashion are available in Paul Nystrom, *The Economics of Fashion* (New York: Ronald Press, 1928), 309–339; Kenneth Dameron, *Men's Wear Merchandising* (New York: Ronald Press, 1930), 73–80; and H. Schramm, "Male Dress From the French Revolution to 1850" and "Fops and Dandies" in *CIBA Review* 11 (January 1958), 7–14 and 20–23. For reservations about use of the term similar to my own, see Elizabeth Wilson, "These New Components of Spectacle: Fashion and Postmodernism," in *Postmodernism and Society*, ed. Roy Boyle and Ali Rattansi (Houndsmills, England: Macmillan, 1990), 218; and Anne Hollander, *Sex and Suits: The Evolution of Modern Dress* (New York: Kodansha International, 1994), 22.

15. Elliott J. Gorn, *The Manly Art: Bare-Knuckle Prize Fighting in America* (Ithaca, N.Y.: Cornell University Press, 1986), 193; Arnaldo Testi, "The Gender of Reform Politics: Theodore Roosevelt and the Culture of Masculinity," *Journal of American History* 84, no. 1 (March 1995): 1523.

16. Godey's Fashions, *Godey's* (June 1893): 783–786.

17. Cynthia E. Russett, *Sexual Science: The Victorian Construction of Womanhood* (Cambridge, Mass.: Harvard University Press, 1989), 140–144.

18. "Biology and 'Woman's Rights,'" *Popular Science Monthly* 14 (1878–79): 211, 213; Herbert Spencer, *Principles of Sociology*, vol. 1 (New York: D. Appleton, 1882): 792; LeConte quoted in Lester Stephens, "Evolution and Women's Rights in the 1890s," *Historian* 38, no. 2 (February 1976): 245.

19. George H. Darwin, "Development in Dress," *Popular Science Monthly* (November 1872): 40–50. This article first appeared in *Macmillan's Magazine* in England and later appeared in *Every Saturday, Littell's Living Age,* and *Eclectic Magazine* in the United States in addition to *Popular Science Monthly*.

20. The term "Darwinian" is used somewhat loosely here, but no more loosely than it was used by Finck and Gilman themselves. Darwin's theories were subject to various interpretations and modifications that waxed and waned in popularity in nineteenth-century America. Some of these interpretations should probably be deemed "evolutionary theory" rather than Darwinian theory since their relationship to Darwin's own writings could be tenuous, but even proponents of these theories very often considered themselves to be working in a Darwinian tradition. This was certainly true of Finck and Gilman. The strand of evolutionary theory that influenced them, and exercised wide influence in the very late nineteenth and very early twentieth centuries, stressed an inevitable progress of civilization that placed Anglo-Saxon middle-class culture at its apex, thus validating its social practices and justifying its continued expansion. "Natural selection," a key Darwinian concept, did not necessarily play a part in this thinking. An overview of the historiographical debates about social Darwinism can be found in Mike Hawkins, *Social Darwinism in European and American Thought, 1860–1940* (Cambridge: Cambridge University Press, 1997), 3–20. A good range of assessments of Darwinism in the United States can be found in Robert Bannister, *Social Darwinism: Science and Myth in Anglo-American Thought* (Philadelphia: Temple University Press, 1979); Cynthia Russett, *Darwinism in America: The Intellectual Response, 1865–1912* (San Francisco: W. H. Freeman, 1976); Edward Pfeifer, "The United States," in *The Comparative Reception of Darwinism,* ed. Thomas Glick (Austin: University of Texas Press, 1974), 168–206; Richard Hofstadter, *Social Darwinism in American Thought, 1860–1915* (1944; Boston: Beacon Press, 1955).

21. [H. T. Finck], "The Poison in Our Food," *Nation* (May 25, 1899): 390–391; Charlotte Perkins Gilman, "Impure Food," *Woman's Journal* (October 1, 1904): 322.

22. Besides many books on music, other examples of Finck's wide-ranging output include *Food and Flavor: A Gastronomic Guide to Health and Good Living; Spain and Morocco: Studies in Local Color; Gardening with Brains;* and *Girth Control for Womanly Beauty, Manly Strength, Health and a Long Life for Everybody.* See Albert Marquis, ed., *Who's Who in America,* vol. 14, 1926–27 (Chicago: A. N. Marquis, 1926), 704; "American Musical Critics," *Bookman* 75 (March 1905): 77.

23. The *Independent* began publication in 1848 under the auspices of the Congregational church but had evolved by the end of the century into a "general illustrated miscellany" of the same sort as *Harper's Weekly, Colliers,* and *Century.* "It printed some fiction, much comment on public affairs, and departments devoted to the fine arts, literature, music, education, science and so on." See Frank Luther Mott, *A History of American Magazines,* vol. 2 (Cambridge, Mass.: Harvard University Press, 1938), 367–379; idem, vol. 4 (Cambridge, Mass.: Harvard University Press, 1957), 10, 50, 288.

24. Henry T. Finck, "Are Womanly Women Doomed?" *The Independent* 53 (January 31, 1901): 267; idem, "The Evolution of Sex in Mind," *The Independent* 53 (December 26, 1901): 3062, 3059.

25. Henry T. Finck, "Will Women Ever Dress Like Men?" *The Independent* 62 (May 30, 1907): 1251–1255.

26. Cynthia Russett, *Sexual Science*, 14.

27. Quoted in Gary Scharnhorst, *Charlotte Perkins Gilman* (Boston: Twayne, 1985), 25.

28. Charlotte Perkins Gilman, "The Dress of Women," *Forerunner* 6, no. 1 (January 1915): 20; idem, "The Dress of Women," *Forerunner* 6, no. 2 (February 1915): 49.

29. Gilman, *Living*, 263, 290.

30. Russett, *Sexual Science*, 151–154. As Gail Bederman shows, Gilman's understanding of evolution led her to see the key hierarchical developments in terms of race, not sex. This allowed her to make radical claims on behalf of women, but in a manner that "was inextricably rooted in the white supremacism of 'civilization.'" See Gail Bederman, *Manliness and Civilization* (Chicago: University of Chicago Press, 1995), 121–169.

31. Charlotte Perkins Gilman, "Why These Clothes?" *The Independent* 58 (March 2, 1905): 467; idem, "Symbolism in Dress," *The Independent* 58 (June 8, 1905): 1295; idem, "Modesty: Feminine and Other," *The Independent* 58 (June 29, 1905): 1448.

32. Gilman, "Modesty: Feminine and Other," 1449.

33. Charlotte Perkins Gilman, "The Dress of Women," *Forerunner* 6, no. 9 (September 1915): 246–247; idem, "The Dress of Women," *Forerunner* 6, no. 2 (February 1915): 49.

34. Gilman, "Modesty: Feminine and Other," 1448.

35. Mary Douglas, *Natural Symbols: Explorations in Cosmology* (New York: Pantheon, 1982), 70. See also her discussion in *Purity and Danger: An Analysis of the Concepts of Pollution and Taboo* (1966; reprint, London: Routledge, 1992), 121. Douglas's work drew part of its inspiration from Marcel Mauss, "Techniques of the Body," *Economy and Society* 2, no. 1 (February 1973): 70–87; this essay is based on a lecture given in 1934. Various theories of the socially constructed body can be found in Michel Foucault, *Discipline and Punish: The Birth of the Prison*, trans. Alan Sheridan (New York: Vintage Books, 1979), 137, 139, 153; Pierre Bourdieu, *Distinction: A Social Critique of the Judgment of Taste*, trans. Richard Howard (Cambridge, Mass.: Harvard University Press, 1984), 190–225; Anthony Giddens, *Modernity and Self-Identity* (Stanford, Calif.: Stanford University Press, 1991), 56–63, 99–100. Good overview discussions of this type of body politics and its influence on feminist thought include Susan Bordo, "Feminism, Foucault, and the Politics of the Body" in *Reconstructing Foucault: Essays in the Wake of the '80s*, ed. Ricardo Miguel-Alfonso and Silvia Caporale-Bizzini (Amsterdam: Rodopi, 1994): 219–243; and Moira Gatens, "Powers, Bodies, Difference," in *Destabilizing Theory: A Contemporary Feminist Debate*, ed. Michele Barrett and Anne Phillips (Cambridge: Polity Press, 1992), 128–132.

36. Gilman, "Symbolism in Dress," 1296; idem, "Modesty: Feminine and Other," 1448. G. Stanley Hall expressed a similar view in 1898 when he wrote that "man's primitive body consciousness has been largely disguised and transformed into clothes consciousness." See Ross, *G. Stanley Hall*, 369.

37. Bederman, *Manliness and Civilization*, 8, 20.

38. Carroll Smith-Rosenberg, "The New Woman as Androgyne: Social Disorder

and the Gender Crisis, 1870–1936," in *Disorderly Conduct: Visions of Gender in Victorian America* (New York: Oxford University Press, 1985), 258–261.

39. Russett, *Sexual Science*, 6; Smith-Rosenberg, "New Woman as Androgyne," 270–272.

40. On wired collars, see, for example, Isabel Mallon, "The Morning-Jacket and the Tea Gown," *LHJ* (July 1891): 23; on puffed sleeves, see idem, "Costumes of Early Autumn," *LHJ* (October 1892): 21; on boned bodices, see idem, "The Gowns of Spring," *LHJ* (March 1895): 19; on wired skirts, see Empress Skirt advertisement, *WHC* (August 1898): 16.

41. Isabel Mallon, "The Art of Street Dressing," *LHJ* (December 1893): 23; idem, "The Gowns to Be Worn This Winter," *LHJ* (September 1897): 35; Mary Katharine Howard, "Problems in Dressmaking," *WHC* (March 1899), 33; idem, "Practical Lessons in Dressmaking," *WHC* (May 1897): 11.

42. Amelia Des Moulins, "The Dressmaker's Life Story," *The Independent* 56 (April 28, 1904): 945–946.

43. Mary Katharine Howard, "Practical Lessons in Dressmaking," *WHC* (September 1897): 11; Maud Cooke, *Twentieth-Century Handbook of Etiquette* (Philadelphia: Co-Operative Publishing, 1899), 390; Editorial, *CDGR* (January 8, 1898): 9.

44. Weston and Wells Mfg. Co. advertisement, *LHJ* (December 1898): 46; W. B. Corset advertisement, *LHJ* (July 1895): 21; Sahlin Distender advertisement, *LHJ* (October 1899): 40 (emphasis added); Aquamiel advertisement, *WHC* (March 1, 1895): 11.

45. Mallon, "Costumes of Early Autumn," 21; idem, "For Woman's Wear," *LHJ* (January 1891): 22; Katharine Eggleston Junkermann, "Physical Culture for Girls," *WHC* (March 1898): 15; Florence Howe Hall, *Social Customs* (Boston: Estes and Lauriat, 1887), 215.

46. Judith Butler, *Gender Trouble: Feminism and the Subversion of Identity* (New York: Routledge, 1990), 33, 136.

47. Alice E. Ives et al., *Our Society* (Detroit: Darling Publishing, 1893), 14; Frances Evans, "About Men," *LHJ* (October 1898): 15; Mary Katharine Howard, "Some Charming Spring Gowns," *WHC* (April 1898): 20; idem, "The Well-Dressed Woman," *WHC* (August 1898): 18; editorial, *Godey's* (June 1894): 753.

48. Eva Wilder McGlasson, "The Aesthetics of Dress," in *The Woman's Book* (New York: Charles Scribner's Sons, 1894), 185.

49. Anne Hollander has argued that an era's pictorial conventions establish what is considered "natural" for the human body. I am expanding on her idea somewhat by contending that late nineteenth-century body ideals were created by visual (not just pictorial) conventions. In other words, the standards were set by the fashionable silhouette, whether viewed in an illustration or in the person of a well-dressed woman. See Anne Hollander, *Seeing Through Clothes* (Berkeley: University of California Press, 1993), xii–xiii, 311–312.

50. Chas. A Stevens & Bros., *Special Catalogue of Fine Cloaks and Silks: Fall and Winter, 1895–96* (Chicago, 1895); idem, *Special Catalogue of Fine Cloaks and Silks: Fall and Winter, 1896–97* (Chicago, 1896).

51. I am appreciative to Patricia Warner for pointing out this precedent to me based on her own collection of fashion plates. It has not been discussed in secondary work as far as I am aware.

52. "Photography in Advertising," *Ad Sense* (April 1898): 30.

53. William Ewing believes modern fashion photography, which he dates from 1927, represents a fusion of portraiture, snapshot, and surrealistic art aesthetics, while Richard Pollay's survey of magazine ads indicates photographs

did not become an important form of advertising illustration until the 1930s. Jackson Lears suggests that the hiring of photographer Edward Steichen by the J. W. Thompson advertising agency in the 1920s was the turning point in the development of advertising photography. See William Ewing, "Perfect Surface," in *Aperture* no. 122 (Winter 1991): 6–19; Richard W. Pollay, "The Subsiding Sizzle: A Descriptive History of Print Advertising, 1900–1980," *Journal of Marketing* 49, no. 3 (Summer 1985): 24–37; Jackson Lears, *Fables of Abundance: A Cultural History of Advertising in America* (New York: Basic Books, 1994), 322–329.

54. Isabel Mallon, "Some Types in Dress," *LHJ* (February 1893): 21.

55. "What to Wear and How to Make It," *WHC* (November 15, 1895): 11; Isabel Mallon, "Dress Notes for November," *LHJ* (November 1891): 26; Emma Hooper, "Gowns for Unusual Figures," *LHJ* (February 1899): 25; Florence Howe Hall, *Social Customs*, 246.

56. Mary Katharine Howard, "Spring and Summer Costumes," *WHC* (April 1897): 14; "What to Wear and How to Make It," *WHC* (February 15, 1895): 12; Emma Hooper, "The Summer Designs in Dresses," *LHJ* (May 1897): 24; idem, "The New Skirts and Waists," *LHJ* (May 1898): 24; Mary Katharine Howard, "Suitable Street Costumes," *WHC* (January 1897): 18; Mallon, "The Gowns to Be Worn This Winter," 35.

57. Gilman, *Living*, 244; Dinah Sturgis, "What to Wear and How to Make It," *WHC* (February 1, 1895): 14; Emily French, *The Diary of a Hard-Worked Woman*, ed. Janette LeCompte (Lincoln: University of Nebraska Press, 1987), 95, diary entry dated August 22, 1890; men are mocked for their lack of fashion sense in Dinah Sturgis, "What to Wear and How to Make It," *WHC* (February 1, 1895): 14 (subtitled "The Women Men Admire") as well as "What to Wear and How to Make It," *WHC* (April 1, 1895): 12 (subtitled "How Some Masculine Authors Dress Women"). Susan Lanser argues that household routines can encode female resistance or self-expression, but she focuses exclusively on professed or demonstrated incompetence at domestic tasks, apparently not considering the possibilities that pleasure, self-worth, and individual assertion could flow from mastery of them as well. See "Burning Dinners: Feminist Subversions of Domesticity," in *Feminist Messages: Coding in Women's Folk Culture*, ed. Joan Newlon Radner (Urbana: University of Illinois Press, 1993), 37–53.

58. Edward Bok, "At Home with the Editor," *LHJ* (May 1894): 12.

59. Writers of etiquette books frequently came from fashionable society, although journalists, magazine editors, and other writers also were successful contributors to the genre. The publishing history of these volumes—which often were reprinted in dozens of editions, sometimes with different titles and authors fronting the same text—indicates that their readership extended far beyond the elite classes. Most scholars have concluded that such writing appealed most strongly to the middle class and those who aspired to it. See Arthur Schlesinger, *Learning How to Behave: A Historical Study of American Etiquette Books* (New York: Macmillan, 1946), 19; John Kasson, *Rudeness and Civility: Manners in Nineteenth-Century Urban America* (New York: Hill and Wang, 1990), 51–54; Karen Halttunen, *Confidence Men and Painted Women: A Study of Middle-Class Culture in America, 1830–1870* (New Haven: Yale University Press, 1982), xvi, 1, 110–116; Sarah Newton, *Learning to Behave: A Guide to American Conduct Books Before 1900* (Westport, Conn.: Greenwood Press, 1994), 3.

60. Harold de Fountenoy Vincent, *The Well-Groomed Man* (Chicago: M. B. Hilly, 1895), 2; Censor [Oliver Bunce], *Don't: A Manual of Mistakes and Improprieties More or Less Prevalent in Conduct and Speech* (New York: D. Appleton, 1884), 27.

61. John Kasson, *Rudeness and Civility*, 118–121.

62. Edward Bok, "What Makes a Gentleman," *LHJ* (July 1898): 14; idem, "The Offense of the Colored Shirt," *LHJ* (June 1897): 14; idem, "At Home with the Editor," *LHJ* (November 1892): 16.

63. Finck, *Romantic Love*, 392–393.

64. Gilman, "Symbolism in Dress," 1297. On the same page, Gilman reminds us that the dressmaker "sees to it that the woman shall have a small waist and large hips, quite regardless of her protesting bones and body."

65. Hart, Schaffner and Marx, *Hand-Book of Styles* (Chicago, 1902), n.p. [8]; W. S. Peck, *Fine Clothing for Fall and Winter 1901 and 1902* (Syracuse, N.Y., 1901), 3; Stein-Bloch Co., *Smartness* (Rochester, N.Y., 1903), n.p. [6]. The latter catalog, a sixteen-page pamphlet, was issued by G. N. Vincent, a New York City clothier, but its contents were copyrighted by Stein-Bloch, so presumably the manufacturer produced the booklet and the merchant simply imprinted his name on a couple of key pages.

66. Christopher Breward, "Renouncing Consumption: Men, Fashion, and Luxury, 1870–1914," in *Defining Dress: Dress as Object, Meaning and Identity*, ed. Amy de la Haye and Elizabeth Wilson (Manchester: Manchester University Press, 1999), 50.

67. Linda Kerber makes some of these points in "Separate Spheres, Female Worlds, Woman's Place: The Rhetoric of Women's History," *Journal of American History* 75, no. 1 (June 1988), 9–39. For a more recent and more thorough renunciation of the concept, see Cathy N. Davidson, "Preface: No More Separate Spheres," *American Literature* 70, no. 3 (September 1998): 443–463.

68. Michael Zakim has argued that the schism between men's and women's fashion development in the late nineteenth century demonstrates the manner in which "sex replaced class as the great social divide in industrial democracies." Michael Zakim, "Sartorial Ideologies," *American Historical Review* 106, no. 5 (December 2001): 1580. On this point see also Gilles Lipovetsky, *The Empire of Fashion: Dressing Modern Democracy*, trans. Catherine Porter (Princeton, N.J.: Princeton University Press, 1994), 109–110; and Kaja Silverman, "Fragments of a Fashionable Discourse," in *Studies in Entertainment: Critical Approaches to Mass Culture*, ed. Tania Modleski (Bloomington: Indiana University Press, 1986), 147. The Silverman essay also appears in *On Fashion*, ed. Shari Benstock and Suzanne Ferriss (New Brunswick, N.J.: Rutgers University Press, 1994), 191.

69. Gilman, "Symbolism in Dress," 1297; Teresa de Lauretis, "The Technology of Gender," in *Technologies of Gender* by Teresa de Lauretis (Bloomington: Indiana University Press, 1987), 3.

70. Samuel Butler, *The Note-Books of Samuel Butler*, ed. Henry Festing Jones (New York: E. P. Dutton, 1917), 243.

Chapter 4. Clothing and Citizenship

1. See for example, the Gage-Downs Co. advertisement with the headline: "The Winning Candidate: Major William McKinley; The Winning Corset Waist: The G-D Chicago Waist," *CDGR* (November 7, 1896); 42; a column on how to make a dry goods window display to commemorate Washington's birthday, "Window Dressing," *CDGR* (February 12, 1898): 61; and David Marks & Sons advertisement headlined "The New Declaration of Independence," *CG* (July 1894): 3.

2. William C. Browning, "The Clothing and Furnishing Trade," in *One Hundred Years of American Commerce,* vol. 2, ed. Chauncey M. Depew (New York: D. O. Haynes, 1895), 564.

3. Charles Tilly, "Citizenship, Identity and Social History," in *Citizenship, Identity and Social History,* ed. Charles Tilly (Cambridge: Cambridge University Press, 1995), 5–9; David Kertzer, *Ritual, Politics, and Power* (New Haven: Yale University Press, 1988), 6.

4. Michael Walzer, "What Does It Mean to Be an 'American'?" *Social Research* 57, no. 3 (Fall 1991): 602; Philip Gleason, "American Identity and Americanization" in *Harvard Encyclopedia of American Ethnic Groups,* ed. Stephan Thernstrom (Cambridge, Mass.: Harvard University Press, 1980), 31–34. All nationalities are constructed, but the newness of United States means the invented aspects of its nationalism lie closer to the surface than in many other countries.

5. John Bodnar, "Introduction: The Attractions of Patriotism," in *Bonds of Affection: Americans Define Their Patriotism,* ed. John Bodnar (Princeton, N.J.: Princeton University Press, 1996), 13. On the changing cultural significance of the American flag, see Stuart McConnell, "Reading the Flag: A Reconsideration of the Patriotic Cults of the 1890s," in *The Bonds of Affection: Americans Define Their Patriotism,* ed. John Bodnar (Princeton, N.J.: Princeton University Press, 1996), 102–119.

6. On populist nationalism, a sense of the key issues and their key supporters can be obtained from Michael Kazin, *The Populist Persuasion: An American History* (New York: Basic Books, 1995), 27–46, and Nell Irvin Painter, *Standing at Armageddon: The United States, 1877–1919* (New York: W. W. Norton, 1987), 44–71. On progressive nationalism, see the summary in Michael Sandel, *Democracy's Discontent: America in Search of a Public Philosophy* (Cambridge, Mass.: Belknap Press of Harvard University Press, 1996), 209–227. On multicultural nationalism, see Leslie Vaughn, "Cosmopolitanism, Ethnicity and American Identity: Randolph Bourne's 'Trans-National America,'" *Journal of American Studies* 25, no. 3 (December 1991), 443–459. These categories are sketched very broadly; each could be subdivided into a number of variants.

7. On the Republican campaign of 1896, see Stanley Jones, *The Presidential Election of 1896* (Madison: University of Wisconsin Press, 1964), 291–293; and Lawrence Goodwyn, *Democratic Promise: The Populist Moment in America* (Oxford: Oxford University Press, 1976), 528–529. On the limited impact of multiculturalism, see Philip Gleason, "American Identity and Americanization," 43–44, and John Higham, "Ethnic Pluralism in Modern American Thought," in *Send These to Me: Jews and Other Immigrants in Urban America* (New York: Atheneum, 1975), 211–212.

8. Benedict Anderson, *Imagined Communities,* rev. ed. (London: Verso, 1991), 6.

9. "Editorial," *CDGR* (February 26, 1898): 9; "Window Dressing," *CDGR* (March 5, 1898): 41.

10. For the linkages between business interests, social Darwinism, progressivism, and imperialism, see Emily Rosenberg, *Spreading the American Dream: American Economic and Cultural Expansion, 1890–1945* (New York: Hill and Wang, 1982), 38–42. Economic motivations for the war are emphasized in Philip Foner, *The Spanish-Cuban-American War and the Birth of American Imperialism, 1895–1902* (New York: Monthly Review Press, 1972). The war and its relation to political parties are covered in Walter Karp, *The Politics of War* (New York: Harper & Row, 1979), 3–116. The concept of manifest destiny is discussed in relation to the war in Anders Stephanson, *Manifest Destiny: American Expansion and the Empire of Right* (New York: Hill and Wang, 1995), 74–111.

11. Thomas Archdeacon, *Becoming American: An Ethnic History* (New York: Free Press, 1983).

12. The cultural stresses involving economic and social changes during this period are covered in Alan Trachtenberg, *The Incorporation of America: Culture and Society in the Gilded Age* (New York: Hill and Wang, 1982). For an argument that relates the 1890s martial zeal to threatened Victorian American values, see Gerald F. Linderman, *The Mirror of War: American Society and the Spanish-American War* (Ann Arbor: University of Michigan Press, 1974). On the divisive rhetoric of the election of 1896, see Jones, *The Presidential Election of 1896*, 276–350.

13. Wanamaker advertisement, *New York Times* (May 18, 1898): 4; Saks & Company advertisement, *Indianapolis News* (May 20, 1898): 7; "Adwriters and the War," *PI* (July 6, 1898): 6; Charles Austin Bates, "Department of Criticism," *PI* (August 10, 1898): 62. The copy in advertisements of this era often mixed a variety of type sizes, fonts, and styles along with various punctuation and capitalization techniques within a single paragraph or sentence. I have not attempted to duplicate these effects in my text.

14. W. C. Loftus advertisement, *New York Tribune* (June 2, 1898): 4; Geo. J. Marott advertisement, *Indianapolis News* (May 4, 1898): 10.

15. "President's Call for 75,000 More Volunteers," *Chicago Tribune* (May 26, 1898): 5; Foreman Shoe Co. advertisement, *Chicago Tribune* (May 26, 1898): 4; The Hub advertisement, *Chicago Tribune* (June 12, 1898): 13; The Hub advertisement, *Chicago Tribune* (June 26, 1898): 15.

16. Sam Whitmire, "War-Time Advertising," *Fame* (July 1898): 275. The definition and influence of yellow journalism are a matter of some historical debate, but contemporary observers and later scholars agree that newspapers in the 1890s broke new ground in the bold use of headlines, illustrations, and page layout to attract readers. For recent interpretations, see W. Joseph Campbell, *Yellow Journalism: Puncturing the Myths, Defining the Legacies* (Westport, Conn.: Praeger, 2001), 6–11; John D. Stevens, *Sensationalism and the New York Press* (New York: Columbia University Press, 1991), 77–78, 87–88, 91–100.

17. *PI* (May 18, 1898): 34.

18. Sam Whitmire, "War-Time Advertising," 275; "War Relics as Window Ads," *Fame* (October 1898): 416–417.

19. "Hints to Retailers and State Street Observations," *CDGR* (October 1, 1898): 61; Hester M. Poole, "Notions and Novelties," *GH* (December 1898): 208; "Patriotic Novelties for Dry Goods Trade," *CDGR* (May 7, 1898): 15, 17; J. Floersheim, Kunstadter & Co. advertisement with headline: "Souvenirs of the War," *CDGR* (May 7, 1898): 12–13; Ryan & Cannon advertisement, *St. Louis Post-Dispatch* (May 12, 1898): 5; "Cloaks and Suits," *DGE* (May 7, 1898): 39; "Wide-Awake Retailing," *DGE* (May 28, 1898): 53.

20. "Flag Represents the Heart," *New York Tribune* (May 19, 1898): 7; "The Flag an Object Lesson," *New York Tribune* (May 30, 1898): 9; "Opinions About the Flag," *New York Tribune* (May 19, 1898): 7.

21. Sam Whitmire, "War-Time Advertising," 275; J. Floersheim, Kunstadter & Co. advertisement, *CDGR* (May 7, 1898): 12–13; "Editorial," *CDGR* (May 14, 1898): 10; "Editorial," *CDGR* (September 3, 1898): 11–12; "Cloaks and Suits," *DGE* (May 7, 1898): 39; "Dress Accessories," *Designer* (August 1898): 55; "Dress Accessories," *Designer* (October 1898): 58.

22. "Ladies' Costume," *Designer* (August 1898): 22; Carson Pirie Scott & Co. advertisement, *LHJ* (September 1898): 27; "Ladies' Military Collars," *Designer* (October 1898): 36–38; "Dress Accessories," *Designer* (October 1898): 57; Spear

& Co. advertisement, *Clothier and Furnisher* (May 1898), 32; Arlington Mills advertisement, *LHJ* (July 1898), 17; "Fashions and Fabrics," *Designer* (August 1898): 51; ibid.; "Fashions and Fabrics," *Designer* (September 1898): 53; "Fashions and Fabrics," *Designer* (November 1898): 54; "Dress Accessories," *Designer* (October 1898): 57–59; editorial, *CDGR* (May 14, 1898): 10. For the popularity of the "Spanish flounce," see "Fashions and Fabrics," *Designer* (March 1898): 53; for its new incarnation as the "Dewey flounce," see "Cloaks and Suits," *DGE* (June 25, 1898): 37; "Fashions and Fabrics," *Designer* (September 1898): 53; "Dress Accessories," *Designer* (October 1898): 57—the latter two articles also contain references to the "Dewey vest"; for "Dewey hats," see *Fame* (October 1898): 403; for "Roosevelt cloth," see "Fashions and Fabrics," *Designer* (November 1898): 54.

23. Ethel Spencer, *The Spencers of Amberson Avenue: A Turn-of-the-Century Memoir* (Pittsburgh: University of Pittsburgh Press, 1983), 42; "At the Hub," *PI* (May 25, 1898): 39.

24. "National Dress for Masquerade and Fancy Dress Parties," *Delineator* (October 1898): 503–504.

25. "Patriotic Women Will Make France's Sympathy for Spain Cost Her Dear," *New York Journal* (May 27, 1898): 5; editorial cartoon, *Indianapolis News* (May 24, 1898): 2; "Patriotic Women. They Will Not Buy Anything That Is Manufactured in France," *Indianapolis News* (May 7, 1898): 5; "Cause for Boycott," *Chicago Tribune* (June 11, 1898): 16; "New York Women Taboo Paris," *Chicago Tribune* (May 29, 1898): 36; "Will American Women Make France Pay $50,000,000 Indemnity for Sympathy with Spain?" *New York Journal*, (May 22, 1898): 18.

26. George Mosse, *Nationalism and Sexuality: Respectability and Abnormal Sexuality in Modern Europe* (New York: Howard Fertig, 1985); Mary G. Dietz, "Context is All: Feminism and Theories of Citizenship," *Daedalus* 116, no. 4 (Fall 1987): 24; Ruth Lister, "Tracing the Contours of Women's Citizenship," *Policy and Politics* 21, no. 1 (January 1993): 3–16; Sylvia Walby, "Is Citizenship Gendered?" *Sociology* 28, no. 2 (May 1994): 379–395; Eileen Boris, "The Racialized Gendered State: Construction of Citizenship in the United States," *Social Politics* 2, no. 2 (Summer 1995): 160–180.

27. Linda Kerber, *No Constitutional Right to Be Ladies: Women and the Obligations of Citizenship* (New York: Hill and Wang, 1998), 236–251; Margaret Higonnet, Jane Jenson, Sonya Michel, and Margaret Collins Weitz, introduction, in *Behind the Lines: Gender and the Two World Wars*, ed. Margaret Higonnet et al. (New Haven: Yale University Press, 1987), 4.

28. Matthew Jacobson, *Special Sorrows: The Diasporic Imagination of Irish, Polish, and Jewish Immigrants in the United States* (Cambridge, Mass.: Harvard University Press, 1995), 161; Kristin L. Hoganson, *Fighting for American Manhood: How Gender Politics Provoked the Spanish-American and Philippine American Wars* (New Haven: Yale University Press, 1998), 125–130; Sybil Lanigan, "Old-Fashioned Plain Sewing," *LHJ* (June 1894): 12.

29. "Fashions and Fabrics," *Standard Designer* (July 1898): 53; "Will American Women Make France Pay?" 18; "Editorial," *CDGR* (September 1898): 12; "Fashion and Fabrics," *Designer* (August 1898): 51; "Dress Accessories," *Designer* (November 1898): 55.

30. Michael Zakim notes the long association of clothing and citizenship ideals in the United States and mentions the significant lack of early development in the women's ready-made sector in "Sartorial Ideologies: From Homespun to Ready-Made," *American Historical Review* 106, no. 5 (December 2001): 1580–1582.

31. "The Clothing Trade," *CG* (January 1893): 63; N. Snellenburg advertisement in "Modern Clothing Advertising," *CG* (June 1895): 63; "The Americans Are Best Dressed," *CG* (January 1895): 107; "Wide-Awake Retailing," *DGE* (April 9, 1898): 81; "Premier Clothier of America," *CG* (February 1895): 9.

32. House of Kuppenheimer, *High-Bred Clothes* (Chicago, 1905); n.p.; N. Snellenburg and Co. advertisement in "Examples of Advertising," *CG* (December 1895): 19; Browning, "Clothing and Furnishing Trade," 564; The Hub advertisement, *Chicago Tribune* (May 15, 1898): 39.

33. Arnheim advertisement, *New York Journal* (May 22, 1898): 36.

34. "Wanamaker as Warrior," *Fame* (May 1898): 192. Wanamaker persisted with his plans but the unit, like practically all volunteer regiments, was never activated. Information on his actions can be found in Herbert Adams Gibbons, *John Wanamaker*, vol. 1 (New York: Harper and Brothers, 1926): 370–376.

35. "At the Hub," *PI* (May 25, 1898): 39.

36. W. S. Peck and Co., *Fine Clothing for Fall and Winter 1901 and 1902* (Syracuse, N.Y., 1901), 5; Hart, Schaffner & Marx, *Hand-Book of Styles* (Chicago, 1902), n.p. [6]; "Foreshadowings," *American Ladies' Tailor* (September 1903): 163; Snellenburg advertisement quoted in Arnold Karr, *Two Centuries of American Men's Wear* (Washington, D.C.: Apparel Retailers of America, 1989), 14–15.

37. Archdeacon, *Becoming American*, 115.

38. The remarks here refer mainly to European immigrants. The experiences of Asians and Mexicans were quite different, perhaps because their continued attachments to their home countries were stronger and their intentions to remain in the United States much weaker. The tendencies of various European immigrant groups varied too, of course, according to their own intentions toward the new world and attachments to the old. See Andrew Heinze, *Adapting to Abundance: Jewish Immigrants, Mass Consumption and the Search for American Identity* (New York: Columbia University Press, 1990), 92–93. Besides Heinze, other good secondary sources on the subject of immigrants and clothing include Elizabeth Ewen, *Immigrant Women in the Land of Dollars: Life and Culture on the Lower East Side, 1890–1925* (New York: Monthly Review Press, 1985); Susan Glenn, *Daughters of the Shtetl: Life and Labor in the Immigrant Generation* (Ithaca, N.Y.: Cornell University Press, 1990); and Barbara Schreier, *Becoming American Women: Clothing and the Jewish Immigrant Experience, 1880–1920* (Chicago: Chicago Historical Society, 1994).

39. Heinze, *Adapting to Abundance*, 93–96; Schreier, *Becoming American Women*, 30–39.

40. Abraham Cahan, *The Rise of David Levinsky* (1917; reprint, New York: Harper & Row, 1960), 93. Cahan himself had emigrated to the United States from Russia in 1882, just three years before his character's arrival in *David Levinsky*.

41. Sydelle Kramer and Jenny Masur, eds., *Jewish Grandmothers* (Boston: Beacon Press, 1976), 130. The comment comes from an oral history interview with Ida Richter, who came to the United States with her family in 1907.

42. Heinze, *Adapting to Abundance*, 9.

43. Margaret F. Byington, *Homestead: The Households of a Mill Town* (1910; reprint, Pittsburgh: University Center for International Studies, 1974), 150 (emphasis added).

44. Archdeacon, *Becoming American*, 145–166; Morton Keller, *Affairs of State: Public Life in Late Nineteenth-Century America* (Cambridge, Mass.: Harvard University Press, 1977), 441–447; Matthew Frye Jacobson, *Whiteness of a Different Color: European Immigrants and the Alchemy of Race* (Cambridge: Harvard University Press, 1998), 32–33.

45. "Among Ourselves," *Designer* (January 1898): 61; "Wide-Awake Retailing," *DGE* (April 9, 1898): 81; Gage-Downs Co. advertisement, *CDGR* (November 25, 1899): 40.

46. Louise Odencrantz, *Italian Women in Industry: A Study of Conditions in New York City* (New York: Russell Sage Foundation, 1919), 228–229. For more examples on the same line, see Rose Laub Coser, Laura S. Anker, and Andrew J. Perrin, *Women of Courage: Jewish and Italian Immigrant Women in New York* (Westport, Conn.: Greenwood Press, 1999): 29.

47. Quoted in Schreier, *Becoming American Women*, 4.

48. Mary Antin, *The Promised Land* (Boston: Houghton Mifflin, 1912), 187.

49. Pierre L. van den Berghe, "Ethnic Cuisine: Culture in Nature," *Ethnic and Racial Studies* 7, no. 3 (July 1984): 387; see also Harvey Levenstein, "The American Response to Italian Food, 1880–1930," *Food and Foodways* 1, no. 1 (1985): 7–8.

50. Melford E. Spiro, "The Acculturation of American Ethnic Groups," *American Anthropologist* 57, no. 6 (December 1955): 1249–1250.

51. Good overviews of women in the garment industry (where the workforce was overwhelmingly female and foreign-born) and department stores (where employees were mainly women but less likely to be immigrants) can be found in Glenn, *Daughters of the Shtetl,* and Susan Porter Benson, *Counter Cultures: Saleswomen, Managers and Customers in American Department Stores, 1890–1940* (Urbana: University of Illinois Press, 1986). For the need to "look American" to get a factory job, see also Ewen, *Immigrant Women,* 25–26, and for the same pressure on sales clerks, see Heinze, *Adapting for Abundance,* 98.

52. Quoted in Ewen, *Immigrant Women,* 68.

53. John F. McClymer, "Gender and the 'American Way of Life': Women in the Americanization Movement," *Journal of American Ethnic History* 10 no. 3 (Spring 1991): 3–20. Quoted material is on p. 12.

54. These anecdotes refer to Ludmilla Foxlee's work with the Department for Foreign-born Women and Immigration of the YWCA. The information is taken from Schreier, *Becoming American Women,* 93–96.

55. Kathie Friedman-Kasaba, *Memories of Migration: Gender, Ethnicity, and Work in the Lives of Jewish and Italian Women in New York, 1870–1920* (Albany: State University of New York Press, 1996), 110–112 (emphasis added); Edward Bok, "Back to First Principles," *LHJ* (November 1897): 14; Olivia Howard Dunbar, "Teaching the Immigrant Woman," in *Americanization,* ed. Winthrop Talbot (New York: H. W. Wilson, 1917), 254. The latter article was first published in *Harper's Bazaar* in 1913.

56. Glenn, *Daughters of the Shtetl,* 68, 77; Paula Hyman, "Culture and Gender: Women in the Immigrant Jewish Community," in *The Legacy of Jewish Migration: 1881 and Its Impact,* ed. David Berger (New York: Brooklyn College Press, 1983), 161–163.

57. Abraham Cahan, *Yekl and the Imported Bridegroom and Other Stories of Yiddish New York* (New York: Dover, 1970), 34, 83.

58. Faina Burko, "The American Yiddish Theater and its Audience Before World War I," in *The Legacy of Jewish Migration: 1881 and Its Impact,* ed. David Berger (New York: Brooklyn College Press, 1983), 92–93.

59. S. P. Breckinridge, *New Homes for Old* (New York: Harper Brothers, 1921), 172. For more on conflict over clothing, see Ewen, *Immigrant Women,* 68–69, 197–201, and Schreier, *Becoming American Women,* 121–148.

60. Viola Paradise, "The Jewish Immigrant Girl in Chicago," *Survey* (April–September 1913): 704; Jane Addams, "The Subtle Problems of Charity," *Atlantic* (February 1899): 169.

61. Stuart Ewen and Elizabeth Ewen, *Channels of Desire: Mass Images and the Shaping of American Consciousness,* 2nd ed. (Minneapolis: University of Minnesota Press, 1992), 154–160; Heinze, *Adapting to Abundance.*

62. Clara Moore [Mrs. H. O. Ward, pseud.], *Sensible Etiquette of the Best Society* (Philadelphia: Porter and Coates, 1878), 251–252.

63. "Advice to Working Women," *Yiddishes Tageblatt* (December 2, 1898): 8. The *Yiddishes Tageblatt* was an eight-page Yiddish daily of which one page each day (labeled *The Jewish Daily News*) was in English. The textual citations in this chapter come from the English-language page.

64. Gertrude Haines, "Dame Fashion's Thumb," *Arena* 26 (December 1901): 624. An argument concerning the cultural agency of dress is advanced in Kathy Peiss, *Cheap Amusements: Working Women and Leisure in Turn-of-the-Century New York* (Philadelphia: Temple University Press, 1986), 62–67; and Schreier, *Becoming American Women,* 108–110, 132.

65. Florence Howe Hall, *Social Customs* (Boston: Estes and Lauriat, 1887), 304, 248.

66. Annie White, *Polite Society Here and Abroad,* (Chicago: Monarch Book, 1891), 279–280; Walter Houghton, et al., *American Etiquette and Rules of Politeness,* 7th ed. (New York: Standard Publishing House, 1883), 258.

67. The *Tageblatt* remained a powerful presence in the Jewish community into the twentieth century, although in the early 1900s it was passed in circulation by the rival *Forverts,* which was edited by Abraham Cahan starting in 1902. See Heinze, *Adapting to Abundance,* 150–152.

68. The manner in which "the weight of emigrant cultures" continually shaped a distinctive immigrant nationalism in the late nineteenth and early twentieth centuries is the focus of Matthew Frye Jacobson, *Special Sorrows: The Diasporic Imagination of Irish, Polish, and Jewish Immigrants in the United States.*

69. "Cuba Libre," *Yiddishes Tageblatt* (July 1, 1898): 8; M. Yachnin advertisement, *Yiddishes Tageblatt* (July 27, 1898): 2; "Life of Orthodox Jewish Girls in the Smaller Cities," *Yiddishes Tageblatt* (March 25, 1898): 8; "The Fashions," *Yiddishes Tageblatt* (August 31, 1898): 8 (emphasis added). On the early adoption of American techniques by the paper's clothing advertisers, see Heinze, *Adapting to Abundance,* 155.

70. This typology of assimilation was devised by Milton Gordon, *Assimilation in American Life: The Role of Race, Religion, and National Origin* (New York: Oxford University Press, 1964). It has been restated and refined by Philip Gleason, "American Identity and Americanization," 38–47, although Gleason subdivides the Anglo-conformity model into "Americanization" and "Anglo-Saxon racialism"; and Russell Kazal, "Revisiting Assimilation: The Rise, Fall, and Reappraisal of a Concept in American Ethnic History," *American Historical Review* 100, no. 2 (April 1995): 442.

71. "Among Ourselves," *Designer* (March 1898): 60.

72. Susan Voso Lab, "'War'Drobe and World War I," in *Dress in American Culture,* ed. Patricia Cunningham and Susan Voso Lab (Bowling Green, Ohio: Bowling Green State University Popular Press, 1993), 200–219.

73. Kathleen Neils Conzen et al., "The Invention of Ethnicity: A Perspective from the U.S.A.," *Journal of American Ethnic History* 12, no. 1 (Fall 1992), 8; see also John Higham, "Ethnic Pluralism," 199.

74. Frances E. Russell, "Woman's Dress," *Arena* 3, no. 15 (February 1891), 359.

75. Jeanette Lauer and Robert Lauer, *Fashion Power: The Meaning of Fashion in American Society* (Englewood Cliffs, N.J.: Prentice-Hall, 1981), 171–201. *New York Post* quoted on p. 182.

76. B. O. Flower, "Fashion's Slaves," *Arena* 4, no. 22 (September 1891): 427.

77. "The Clothing Trade," 63; "What Are Fashions?" *CC* (February 1897): 24.

78. "The American Jewess," *Yiddishes Tageblatt* (June 12, 1898): 8 (emphasis added).

79. Cahan, *The Rise of David Levinsky*, 101.

Chapter 5. Ad Experts and Clothiers

1. Joseph A. Appel, *The Business Biography of John Wanamaker* (New York: Macmillan, 1930), 41–42. Appel believes Wanamaker's memory was faulty in some details, but he appears to document the essence of this story. This is one of the many tales about Wanamaker's life that were often repeated in slightly different versions. See Russell H. Conwell, *The Romantic Rise of a Great American* (New York Harper & Brothers, 1924), 102; *Golden Book of the Wanamaker Stores*, vol. 1 (n.p., 1911), 27; and "Wanamaker Put New Ideas in Trade," *New York Times* (December 13, 1922): 12.

2. "Fifty Years," *PI* (July 28, 1938): 11, 72; Alan Trachtenberg, *The Incorporation of America: Culture and Society in the Gilded Age* (New York: Hill and Wang, 1982), 136.

3. "Essays on Advertising," *CG* (June 1890): 43; "The Science of Advertising," *CG* (February 1890): 61; "A Talk on Advertising," *CG* (April 1893): 54–55; "Modern Advertising," *CG* (December 1893): 52–53; "A Little Chat on Advertising," *CG* (January 1895): 121–122; "Good Advertising," *CG* (February 1895): 11; "Clever Advertising," *CG* (March 1895): 61–63; "Effective Advertising," *CG* (October 1895): 1 (part of eight-page section paginated separately from rest of issue); "Top-Notch Advertising," *CG* (November 1895): 79.

4. Charles Austin Bates, *Good Advertising* (New York: Holmes, 1896), 512. The "Wanamaker style" was also a well-known term designating a certain informal, conversational approach to advertising. See for example, Addison Archer, "The Wanamaker Style," *PI* (June 19, 1895): 4–5. Some say this should be called the "Powers style," after J. E. Powers, the man Wanamaker hired in 1880 to implement his advertising strategy, but at any rate it was strongly identified with the Wanamaker store. By 1890, Wanamaker management estimated more than fifty other stores were imitating it. See James Norris, *Advertising and the Transformation of American Society, 1865–1920* (New York: Greenwood Press, 1990), 17; Daniel Pope, *The Making of Modern Advertising* (New York: Basic Books, 1983), 134–135.

5. Surveys at the end of the nineteenth century ranked clothing as either the third or fourth largest category of magazine advertising, although these rankings apparently included a wide array of accessories, furnishings, and underwear as well as basic garments. Results of an 1898 survey by *Press and Printer* are cited in Frank Presbrey, *The History and Development of Advertising* (1929; reprint, New York: Greenwood Press, 1968), 362–363.

6. Curtis Publishing Company advertisement, *CDGR* (February 5, 1898): 15.

7. Among works that focus on the 1920s as the decade when advertising came of age are Stuart Ewen, *Captains of Consciousness: Advertising and the Social Roots of Consumer Culture* (New York: McGraw-Hill, 1976); T. J. Jackson Lears, "Some Versions of Fantasy: Toward a Cultural History of American Advertising, 1880–1930," *Prospects* 9 (1984): 349–405; Roland Marchand, *Advertising the American Dream: Making Way for Modernity, 1920–1940* (Berkeley: University of California Press, 1985); William Leiss, Stephen Kline, and Sut Jhally, *Social Communication*

in Advertising: Persons, Products and Images of Well-Being, 2nd ed. (New York: Routledge, 1990).

8. For works that attribute similar significance to late nineteenth-century
developments, see Richard Ohmann, *Selling Culture: Magazines, Markets, and Class
at the Turn of the Century* (London: Verso, 1996), 216–218; and Pope, *Making of
Modern Advertising,* 8.

9. "Severn's Advertising Points," *Ad Sense* (April 1898): 42; "Pertinent Business Proverbs," *Ad Sense* (April 1898): 42–43.

10. William Leach described *Fame* as "a fleeting but influential advertising
magazine," although with a publication run from 1892 to 1938, it outlasted
many of its contemporaries among advertising trade publications. See William
Leach, *Land of Desire: Merchants, Power, and the Rise of a New American Culture* (New
York: Pantheon, 1993).

11. Artemas Ward, "Stray Shots," *Fame* (September 1892): 196; Will B. Wilder,
"Hypnotism in Advertising," *Fame* (September 1892): 196. *Printers' Ink* published
a similar article the same year. See A. L. Kinkead, "Advertising a Kind of Hypnotism," *PI* (March 16, 1892): 358.

12. J. F. Place, "Honest Advertising Is Best," *PI* (August 17, 1892): 164.

13. Charles Austin Bates, *Short Talks on Advertising* (New York: Charles Austin
Bates, 1898), 41; idem, "Creating a Demand," *Charles Austin Bates Criticisms* (May
1897): 65, 67. Bates evidently believed in both advertising and patent medicine
so strongly that he risked his considerable reputation and fortune on a nostrum
called Laxacola around the turn of the century. The product failed, and Bates
went bankrupt and dropped from view. See Stephen Fox, *The Mirror Makers:
A History of American Advertising and Its Creators* (New York: William Morrow,
1984), 37.

14. P. T. Barnum entered the public limelight in the 1830s, when he began
promoting attractions such as a slave who purported to have been George Washington's nursemaid (she turned out to be about eighty years younger than she
claimed) and the "Feejee Mermaid," a curiosity concocted out of the carcasses
of a fish and a monkey. During a long and successful career, his name became
synonymous with flamboyant promotional activities. Barnum himself ascribed
his success to having "advertising more audacious . . . posters more glaring . . .
pictures more exaggerated . . . flags more patriotic, and . . . transparencies more
brilliant" than his competitors. His reputation for outlandish publicity stunts
and exaggerated claims did not endear him to the 1890s ad professional
attempting to craft a self-image that merged Victorian dignity and scientific professionalism. For comments on the manner in which later advertisers attempted
to distance themselves from Barnum's legacy, see Marchand, *Advertising the
American Dream,* 7–8; and Jackson Lears, *Fables of Abundance: A Cultural History of
Advertising in America* (New York: Basic Books, 1994), 213–215. For a recent biography, see A. H. Saxon, *P. T. Barnum: The Legend and the Man* (New York: Columbia University Press, 1989), in which the quotation from Barnum cited above
appears on p. 114.

15. Charles Austin Bates, "Advertising for Retailers," *PI* (June 13, 1894): 732;
"Pyrotechnic Advertising Talk," *Ad Sense* (April 1898): 43.

16. Artemas Ward, "Stray Shots," *Fame* (June 1894): 147; Joel Benton, "Salpi-
con," *Fame* (July 1894): 211.

17. On the development of "possession-reading skills," see Ellen Garvey, *The
Adman in the Parlor: Magazines and the Gendering of Consumer Culture, 1880s to
1910s* (New York: Oxford University Press, 1996), 14–15. Thomas Schlereth
noted that mail order catalogs served as a "guide to social conduct, proper

fashion, and acceptable personal behavior," although he did not develop this comparison. See Thomas Schlereth, "Mail-Order Catalogs as Resources in Material Culture Studies," in *Cultural History and Material Culture: Everyday Life, Landscapes, Museums* (Charlottesville: University Press of Virginia, 1990), 65. In a way, my argument is similar to the claim Raymond Williams made when he asserted that advertising gained so much cultural influence because of a "social failure to find [other] means of public information and decisions over a wide range of everyday economic life." See Raymond Williams, "Advertising: The Magic System," in *Problems in Materialism and Culture: Selected Essays* (London: Verso, 1980), 185, 193.

18. Helen Mar Shaw, "The Ad for Woman's Eye," *Judicious Advertising* (November 1902): 27. For examples on "dignity," see A. L. Teele, "Sympathetic Advertising," *Fame* (May 1892): 84; on "taste," see Joel Benton, "Olla Podrida," *Fame* (May 1892): 70; on "refinement," see "The Artistic in Advertising," *Profitable Advertising* (December 15, 1893): 197.

19. John H. Young, *Our Deportment* (Detroit: F. B. Dickerson, 1881), 17; Clara Moore [Mrs. H. O. Ward, pseud.], *Sensible Etiquette of the Best Society* (Philadelphia: Porter and Coates, 1878), 250; Artemas Ward, "Stray Shots," *Fame* (October 1892): 227.

20. Thomas Balmer, "The Gospel of Advertising," *Advertising Experience* (June 1897): 7–8.

21. Artemas Ward, "Stray Shots," *Fame* (May 1892) 67; idem, "Stray Shots," *Fame* (November 1892): 259.

22. "Not a Correction," *Fame* (September 1892): 208; "At Random," *Fame* (December 1895): 367.

23. Burton Bledstein, *The Culture of Professionalism: The Middle Class and the Development of Higher Education in America* (New York: W. W. Norton, 1976).

24. *Profitable Advertising* (November 15, 1895): 176; "An Artistic Doctor of Publicity," *CG* (September 1895): 50; "The Publicity Professor," *CG* (June 1895): 59.

25. Claude Hopkins, "Powers and Fowler Score for Modesty," *Fame* (April 1896): 55. Daniel Pope called Hopkins the "premier copywriter of his era" in *The Making of Modern Advertising*, 221.

26. *Profitable Advertising* (May 15, 1894): 373 (emphasis in original).

27. "The Literary Art of Putting Things," *PI* (August 15, 1894): 247. See also James Moffett, "Shall Advertisements Be Signed?" *Fame* (June 1892): 101–102; *PI* (September 12, 1894): 384; J. W. Schwartz, "Advertising in General," *PI* (March 2, 1898): 4. Jackson Lears cites attorney comparisons and the move for signed bylines as much later developments (occurring in 1915 and 1930, respectively) in "Some Versions of Fantasy," 360, 365.

28. Eliot Friedman, "Are Professions Necessary?" in *The Authority of Experts: Studies in History and Theory*, ed. Thomas Haskell (Bloomington: Indiana University Press, 1984), 8–10; Nathaniel Fowler, *About Advertising and Printing: A Concise, Practical, and Original Manual in the Art of Local Advertising* (Boston: L. Barta, 1889), 6; "A Wail on Advertising," *CG* (March 1895): 16; Quentin J. Schultze, "'An Honorable Place': The Quest for Professional Advertising Education, 1900–1917," *Business History Review* 56, no. 1 (Spring 1982), 16–32.

29. Thomas Haskell, "Introduction," in *The Authority of Experts: Studies in History and Theory*, ed. Thomas Haskell (Bloomington: Indiana University Press, 1984), xi–xii; William Leach views these developments as entirely negative. He describes the creation of "a century of intermediaries" that "helped inject into American culture a new amoralism essentially indifferent to virtue"; see *Land of Desire*, 15.

30. Nathaniel Fowler, *Building Business: An Illustrated Manual for Aggressive Business Men* (Boston: Trade Company, 1893) 14.

31. "A Wail on Advertising," 16; C. B. De La Vergne, Jr., "The Science of Advertising," *CG* (June 1890): 44.

32. "Trade Truths and Tattle," *CG* (January 1895): 16; Stein-Bloch Co. advertisement, *CG* (January 1895): 8; John S. McKeon advertisement, *CG* (January 1895): 141.

33. "The Light That Attracts Them," *Ad Sense* (March 1898), 5; Fowler, *About Advertising*, 8. Frank Presbrey, who worked as an ad man beginning in the 1890s and later wrote a history of the field, credited Fowler with writing the first book of advertising advice. He was probably referring to this work, which was published in 1889. See Presbrey, *The History and Development of Advertising*, 310.

34. W. G. Watrous, "Advertising Wholesale Clothing," *Judicious Advertising* (November 1902): 16; Arthur B. Chivers, "Illustrating Retail Advertising," *Advertising Experience* (December 1896): 9. Conne was advertising manager for The Hub, a prominent Chicago department store.

35. "Shoddy" originally referred to fabric woven out of a combination of new and waste wool fibers—it was used with embarrassing results in some Civil War uniforms. See "History of the Men's Wear Industry," *Men's Wear* (February 10, 1950), 204.

36. J. S. Appel, "Advertising as a Trade Factor," *CG* (October 1890): 34.

37. D. J. McDonald, "How to Write Advertisements," *CG* (July 1890): 55; "The Science of Advertising," *CG* (February 1890): 61. Trade journals frequently singled out Rogers, Peet & Co. advertisements for praise. *Printers' Ink*, in a typical reference, described the firm's advertising as "uniformly clever and readable." See *PI* (October 12, 1892): 462. Here Chambers appears specifically to be distancing himself from Barnum-style ads, although P. T. Barnum apparently never uttered the phrase, "There's a sucker born every minute," which is so often attributed to him. See Saxon, *P. T. Barnum*, 334–337.

38. Many references to this "crusade" appeared throughout the first half of the 1890s. For a listing of "abuses" from around the country, see "The Sentiment Against Fire Sale Frauds," *CG* (February 1890): 44–45; for a call to collective action, see "The Bankrupt Stock and Fire Sale Evil," *CG* (July 1894): 59–60; for a report on related legal action in which an antipeddler ordinance was declared unconstitutional ("The decision may be considered good law, but it is clearly not good common sense"), see "Itinerant Merchants," *CG* (February 1895): 16. Jackson Lears has noted the ideology of a WASPish "ethnic solidarity" embedded in these campaigns. Combining "Protestant plain speech and professional probity," they often dealt in anti-Semitic stereotypes. See Lears, *Fables of Abundance*, 205.

39. Edward Hamilton Bell, "The Development of Our Modern Costume," *CG* (February 1890): 47; "Here, There and Everywhere," *CG* (January 1895): 40; "The Prince's Clothes," *CG* (May 1895): 50; "Dress of Men of Genius," *CG* (May 1890): n.p.; "Wall Street's Beau Brummels," *CG* (November 1890): 32–34; "Old World Notorieties and Their Dress," *CG* (January 1890): 63.

40. "A Little Chat on Advertising," 122; "New Goods for Your Furnishing Department," *CG* (January 1895): 123; L. Golland's Sons advertisement, *CG* (January 1895): 5; Fechheimer, Fishel & Co. advertisement, *CG* (April 1895): 1.

41. "A Successful House," *CG* (April 1893): 59; *PI* (June 27, 1894): 808; *The Wanamaker System* (Philadelphia: John Wanamaker, 1899).

42. "Hints to Retailers," *CDGR* (January 4, 1896): 67; Archer, "Wanamaker Style," 5; "Iron City Clothiers," *CG* (April 1893): 60.

43. "Friendly Chats with Clerks," *CG* (February 1895): 30–31; E. C. Almy advertisement, *CG* (November 1895): 12.

44. Warren Susman argued for a transformation at the turn of the century from the "culture of character" to the "culture of personality" in a 1979 essay called "'Personality' and the Making of Twentieth-Century Culture" that was reprinted in *Culture as History: The Transformation of American Society in the Twentieth Century* (New York: Pantheon, 1984), 271–285. Franklin, in his autobiography, recalled his early attempts to craft a businesslike image: "In order to secure my credit and character as a tradesman, I took care not only to be in *reality* industrious and frugal, but to avoid all appearances of the contrary. I dressed plainly; I was seen at no places of idle diversion." *Benjamin Franklin's Autobiography*, ed. J. A. Leo Lemay and P. M. Zall (New York: W. W. Norton, 1986), 54 (emphasis in original).

45. "Rounding the Turn," *CG* (January 1895): 128; Charles Austin Bates, *Short Talks on Advertising*, 8; "Church Advertising," *PI* (September 7, 1892): 281; "Advertising a Blessing—Its Suppression a Calamity," *Fame* (April 1893): 74.

46. "Banner Bros.' New Home," *CG* (January 1893): 59; "A Talk on Advertising," 55; Charles Austin Bates, "Advertising for Retailers," *PI* (August 29, 1894): 310.

47. James Marston Fitch, *American Building: The Historical Forces that Shaped It*, 2nd ed. (New York: Schocken Books, 1966), 168–210; John Burchard and Albert Bush-Brown, *The Architecture of America: A Social and Cultural History* (Boston: Little, Brown, 1966), 81–84; Trachtenberg, *The Incorporation of America*, 118–121; Daniel Bluestone, *Constructing Chicago* (New Haven: Yale University Press, 1991), 104–151; "Trade Topics," *CG* (March 1895): 46; "A Great Clothing House," *CG* (January 1895): 11.

48. Bledstein, *The Culture of Professionalism*, 53–54. Jackson Lears characterizes this balancing act as a tension between a new "professional-managerial worldview" and an older "carnivalesque tradition" of "enchantment." Lears sees this dilemma as a stark dichotomy and "fundamental conflict." Rather than a genuine attempt to amalgamate old and new values, he interprets the espousal of old verities as a "veneer" for a "deeper structure of belief" that is cynical and manipulative. My analysis suggests a less orderly shuffling and reshuffling of values, a deeper structure that is kaleidoscopic rather than Manichean. See Lears, *Fables of Abundance*, 212, 230, and all of Part II.

49. Henry R. Plomer, *English Printers' Ornaments* (New York: Burt Franklin, 1924).

50. Historian Daniel Pope argues against interpretations of advertising that uncover intricate networks of cultural meanings while ignoring the fundamental reality that advertising was primarily a business tool. See *The Making of Modern Advertising*, 7–11.

51. M. D. McDonald, "All-Around Advertising," *CG* (August 1890): 49 (McDonald was advertising manager for the J. L. Hudson's store in Cleveland); Alfred Bersbach, "Illustrations in Advertising," *Ad Sense* (March 1898): 13; David Phillips, "Tracing Results," *The Advisor* (June 1899): 4.

52. Will B. Wilder, "Years and Cycles," *Fame* (February 1893): 452.

53. Several authors have argued that even advertising that is unsuccessful (in terms of product sales) still effectively promotes the values of capitalism and large-scale consumption. See, for example, Christopher Lasch, "The Culture of Consumption," in *The Encyclopedia of American Social History*, vol. 2, ed. Mary Kupiec Clayton, Elliott J. Gorn, and Peter W. Williams (New York: Charles Scribner's

Sons, 1993), 1386–1387; and Leach, *Land of Desire*, xv. Clothing advertisements, in this regard, had the added impact of promoting "the need to be fashionable" even when they failed to popularize a specific fashion. See Norris, *Advertising and the Transformation of American Society*, 106.

54. "Do Trade Papers Pay?" *Charles Austin Bates Criticisms* (November 1897): 170; David Phillips, "The Country Advertiser," *The Advisor* (March 1899): 7; Harvey Morris, *The Story of Men's Clothes* (Rochester: Hickey-Freeman, 1926), 23; Joel Benton, "The 'One-Price' Plea," *Fame* (November 1898): 464; *The Wanamaker System*, n.p. [1]; Chas. Jones, "Store Management," *PI* (December 7, 1898): 23, Susan Strasser, *Satisfaction Guaranteed* (New York: Pantheon, 1989), 74, 230.

55. Stuart Ewen and Elizabeth Ewen, *Channels of Desire: Mass Images and the Shaping of American Consciousness*, 2nd ed. (Minneapolis: University of Minnesota Press, 1992), 33. The Ewens refer to the idea of money as a mass medium within which a new worldview was embedded. They do not discuss it in relation to the one-price system.

56. "Talks on Advertising," *CG* (June 1893): 73; William H. Maher, "Who Shall Write the Advertisement?" *PI* (January 11, 1893): 84; *PI* (August 22, 1894): 284 (emphasis added). Roland Marchand discusses the simulated personalism of ads in later advertising in *Advertising the American Dream*, 9.

57. John Manning, "The Advertisement and Its Relation to the Elementary Laws of Trade," *Fame* (February 1893): 486. *Fame* liked this advice so much it published it again verbatim under a different title and byline a year and a half later in W. E. Carson, "Passing Notes," *Fame* (September 1894): 290, 292.

58. H. B. Howard, "The Beifeld Cloak," *PI* (November 9, 1898): 46–47. Marketing to consumers was a major change in business strategy. In the 1880s the company expressed distress that its catalogs should ever "find their way into the hands of consumers (non-dealers)" and deliberately omitted prices in these publications so as to avoid inadvertently revealing wholesale secrets to retail customers. See Beifeld Brothers, *Illustrated Catalogue of Ladies' and Children's Cloaks, Etc.* (Chicago, 1881): inside front cover.

59. Howard, "The Beifeld Cloak," 46–47.

60. Addison Archer, "What an Expert Is," *PI* (October 23, 1895): 3–4 (emphasis added); Fowler, *Building Business*, 425 (emphasis added); *PI* (June 13, 1894): 728; "Philadelphia Advertising," *CG* (April 1893): 55; Addison Archer, "Bates on Bates," *PI* (August 14, 1895): 9.

61. "Hits and Misses," *Advertising Experience* (May 1897): 20; "The Sin of Over-Illustration," *Fame* (August 1898): 318; Neil Harris, "Pictorial Perils: The Rise of American Illustration," in *Cultural Excursions: Marketing Appetites and Cultural Tastes in Modern America* (Chicago: University of Chicago Press, 1990), 339.

62. Edward Bok, "At Home with the Editor," *LHJ* (April 1894): 14; C. B. De La Vergne Jr., "The Science of Advertising," 44–45—De La Vergne worked for Smith, Gray & Co. in Brooklyn.

63. Joseph Hamlin Phinney, "A Cut Argument," *PI* (June 15, 1898): 3; "Factors in Advertising," *PI* (June 19, 1895): 28; "Pictures in Advertising," *Advertising Experience* (December 1896): 11. Among many other pertinent discussions of these issues, see Bersbach, "Illustrations in Advertising," 12–14; "Type Ads vs. Picture Ads," *Ad Sense* (April 1898): 41; Chivers, "Illustrating Retail Advertising," 8–10; "Do Justice to the Cuts," *Fame* (November 1892): 293–294; Will B. Wilder, "The Use of Cuts," *Fame* (July 1896): 167–168; Watrous, "Advertising Wholesale Clothing," 16–17; Charles Austin Bates, "Magazine Advertising," *PI* (August 8, 1894): 187–188; "Pictorial Ads," *PI* (October 30, 1895): 26; "The Artistic in Advertising," 193–197.

64. Howard, "The Beifeld Cloak," 46; Frank Drake, "How Newspaper Illustration was Evolved," *PI* (March 2, 1898): 66–69; "Rate Cards and Extras of Daily Papers," *Advertising Experience* (May 1897): 3; "One Surrenders—Push the Limit," *Fame* (December 1892): 327; "Setting the Type," *Fame* (July 1894): 211; "Cuts and Display Type in the 'Herald,'" *PI* (November 30, 1892): 710; *PI* (July 4, 1894): 11; *PI* (December 7, 1892): 765; "An 'Old Fogy' Idea," *The Advisor* (March 1899): 9.

65. A sampling of stock cuts offered for sale was displayed in *CG* (September 1895) and referred to in the *CDGR* (September 25, 1897): 37. Some sold for as cheaply as 25 cents each, and by the last half of the 1890s many manufacturers began making cuts of their goods available free to merchants. One advertising manager was able to acquire a collection of more than 3,000 cuts in less than a month by seeking them from his suppliers. See Sam Whitmire, "Getting and Keeping Cuts," *PI* (June 8, 1898): 22.

66. "An Artistic Doctor of Publicity," 50; Chivers, "Illustrating Retail Advertising," 9; "The Artistic in Advertising," 193.

67. "Fifty Years," 84; M. M. Gillam, "The Wanamaker Advertising Idea," *PI* (January 6, 1892): 7; "At Random," *Fame* (April 1893): 82; "Up-to-Date Advertising," *CDGR* (October 2, 1897): 43.

68. Richards, *The Commodity Culture of Victorian England*, 59–60.

69. Artemas Ward, "Stray Shots," *Fame* (June 1894): 147; idem, "Stray Shots," *Fame* (March 1892): 3.

70. On advertising's failure to influence fashion, see Paul Nystrom, *The Economics of Fashion* (New York: Ronald Press, 1928), 13; and Norris, *Advertising and the Transformation of American Society*, 100, 106.

71. "The Mixing of Commerce and Art," *Ad Sense* (April 1898): 35; the story from *Printers' Ink* (November 26, 1914) was reprinted in Paul Terry Cherington, *The First Advertising Book* (New York: Doubleday, Page, 1917), 109–112; Susan Strasser offers evidence that the meaning of brand names underwent a similar process of experimentation in *Satisfaction Guaranteed*, 37–43.

72. "Make It to Their Interest," *Ad Sense* (March 1898): 18.

73. *PI* (September 5, 1894): 353; S. H. & M. advertisement, *LHJ* (January 1895): 22.

74. One such incident is described in "A Distinction—Or a Difference," *Charles Austin Bates Criticisms* (March 1898): 295–296.

75. *PI* (October 17, 1894): 633; "The Curse of Cheapness," *CG* (July 1895): 13; Oscar Herzberg, "Women and Advertising," *PI* (October 30, 1895): 20; "Advertising Clothing," *PI* (July 13, 1892) 28; "The Science of Advertising," *CG* (February 1890): 61; "The Artistic in Advertising," 197.

76. "Advertising Clothing," 27–28; George Gardner, "The Logic of Advertising," *CG* (September 1890): 34.

77. Charles Austin Bates, "Department of Criticism," *PI* (October 9, 1895): 63 (emphasis added); John T. Burgess, "Practical Advertising," *Fame* (January 1893): 389; Will B. Wilder, "The Aerating Power of Advertising," *Fame* (November 1892): 261.

78. "English Advertisers," *CG* (November 1894): 25; H. I. Cleveland, "The American Advertiser's Untouched Field," *Judicious Advertising* (January 1903): 18.

79. Will B. Wilder, "The Advertiser as Missionary," *Fame* (October 1894): 309.

80. "An Old, Old House," *CG* (April 1895): 46; editorial, *Dry Goods Economist* (February 5, 1898): 13; *The Wanamaker System*, n.p. [4]; Putnam advertisement, *CG* (July 1895): 14; "The Americans Are Best Dressed," *CG* (January 1895): 107.

81. *Joseph Schaffner 1848–1918: Recollections and Impressions of His Associates* (Chicago: n.p., 1920), 5, 13, 19, 50–51.

82. *Joseph Schaffner,* 39–49. Like Wanamaker's, Schaffner's firm hired talented advertising writers who contributed greatly to the company's advertising success, although the top managers undoubtedly deserve credit for the businesses' overall strategy. In the case of Hart, Schaffner & Marx, the key advertising professional was George L. Dyer, who directed the company's publicity starting in the 1890s. *Printers' Ink* later claimed Dyer's ads were able to "inaugurate a new era of clothes making and practically revolutionize the industry." See "Fifty Years," 151.

83. Hart, Schaffner & Marx advertisement, *LHJ* (March 1899): 41; Alfred Chandler, *The Visible Hand: The Managerial Revolution in American Business* (Cambridge, Mass.: Harvard University Press, 1977), 505.

84. *Joseph Schaffner,* 7.

Conclusion

1. The ideas in this section on the cultural function of stories and symbols are adapted in part from Clifford Geertz, "Deep Play: Notes on the Balinese Cock Fight," in *The Interpretation of Cultures* (New York: Basic Books, 1973), 443–453.

2. Sharlot Mabridth Hall, "Fitness and Unfitness in Dress," *GH* (March 1896): 104–106.

3. "A Clothing Conversation," *Browning, King & Co.'s Illustrated Monthly* (January 1898): 10.

4. Hester M. Poole, "Notions and Novelties," *GH* (December 1898): 208; Susan Porter Benson, *Counter Cultures: Saleswomen, Managers, and Customers in American Department Stores 1890–1940* (Urbana: University of Illinois Press, 1988), 76. See also William Leach, "Transformations in a Culture of Consumption: Women and Department Stores, 1890–1925," *Journal of American History* 71 no. 2 (September 1984): 319–342.

5. "A Clothing Conversation," 10.

6. Vivian C. Hopkins, ed., "Diary of an Iowa Farm Girl: Josephine Edith Brown, 1892–1901," *Annals of Iowa* 3rd Series 42, no. 1 (Summer 1973), 128, diary entry dated September 14, 1892; Lela Barnes, ed., "North Central Kansas in 1887–1889: From the Letters of Leslie and Susan Snow of Junction City—Concluded," *Kansas Historical Quarterly* 29, no. 4 (Winter 1963): 417, letter dated March 20, 1889; Isabella Maud Rittenhouse, *Maud,* ed. Richard Lee Strout (New York: Macmillan, 1939), 13, diary entry dated May 26, 1881; Rose Pastor Stokes, *I Belong to the Working Class: the Unfinished Autobiography of Rose Pastor Stokes,* ed. Herbert Shapiro and David L. Sterling (Athens: University of Georgia Press, 1992), 80. Stokes wrote this memoir in the 1930s. The quoted material refers to incidents that happened between 1900 and 1901.

7. George Marcus and Michael Fischer, *Anthropology as Cultural Critique: An Experimental Moment in the Human Sciences* (Chicago: University of Chicago Press 1986), 78 (emphasis in original).

8. Jeanette Lauer and Robert Lauer, *Fashion Power: The Meaning of Fashion in American Society* (Englewood Cliffs, N.J.: Prentice-Hall, 1981), 246.

9. Ruth Ashmore, "The Girl Who Uses Slang," *LHJ* (November 1893): 20.

Index

Acknowledgments

In any study such as this, one acquires almost innumerable debts to archivists, colleagues, teachers, friends, and family. I certainly acquired more than my fair share, and I can only hint at the assistance I have received from various quarters.

My most extended period of research took place at the Winterthur Museum and Library. The cooperation of the entire staff, especially librarian-in-charge Neville Thompson, made my time there enormously productive. I also paid several visits to the Warshaw Collection at the National Museum of American History, the Business Reading Room at the Library of Congress, and the Hagley Museum and Library. Staff members at each location did whatever they could to assist me. Shorter trips to the Historical Society of Pennsylvania in Philadelphia, the Cincinnati Historical Society, and the Steenbock Library at the University of Wisconsin—Madison also elicited friendly assistance and yielded useful material. The staff at the interlibrary loan department at Indiana University went beyond the call of duty on my behalf, sometimes persisting for months to obtain material I needed.

Teachers, friends, and colleagues at Indiana University provided much crucial advice. The insightful and thorough comments of Casey Blake are evident throughout this book. Michael McGerr offered me valued support and suggestions virtually from the first day I set foot on the Bloomington campus; Wendy Gamber generously shared her expertise and advice virtually from the first day she set foot on campus; David Nord provided useful comments on my research and writing from the time this project first began to take shape. Pat Roath, then assistant curator of Indiana University's Elizabeth Sage Costume Collection, on several occasions made time for my questions during the formative stages of this research and continued to take a friendly and encouraging interest in its progress. Also in Bloomington, the management and staff of the *Herald-Times*, and particularly editor Bob Zaltsberg, generously accommodated my academic pursuits while I simultaneously pursued a Ph.D. and worked in the newsroom. I would never have been able to sustain both myself and this project without the cooperation of Bob and others at the *Herald-Times*.

Earlier versions of sections of this book have previously appeared in articles in *American Studies, Dress, Journal of American Culture,* and *The Historian*. The editors and readers at each journal provided helpful commentary. I also owe major thanks to the Costume Society of America, whose Stella Blum Research Fellowship underwrote an important part of my research. Society members also offered a perceptive and receptive audience when I presented preliminary results of my research at one of their annual meetings. At the University of Pennsylvania Press, Robert Lockhart and Samantha Foster offered much appreciated help and advice as they shepherded the book into print, and anonymous readers of the preliminary manuscript contributed many suggestions.

On a personal level, I first must thank my parents, Mary and Tom Schorman. Although their impact on my scholarship is indirect, in many ways their example and encouragement are responsible for my willingness and ability to undertake a project such as this one. My biggest debt and greatest thanks are to my wife, Judi Hetrick. Besides being the best editor I have ever known, she gave me unwavering support and assistance throughout my research and writing and helped in countless ways while at the same time pursuing her own scholarly and teaching goals. This book is certainly a better one because of her, and without her it might not exist at all.